Discovering the News

DISCOVERING THE NEWS

A Social History of American Newspapers

MICHAEL SCHUDSON

BASIC BOOKS

A Member of the Perseus Books Group

Excerpt from "For Eugene McCarthy" from *History* by Robert Lowell. Copyright © 1967, 1969, 1970, and 1973 by Robert Lowell. Reprinted with the permission of Farrar, Straus & Giroux, Inc.

Library of Congress Cataloging in Publication Data

Schudson, Michael.

  Discovering the news : a social history of American
newspapers.

  Includes bibliographical references and index.

  1. Journalism—United States—History. 2. Journalism
—Objectivity. I. Title.

PN4855.S3   071'.3   78–54997

ISBN: 0-465-01669-3 (cloth)

ISBN-10: 0-465-01666-9   ISBN-13: 978-0-465-01666-2 (paper)

To my father

and in memory of

my mother

CONTENTS

CHAPTER 4

CHAPTER 5

ACKNOWLEDGMENTS

THIS BOOK had its origin in a discussion with David Riesman five years ago. In that conversation, I expressed my interest in tracing the social history of important modern values. If there is a history of ideas and a sociology of knowledge, is there not also a history of ideals and a sociology of values? It is a long way from that general question to a specific study of objectivity in American journalism. But it was David Riesman's sensitive response to my first, tentative articulation of an idea that helped me take the idea seriously. I am indebted to him for the unceasing generosity of his mind and spirit.

In an earlier version, this work was a doctoral dissertation in the Department of Sociology at Harvard University. It concerned the history of the ideal of objectivity in American law and in American journalism. While the work on the legal profession is not represented here, the discipline of comparing two occupational groups was very important to me, and my discussion of journalism would have been the poorer without it. My dissertation advisers, Daniel Bell and Morton Horwitz, demonstrated a personal interest in my project and in me which was far beyond any call of duty. I am enormously grateful for their intellectual and moral support.

Many others helped me through the dissertation. In reading my manuscript and encouraging my work Cora Brooks, Robert Manoff, and Robert Snow were more helpful than I know how to say. Robert Post's detailed criticism of several chapters was very important. Richard Schuldenfrei's intelligent and infectious enthusiasm for my efforts was indispensable.

As I turned the dissertation into a book, more friends and colleagues came to my aid. For reading the entire manuscript and advising me on it, I acknowledge the help of Morris

Janowitz, Peter Novick, Paul Starr, Gaye Tuchman, and my most thoughtful editor at Basic Books, Martin Kessler. For critical reading of the introduction, I want to thank Herbert Gans; for chapter one, Robert Ferguson; for chapter three, Neil Harris; for chapter four, Ronald Steel; and for chapter five, Paul Hirsch, Robert Manoff, Martha Minow, and Paul Starr. Libby Bruch at Basic Books provided expert copy editing.

Financial support for my research was provided by the Danforth Foundation, the Russell Sage Foundation Residency in Law and Social Science, and the Division of the Social Sciences at the University of Chicago. I am indebted to Alice Ryerson for a week as resident at the Ragdale Foundation in Lake Forest, Illinois, where I drafted the final chapter.

I am grateful to the score of journalists who shared their time and thoughts with me. They will see all too well the shortcomings of this work, knowing as they do the complexity and diversity of American journalism. I hope, nevertheless, that in my focus on main directions of metropolitan daily journalism and main connections between newspapers and society, they will recognize elements of a world they know.

I owe thanks to many libraries and librarians: Widener Library at Harvard University; the American Antiquarian Society in Worcester, Massachusetts; the library of the School of Journalism, Columbia University; the New York Historical Society Library; Sterling Library at Yale University; the Library of Congress; Regenstein Library at the University of Chicago; and the *Chicago Tribune* archives. Many friends, colleagues, and students have led me to books or articles they thought might interest me. To handle a wide-ranging topic the art of browsing is invaluable, and I have been fortunate to have so many friends who share my delight in it.

Why do writers so often acknowledge the obvious fact that none of the people who have helped them are responsible for the errors in the finished work? Because, as I now understand, a work of scholarship is a collective enterprise, even if one's style of working is solitary. When finished, the work is necessarily inadequate to the good wishes and high hopes of so many who helped it along. I remember a friend saying that the best time in pottery is the moment, with the wheel spinning, just before you shape the pot—just before the infinity of possibilities becomes but one of the possible things. The process of writing is guided by hope and ambition; the product must be defined, in part, by its limitations.

A last word of thanks. Among the many things for which I am grateful to my parents, I feel particularly blessed by their encouragement, from my earliest years, to express myself—in painting, in music, in poetry, in prose. With love and gratitude, I dedicate this book to my father and to the memory of my mother.

Discovering the News

INTRODUCTION

THE IDEAL OF OBJECTIVITY

AMERICAN JOURNALISM has been regularly criticized for failing to be "objective." Whether it was Democrats in 1952 complaining of a one-party press biased against Adlai Stevenson or the Nixon-Agnew administration attacking newspapers and television networks for being too liberal, the press has repeatedly been taken to task for not presenting the day's news "objectively."

But why do critics take it for granted that the press *should* be objective? Objectivity is a peculiar demand to make of institutions which, as business corporations, are dedicated first of all to economic survival. It is a peculiar demand to make of institutions which often, by tradition or explicit credo, are political organs. It is a peculiar demand to make of editors and reporters who have none of the professional apparatus which, for doctors or lawyers or scientists, is supposed to guarantee objectivity.

And yet, journalists, as well as their critics, hold newspapers to a standard of objectivity. Not all journalists believe they should be objective in their work, but the belief is widespread,[1] and all journalists today must in some manner confront it. But why? What kind of a world is ours and what kind of an institution is journalism that they sustain this particular ideal, objectivity? That is the problem this book addresses. I shall not ask here the familiar question: are newspapers objective? I shall ask, instead, why that question is so familiar.

The question assumes special interest when one learns that, before the 1830s, objectivity was not an issue. American newspapers were expected to present a partisan viewpoint, not a neutral one. Indeed, they were not expected to report the "news" of the day at all in the way we conceive it—the idea of "news" itself was invented in the Jacksonian era. If we are to understand the idea of objectivity in journalism, the transformation of the press in the Jacksonian period must be examined. That is the task of the first chapter, which will interpret the origins of "news" in its relationship to the democratization of politics, the expansion of a market economy, and the growing authority of an entrepreneurial, urban middle class.

There is an obvious explanation of why the idea of news, once established, should have turned into nonpartisan, strictly factual news later in the century. This has to do with the rise of the first American wire service, the Associated Press. The telegraph was invented in the 1840s, and, to take advantage of its speed in transmitting news, a group of New York newspapers organized the Associated Press in 1848. Since the Associated Press gathered news for publication in a variety of papers with widely different political allegiances, it could only succeed by making its reporting "objective" enough to be acceptable to all of its members and clients. By the late nineteenth century, the AP dispatches were markedly more free from editorial comment than most reporting for single newspapers.[2] It has been argued, then, that the practice of the Associated Press became the ideal of journalism in general.[3]

While this argument is plausible, at first blush, there is remarkably little evidence for it and two good reasons to doubt it. First, it begs a key question: why should a practice, obviously important to the survival of the institution of the wire service, become a guiding ideal in institutions not subject to the same constraints? It would be just as likely, or more likely, that newspapers would take the availability of wire service news as license to concentrate on different kinds of reporting. *If* the AP style became a model for daily journalists, one would still have to account for its affinity with their interests and needs. But this brings us to the second, still more serious problem: objective reporting did *not* become the chief norm or practice in journalism in the late nineteenth century when the Associated Press was growing. As I will show in the second and third chapters, at the turn of the century there was as much emphasis in leading papers on telling a good story as on getting the facts. Sensationalism in its various forms was the chief development in newspaper content. Reporters sought as often to write "literature" as to gather news. Still, in 1896, in the bawdiest days of yellow journalism, the *New York Times* began to climb to its premier position by stressing an "information" model, rather than a "story" model, of reporting. Where the Associated Press was factual to appeal to a politically diverse clientele, the *Times* was informational to attract a relatively select, socially homogeneous readership of the well to do. As in the Jacksonian era, so in the 1890s, changes in the ideals of journalism did not translate technological changes into occupational norms so much as make newspaper ideals and practices consonant with the culture of dominant social classes.

But into the first decades of the twentieth century, even at the *New York Times,* it was uncommon for journalists to see a sharp divide between facts and values. Yet the belief in objectivity is just this: the belief that one can and should separate facts from values. Facts, in this view, are assertions about the world open to independent validation. They stand beyond the distorting influences of any individual's personal preferences. Values, in this view, are an individual's conscious or unconscious preferences for what the world should be; they are seen as ultimately subjective and so without legitimate claim on other people. The belief in objectivity is a faith in "facts," a distrust of "values," and a commitment to their segregation.

Journalists before World War I did not subscribe to this view. They were, to the extent that they were interested in facts, naive empiricists; they believed that facts are not human statements about the world but aspects of the world itself. This view was insensitive to the ways in which the "world" is something people construct by the active play of their minds and by their acceptance of conventional—not necessarily "true"—ways of seeing and talking. Philosophy, the history of science, psychoanalysis, and the social sciences have taken great pains to demonstrate that human beings are cultural animals who know and see and hear the world through socially constructed filters. From the 1920s on, the idea that human beings individually and collectively construct the reality they deal with has held a central position in social thought.[5]

Before the 1920s, journalists did not think much about the subjectivity of perception. They had relatively little incentive to doubt the firmness of the "reality" by which they lived. American society, despite serious problems, remained buoyant with hope and promise. Democracy was a value unquestioned in politics; free enterprise was still widely worshipped in economic life; the novels of Horatio Alger sold well. Few people doubted the inevitability of progress. After World War I, however, this changed. Journalists, like others, lost faith in verities a democratic market society had taken for granted. Their experience of propaganda during the war and public relations thereafter convinced them that the world they reported was one that interested parties had constructed for them to report. In such a world, naive empiricism could not last.

This turning point is the topic of my fourth chapter. In the twenties and thirties, many journalists observed with growing anxiety that facts themselves, or what they had taken to be facts, could not be trusted. One response to this discomfiting view was the institutionalization in the daily paper of new genres of subjective reporting, like the political column. Another response turned the journalists' anxiety on its head and encouraged journalists to replace a simple faith in facts with an allegiance to rules and procedures created for a world in which even facts were in question. This was "objectivity." Objectivity, in this sense, means that a person's statements about the world can be trusted if they are submitted to established rules deemed legitimate by a professional community. Facts here are not aspects of the world, but consensually validated statements about it.[6] While naive empiricism has not disappeared in journalism and survives, to some extent, in all of us, after World War I it was subordinated to the more sophisticated ideal of "objectivity."

Discussion of objectivity as an ideal (or ideology) in science, medicine, law, the social sciences, journalism, and other pursuits tends to two poles: either it seeks to unmask the profession in question or to glorify it. It is either debunking or self-serving. Debunkers show that the claims of professionals about being objective or expert or scientific are really just attempts to legitimate power by defining political issues in technical terms. This is often true. But, first, why is "objectivity" the legitimation they choose, and, second, why is it so often convincing to others? When professionals make a claim to authoritative knowledge, why do they base the claim on their objectivity rather than on, say, divine revelation or electoral mandate? Debunking by itself does not provide an answer.

The opposite stance is to Whiggishly identify objectivity in journalism or in law or other professions with "science," where science is understood as the right or true or best path to knowledge. This is the point at which science, generally understood as opposed to ideology, threatens to become ideology itself. But that, in a sense, is just what interests me here—not the internal development of science as an institution or a body of knowledge and practices, but the reasons the *idea* of science and the *ideal* of objectivity are so resonant in our culture. Even if science, as we know it today, is in some sense getting us nearer to truth than past systems of knowledge, we can still inquire why twentieth-century Western culture should be so wise as to recognize this. And that is a question that glorifications of science and objectivity do not answer.

It should be apparent that the belief in objectivity in journalism, as in other professions, is not just a claim about what kind of knowledge is reliable. It is also a moral philosophy, a declaration of what kind of thinking one should engage in, in making moral decisions. It is, moreover, a political commitment, for it provides a guide to what groups one should acknowledge as relevant audiences for judging one's own thoughts and acts. The relevant audiences are defined by institutional mechanisms. Two mechanisms of social control are frequently said to underwrite objectivity in different fields. First, there is advanced education and training. This is supposed to provide trainees with scientific knowledge and an objective attitude which helps them set aside personal preferences and passions. Thus the training of physicians enables them to sustain detached attitudes at times when persons without such training would submit to panic or despair at the human agony they face. Law students are taught to distinguish "legal" questions (generally understood to be technical) from "moral" issues (generally understood to be outside the proper domain of legal education and legal practice).

A second basic form of social control is insulation from the public. Technical language or jargon is one such insulating mechanism. Others may be institutional. For instance, legal scholars argue that courts are able to be more objective than legislatures because judges are institutionally further removed from the pressures of electoral politics than are legislators. Objectivity in the professions is guaranteed, then, by the autonomy of professional groups—the collective independence of professions from the market and from popular will, and the personal independence of professionals, assured by their training, from their own values.

In this context, the notion of objectivity in journalism appears anomalous. Nothing in the training of journalists gives them license to shape others' views of the world. Nor do journalists have esoteric techniques or language. Newspapers are directly dependent on market forces. They appeal directly to popular opinion. Journalism is an uninsulated profession. To criticize a lawyer, we say, "I'm not a lawyer, but—" and to question a doctor, we say, "I'm no expert on medicine, but—." We feel no such compunction to qualify criticism of the morning paper or the television news. I do not subscribe to the view that journalism is thereby inferior to other professional groups; I simply mean to identify the problem of objectivity in the case of journalism. How is it that in an occupation without the social organization of self-regulated authority there is still passionate controversy about objectivity? Of course, one answer is that the less a profession is seen to be self-evidently objective, the more passionate the controversy will be. But this is not answer enough. Why, in journalism, where none of the features that guarantee objectivity in law or medicine exist or are likely to exist, should objectivity still be a serious issue? Why hasn't it been given up altogether?

By the 1960s, both critics of the press and defenders took objectivity to be the emblem of American journalism, an improvement over a past of "sensationalism" and a contrast to the party papers of Europe. Whether regarded as the fatal flaw or the supreme virtue of the American press, all agreed that the idea of objectivity was at the heart of what journalism has meant in this country. At the same time, the ideal of objectivity was more completely and divisively debated in the past decade than ever before. In the final chapter, I will examine how changing subject matter, sources of news, and audience for the news precipitated this debate in journalism. Government management of the news, which began to concern journalists after World War I, became an increasingly disturbing problem with the rise of a national security establishment and an "imperial" presidency after World War II. In the Vietnam war, government news management collided with a growing "adversary culture" in the universities, in journalism, in the government itself, and in the population at large. The conflagration that followed produced a radical questioning of objectivity which will not soon be forgotten and revitalized traditions of reporting that the objective style had long overshadowed. The ideal of objectivity has by no means been displaced, but, more than ever, it holds its authority on sufferance.

I originally conceived this work as a case study in the history of professions and in the genesis of professional ideology. I saw objectivity as the dominant ideal that legitimates knowledge and authority in all contemporary professions. If I could excavate its foundations in one field, I could hope to expose its structure in all. While this book has not entirely outgrown that ambition, it came to be moved equally by another. I grew fascinated by journalism itself and convinced there were important questions, not only unanswered but unasked, about the relationship of journalism to the development of American society as a whole. Where standard histories of the American press consider the social context of journalism only in passing, this work takes as its main subject the relationship between the institutionalization of modern journalism and general currents in economic, political, social, and cultural life.

With two such ambitions, I know my reach has exceeded my grasp. If I have not achieved as much here as I would like, I hope nonetheless to have engaged the reader's interest in the quest and the questions.

CHAPTER 1

THE REVOLUTION IN AMERICAN JOURNALISM IN THE AGE OF EGALITARIANISM: THE PENNY PRESS

BY BIRTH, education, and marriage, James Fenimore Cooper was an American aristocrat. For him, power and prestige were always near at hand. But he was also an ardent nationalist, a great admirer of Jefferson and even Jackson. His novel *The Bravo* (1831) honored the July Revolution in France. It sought to expose those people in society who were "contending for exclusive advantages at the expense of the mass of their fellow-creatures."[1]

The Bravo was written during Cooper's seven-year sojourn in Europe from 1826 to 1833. In that time Cooper developed "a lofty detachment from the fears natural to his own class, and a warm sympathy for the lower classes that in Europe were, and in America might be, deprived of their political rights."[2] But detachment did not last. The America Cooper found on his return seemed far different from the Republic he remembered. Cooper felt that a new breed of individuals seeking only their own ends was threatening the bonds of community. His growing disaffection led him to attack American newspapers. He did so in an extended series of libel suits; in his characterization of a newspaper editor, the disgusting Steadfast Dodge who appeared in *Homeward Bound* (1838) and *Home As Found* (1838); and in *The American Democrat* (1838), a short work of political criticism. In that work he wrote:

If newspapers are useful in overthrowing tyrants, it is only to establish a tyranny of their own. The press tyrannizes over publick men, letters, the arts, the stage, and even over private life. Under the pretence of protecting publick morals, it is corrupting them to the core, and under the semblance of maintaining liberty, it is gradually establishing a despotism as ruthless, as grasping, and one that is quite as vulgar as that of any christian state known. With loud professions of freedom of opinion, there is no tolerance; with a parade of patriotism, no sacrifice of interests; and with fulsome panegyrics on propriety, too frequently, no decency.[3]

Perhaps this is suggestive of the state of the American press in the 1830s; more surely it represents a protest of established power against a democratized—in this case, middle-class—social order. Cooper expressed a deep anxiety about the moral influence of the press which appeared to him to be "corrupting," "vulgar," and without decency. It had in his eyes the unwelcome characteristics of a middle-class institution: parochialism, scant regard for the sanctity of private life, and grasping self-interest. Most disturbing of all, it had enormous and unwarranted power over the shaping of opinion.

Cooper's fears of a "press-ocracy" were exaggerated, but he was responding to real changes in American journalism. In 1830 the country had 650 weeklies and 65 dailies. The average circulation of a daily was 1,200, so the total daily circulation was roughly 78,000. By 1840 there were 1,141 weeklies and 138 dailies. The dailies averaged 2,200 in circulation for an estimated total daily circulation of 300,000.

Population during the same period was also growing, but more slowly—from 12.9 million to 17.1 million, urban population increasing from .9 million to 1.5 million.[4] But Cooper was not responding to statistics. He knew that newspapers were different, not just more numerous, than the ones he left behind in 1826, and those most different—the "penny papers"—appeared most powerful. The new journals reflected political, social, and technological changes that a thoughtful man might well have been alarmed about. It is now widely agreed that the 1830s, a remarkable decade in so many ways, marked a revolution in American journalism. That revolution led to the triumph of "news" over the editorial and "facts" over opinion, a change which was shaped by the expansion of democracy and the market, and which would lead, in time, to the journalist's uneasy allegiance to objectivity.

The Revolution of the Penny Press

When Cooper left America, as when Tocqueville visited a few years later, the typical American paper was generally a weekly, but there were already many dailies in seaboard cities. The typical daily was four pages long. Its front page was almost exclusively devoted to advertising, and the fourth page likewise was strictly advertising. These outside pages were like the cover of a book or magazine—one turned to the inside to find the content of the paper. Page two carried the editorial columns. Much of page two and page three detailed the arrival of ships in the harbor and the contents of their cargoes, as well as other marine news. On page two one could find an editorial on politics, as well as short "items" of news. Many of the "items" were lifted directly from other newspapers, with credit generally given. Other items were not distinguished, in layout, typography, or style, from editorial—all were expressions of the editor or his party.

Some newspapers were primarily commercial, others were political. The political papers gave greater emphasis to news of national politics. They were financed by political parties, factions of parties, or candidates for office who dictated editorial policy and sometimes wrote the editorials personally. There was nothing deceptive about this—it was standard practice and common knowledge. The party papers were dependent on political leaders, not only for their initial capital and their point of view, but for maintenance through the paid publication of legal notices when the party they backed held power. Edwin Croswell ran the *Albany Argus,* the organ of the Democratic Party in New York, from 1824 to 1840, during which time he was also official state printer. This was the most lucrative post in the state; Croswell estimated it was worth $30,000 a year. Thurlow Weed of the *Albany Evening Journal* succeeded Croswell as state printer. He stated that he and his two partners grossed $50,000 in 1841, though Croswell put the figure at $65,000.[5]

The commercial press and the party press had several important features in common. First, they were expensive. A paper ordinarily cost the reader six cents an issue at a time when the average daily wage for nonfarm labor was less than eighty-five cents. But a person could not buy one issue at a time except at the printer's office. Newspapers were generally sold only by subscription, and annual subscriptions ranged from eight to ten dollars. Not surprisingly, circulation of newspapers was low, usually just one to two thousand for even the most prominent metropolitan papers. Newspaper readership was confined to mercantile and political elites; it is no wonder, then, that newspaper content was limited to commerce and politics.

This is not to say that these papers were staid or sedate. True, dominated as they were by advertising and shipping news, they appear to have been little more than bulletin boards for the business community. But their editorials, in which they took great pride, were strongly partisan, provocative, and ill-tempered. Editors attacked one another ferociously in print, and this sometimes carried over into fist fights or duels. The New York diarist Philip Hone recorded one such incident in 1831:

While I was shaving this morning I witnessed from the front windows an encounter in the streets between William Cullen Bryant, one of the editors of the Evening Post, and Wm L Stone, editor of the Commercial Advertiser. The former commenced the attack by striking Stone over the head with a cowskin; after a few blows the parties closed and the whip was wrested from Bryant and carried off by Stone.[6]

Editing a newspaper was an intensely personal matter. Early newspapers were small operations. One man generally served as editor, reporter (insofar as there was any reporting at all), business manager, and printer. But the personal character of these early papers should not be misunderstood. Many editors were subservient to their political masters and, at the same time, very limited in their views on what was acceptable to put in print. "Journalists," wrote New York editor James Gordon Bennett's contemporary biographer, "were usually little more than secretaries dependent upon cliques of politicians, merchants, brokers, and office-seekers for their position and bread. . . ."[7] Not until the revolution in the press of the 1830s did the editor's ability to express himself in his newspaper grow, and then it grew in new directions—the editor made himself known, not only through editorials, but through the industry, enterprise, and innovation in his news gathering. Paradoxically, the newspaper became a more personal instrument at the same time that it began to emphasize news rather than editorial.

We can trace this development in a makeshift way by examining the names of newspapers in different periods.

Before the 1830s, when newspapers sought the readership of commercial elites, they named themselves accordingly. In Boston, in 1820, the two dailies were *The Boston Daily Advertiser* and the *Boston Patriot and Daily Mercantile Advertiser*. In Baltimore, the dailies in 1820 were the *American and Commercial Daily Advertiser*, the *Federal Gazette and Baltimore Daily Advertiser*, the *Federal Republican and Baltimore Telegraph* (formerly the *Federal Republican and Commercial Gazette*), the *Morning Chronicle and Baltimore Advertiser*, and finally the *Baltimore Patriot and Mercantile Advertiser*. More than half of all newspapers published weekly or more frequently in New York, Boston, Baltimore, Philadelphia, Washington, Charleston, and New Orleans in 1820 had the words "advertiser," "commercial," or "mercantile" in their titles. But, after 1830, few newspapers were founded which bore such names. Instead, there were a great many papers whose names express a kind of *agency*—names like "critic," "herald," "tribune." One might also include as part of this development the papers named "star" or "sun," for both words suggest active objects which illuminate the world. So newspapers, if we can judge from their titles, became less passive, more self-consciously expressive of the editor's personality and convictions after 1830.[8]

The movement from "advertisers" to "heralds" and "suns" in the 1830s has been called the "commercial revolution" in the American press.[9] The "commercial revolution" refers not to all newspapers in the period but to those which most radically broke with tradition and established the model which the mainstream of American journalism has since followed. These were the "penny papers." As the name suggests, what was most obviously original about them is that they sold for a penny, not six cents. Further, rather than selling by annual subscription, they were hawked in the streets each day by newsboys. Their circulation was correspondingly enormous compared to the six-penny journals.

The first penny paper, the *New York Sun,* first published September 3, 1833, had the largest circulation of any paper in the city within a few months—by January, 1834, it claimed a circulation of 5,000. Within two years it was selling 15,000 copies a day. The *Sun* was quickly followed by two other penny papers in New York—the *Evening Transcript* and, on May 6, 1835, James Gordon Bennett's *New York Herald.* In June, 1835, the combined circulation of just these three papers was 44,000; when the *Sun* began in 1833, the combined circulation of all of the city's eleven dailies had been only 26,500.[10]

The penny press spread to the country's other urban, commercial centers—Boston, Philadelphia, and Baltimore. The *Boston Daily Times* appeared February 16, 1836, and within weeks was the city's largest paper, claiming a circulation of 8,000 by the middle of March. In Philadelphia, the *Philadelphia Public Ledger* began March 25, 1836, organized by William Swain and Arunah Abell, New York printers and friends of Benjamin Day, and their partner Azariah Simmons. The *Public Ledger*'s circulation was 10,000 within eight months, and 20,000 after eighteen months, at a time when the largest of the established dailies in the city sold about 2,000. The *Baltimore Sun* was founded in 1837 by Arunah Abell with the backing of his fellow *Public Ledger* proprietors. Within nine months its circulation was over 10,000, more than triple the circulation of any other Baltimore paper.[11]

The penny papers made their way in the world by seeking large circulation and the advertising it attracted, rather than by trusting to subscription fees and subsidies from political parties. This rationalized the economic structure of newspaper publishing. Sources of income that depended on social ties or political fellow feeling were replaced by market-based income from advertising and sales. Sales moved to a cash basis, and the old complaints of editors about subscribers who would not pay declined. Advertising, as well as sales, took on a more democratic cast. First, advertising in the established journals, which heretofore had addressed the reader only insofar as he was a businessman interested in shipping and public sales or a lawyer interested in legal notices, increasingly addressed the newspaper reader as a human being with mortal needs. Patent medicines became the mainstay of the advertising columns.[12] "Want ads" became a more prominent feature of the papers; when P. T. Barnum moved to New York in the winter of 1834–1835 to find a job in a mercantile house, he conducted his job search by reading the "wants" each morning in the *Sun*.[13]

Second, advertising became more strictly an economic exchange, not a moral one: older journals had often refused to print ads for what they believed to be objectionable advertising. The *Journal of Commerce* in New York would not accept advertisements of theaters, lotteries, or "business to be transacted on the Sabbath." The *New England Palladium* in Boston followed a similar policy. The *New York Evening Post* banned lottery advertising and, by the late 1820s, this was fairly common. The penny press, in contrast, was not very fussy about who advertised in its columns. Penny papers were self-righteous in defending their wide-open practices:

Some of our readers complain of the great number of patent medicines advertised in this paper. To this complaint we can only reply that it is for our interest to insert such advertisements as are not indecent or improper in their language, without any inquiry whether the articles advertised are what they purport to be. That is an inquiry for the reader who feels interested in the matter, and not for us, to make. It is sufficient for our purpose that the advertisements are paid for, and that, while we reserve the right of excluding such as are improper to be read, to the advertising public we are impartial, and show no respect to persons, or to the various kinds of business that fill up this little world of ours. One man has as good a right as another to have his wares, his goods, his panaceas, his profession, published to the world in a newspaper, provided he pays for it.[14]

This comment from the *Boston Daily Times* could not better express a policy and a morality of laissez faire. In this, it was representative of the penny press. With an over-the-shoulder nod to propriety, the penny papers appealed to the equal right of any advertiser to employ the public press, so long as the advertiser paid. The self-righteousness of the penny papers, compared to the established press, was peculiarly inverted: they proudly denied their own authority or responsibility for exercising moral judgment in advertising matters and defended this position, without embarrassment, as consistent with their self-interest.

The six-penny papers criticized the penny press for its advertising policies and centered especially on the large number of patent medicine ads. Bennett's *Herald* was the special butt of this criticism. It became the object of abuse from penny papers as well, including Horace Greeley's penny *New York Tribune,* established in 1841, and Henry Raymond's penny *New York Times,* founded in 1851. These papers, it is fair to surmise, coveted Bennett's readership. Greeley criticized the *Sun* and the *Herald* in 1841 for taking the ads of New York's leading abortionist, Madame Restell. On the other hand, the *Tribune*'s columns were themselves filled with patent medicine advertising, and when a reader complained, Greeley wrote: "He should complain to our advertisers themselves, who are not responsible to us for the style or language (if decent) of their advertisements, nor have we any control over them."[15] In 1852 the *Times* wrote that the *Herald* was "the recognized organ of quack doctors."[16] This was, however, the narcissism of small differences: the same issue of the *Times,* for instance, included ads for "The American Mental Alchemist," Dr. Kellinger's Liniment, Doctor Houghton's Pepsin, and Ayer's Cherry Pectoral; both the *Times* and the *Herald* that day ran about two thirds of a column of medical ads. All the penny papers, to greater or lesser degrees, adopted the language and morality of laissez faire.

No less original than the economic organization of the new journalism was its political position. Most of the penny papers, including all of the pioneers in the field, claimed political independence, something that earlier papers rarely pretended to. James Gordon Bennett felt that this was closely tied to the economic design of the penny paper, the "nonsubscriber plan," as he called it, of selling on the streets. Only the penny press could be a free press, he wrote, "simply because it is subservient to none of its readers—known to none of its readers—and entirely ignorant who are its readers and who are not."[17] The penny papers were not only formally independent of political parties but were, relatively speaking, indifferent to political events. The *New York Sun*'s lead on a short item of congressional news was not unusual: "The proceedings of Congress thus far, would not interest our readers."[18] The *Sun* had announced in its first issue that its object was "to lay before the public, at a price within the means of everyone, all the news of the day, and at the same time afford an advantageous medium for advertising." No mention of politics. Early issues of the *New York Transcript* featured fiction on page one and inside focused on local items that rarely included politics. One issue, for instance, included short paragraphs on attempted rape, riot, attempted suicide, mail robbery, stingless bees from Mexico, and even news of an abandoned child left in a basket on a doorstep.[19] A year later, it should be added, articles were longer, there was more court reporting, and there was more news of national politics.

The *Transcript,* like some other penny papers, advertised its divorce from politics. The paper announced in its inaugural issue that, so far as politics goes, *"we have none."* The *Boston Daily Times* claimed to be "neutral in politics" and advised political parties to find the way into the newspaper columns by advertising. The *Baltimore Sun* proclaimed:

We shall give no place to religious controversy nor to political discussions of merely partisan character. On political principles, and questions involving the interests of honor of the whole country, it will be free, firm and temperate. Our object will be the common good, without regard to that of sects, factions, or parties; and for this object we shall labor without fear or partiality.[20]

While some penny papers failed, at least at first, to attend very much to politics at all, others covered politics more completely than the six-penny press, and just as vigorously. But even these papers, like the *New York Herald,* did not identify their mission or their hopes with partisan politics; to some extent, the world of parties became just a part of a larger universe of news. The penny papers were not all determined to be politically neutral. Horace Greeley's aim in establishing the *New York Tribune* in 1841 was to found "a journal removed alike from servile partisanship on the one hand and from gagged, mincing neutrality on the other."[21] But even Greeley's avowal of principled partisan politics supports the general point, for Greeley contrasts the *Tribune* to the "gagged, mincing neutrality" he surely associated with some of his penny rivals.

The penny press was novel, not only in economic organization and political stance, but in its content. The character of this originality is simply put: the penny press invented the modern concept of "news." For the first time the American newspaper made it a regular practice to print political news, not just foreign but domestic, and not just national but local; for the first time it printed reports from the police, from the courts, from the streets, and from private households. One might say that, for the first time, the newspaper reflected not just commerce or politics but social life. To be more precise, in the 1830s the newspapers began to reflect, not the affairs of an elite in a small trading society, but the activities of an increasingly varied, urban, and middle-class society of trade, transportation, and manufacturing.

The six-penny papers responded to the penny newcomers with charges of sensationalism. This accusation was substantiated less by the way the penny papers treated the news (there were no sensational photographs, of course, no cartoons or drawings, no large headlines) than by the fact that the penny papers would print "news"—as we understand it—at all. It was common for penny papers, covering a murder trial, to take a verbatim transcript of the trial and spread it across most, or all, of the front page. What the six-penny press decried as immoral was that a murder trial should be reported at all. The typical news story was the verbatim report, whether it be of a presidential address, a murder trial, or the annual statement of the United States Treasury.

News became the mainstay of the daily paper. The penny papers did not depend on the usual trickle of stale news but sought out the news. They took pride in their activity, as the *New York Transcript* made clear in 1834:

There are eleven large and regularly established daily papers in this city; and with the exception of the *Courier and Enquirer,* and perhaps the *Times,* not one of them employs a news reporter, or takes any other pains to obtain accurate and correct local information—on the other hand there are two small daily NEWS papers, (ourselves and our cotemporary,) and those two employ four reporters, exclusively to obtain the earliest, fullest, and most correct intelligence on every local incident; and two of these latter arise at 3 in the morning, at which hour they attend the police courts, and are there employed, with short intermissions, till the close of the office at 8 in the evening, while others are obtaining correct information about the city.[22]

In 1835 the *Herald* joined the *Transcript* and its "cotemporary" the *Sun* and, by the end of 1837, boasted two Washington correspondents, permanent correspondents in Jamaica and Key West; occasional correspondents in London, Philadelphia, and Boston; two Canadian correspondents during the MacKenzie Rebellion of 1837; and a correspondent roving New York State to report on the wheat crop. This was expensive, the *Herald* noted, but it was done to gratify the public.[23] A year later the *Herald* had hired six European correspondents as regular contributors.[24]

The institution of paid reporters was not only novel but, to some, shocking. Until the late 1820s, New York coverage of Washington politics relied mainly on members of Congress writing occasionally to their home papers. Some regular "letter writers" passed on dull reports and summarized speeches. James Gordon Bennett, writing in 1827 and 1828 for the *New York Enquirer,* initiated more lively reporting with his dispatches on "the court of John Q. Adams."[25] Adams never accommodated himself to the impudence of the new journalism. He wrote with disgust in his diary in 1842 that sons of President Tyler "divulged all his cabinet secrets to a man named Parmalee and John Howard Payne, hired reporters for Bennett's *Herald* newspaper in New York. . . ."[26] His use of "hired" to qualify "reporters" suggests how new, and perhaps disreputable, the institution of a reportorial staff was.

One way to see the dominance of the newspaper by news, which the penny press initiated, is to regard it as the decline of the editorial. This is much less than the whole story, but it was one of the ways in which contemporaries understood the change they were witnessing. In an article in *North American Review* in 1866, Horace Greeley's biographer James Parton sought to explain the phenomenal success and influence of James Gordon Bennett's *New York Herald.* Parton reviewed current opinion about the *Herald.* One view was that the *Herald* rose to prominence because it was a very bad newspaper, pandering to the bad taste of the public. A second view, and Parton's own view, was that the *Herald* succeeded because it was a very good newspaper—but that the newspaper had become something different from what the *Herald*'s critics assumed it to be. Parton argued that people who thought the *Herald* a bad paper spoke mainly of its editorials which, he admitted, were execrable. Bennett was ornery, prejudiced, misanthropic, and opportunistic, and his editorials reflected his nature. But, Parton went on, the editorial is dying and only the news is the "point of rivalry" between papers. The success of a journal had come to depend "wholly and absolutely upon its success in getting, and its skill in exhibiting, the news. The word *newspaper* is the exact and complete description of the thing which the true journalist aims to produce."[27]

News was, indeed, the point of rivalry with the penny papers. We have so completely identified the concept of "news" with the newspaper itself that it may be difficult to understand how dramatic a change the penny press represented. Until the 1830s, a newspaper provided a service to political parties and men of commerce; with the penny press a newspaper sold a product to a general readership and sold the readership to advertisers. The product sold to readers was "news," and it was an original product in several respects. First, it claimed to represent, colorfully but without partisan coloring, events in the world. Thus the news product of one paper could be compared to that of another for accuracy, completeness, liveliness, and timeliness. The *Herald* in 1840 crowed over the accuracy and fullness of its report of a speech by Daniel Webster and ridiculed a Mr. Stansbury, reporting for a six-penny paper, who "knows nothing of stenography and wrote out some thirty or forty pages of small quarto foolscap, in long hand."[28] The *Herald* patted itself on the back, on one occasion, for having had the only reporter on the school-visiting trip of the City Council and School Fund commissioners and, on another, for having been the only paper in the city to print the United States Treasurer's report in full.[29] As for the timeliness of news, the *Herald* and the *Sun* rivaled each other in printing "extras" and praising themselves for it. The *Herald,* for instance, boasted on November 21, 1840, of its extra on the day before announcing the arrival of British forces in Canton: *"No other newspaper establishment in New York had the news at that time, nor could they get it, they are so inefficient and lazy."* [30]

During the first decades of the nineteenth century, newspapers had increasingly tried to be up-to-date, especially in reporting the arrival of ships and in printing the news they brought with them. The New York papers began to send out small boats to incoming ships to gather up news; in the late 1820s, several papers formed an association which bought a fast boat to meet the ships for all association members. But only with the penny press was the competition for news "beats" firmly established as the chief basis of the newspaper business. Thanks to James Gordon Bennett, even advertising became more timely. Until the 1840s advertisers paid a flat fee, often on an annual basis, to place the same notice in a paper day after day. In 1847 Bennett announced that, beginning January 1, 1848, all ads in the *Herald* would have to be resubmitted daily. This encouraged changing ad copy so that Bennett's managing editor, Frederic Hudson, exclaimed in his history of American journalism:

... the advertisements form the most interesting and practical city news. They are the hopes, the thoughts, the joys, the plans, the shames, the losses, the mishaps, the fortunes, the pleasures, the miseries, the politics, and the religion of the people. Each advertiser is therefore a reporter, a sort of penny-a-liner, he paying the penny. What a picture of the metropolis one day's advertisements in the *Herald* presents to mankind![31]

The penny papers' concept of news not only created news as a marketable product whose attributes—particularly timeliness—could be measured, it invented a genre which acknowledged, and so enhanced, the importance of everyday life. In literature until the eighteenth century, aristocratic conventions had dictated that the common aspects of everyday life could receive only comic treatment, if they were dealt with at all.[32] A similar convention appears to have prevailed in journalism—newspapers simply did not report on the lives of ordinary people. Although the War of 1812 ended the almost exclusive dominance of foreign news in the American press, local or hometown news, before the penny papers, remained a minor feature. The commercial press proved less reliable in reporting local prices of commodities or stocks than in reporting foreign news and shipping news.[33] The penny press, in contrast, focused on the nearby and the everyday, and for the first time hired reporters on a regular basis to cover local news. Reporters were assigned to the police, the courts, the commercial district, the churches, high society, and sports. The penny papers made the "human interest story" not only an important part of daily journalism but its most characteristic feature.

The penny papers saw news in ordinary events where no one had seen anything noteworthy before. This is nowhere better indicated than in those moments when even the most aggressive penny papers had a hard time claiming there had been any news. In an item headed "The News of the Week," the *Herald* of March 12, 1837 wrote:

THE NEWS OF THE WEEK

Is not of very much importance. Yet the most insignificant events can be swelled to matters of great moment, if they are traced up eternity to their causes, or down eternity to their consequences. Not a single incident—not the slightest event that does not become a part of the time past or the time to come, and thus mix with the greatest everlasting both in time and in space. The news of a day—of a week—is supposed by the superficial blockheads who conduct newspapers and govern nations—or cheat the public—or sell quack medicine—or stir up politics—or shave in Wall Street, to be of trifling moment. And so it is to them. To the philosopher who dips deeply into things, it is different.[34]

The penny papers inaugurated this democratic attitude toward the happenings of the world: any event, no matter how apparently trivial, might qualify for print in a newspaper.

The attention to everyday life did not necessarily mean attention to the familiar. The penny papers printed much that would appeal to the ordinary middle-class reader precisely because it was exotic—it concerned the everyday lives of other classes. Benjamin Day at the *Sun* pioneered the coverage of the criminal, especially in reporting police news. Bennett, from the *Herald*'s earliest days, reported on the social affairs of the elite of New York and Saratoga. As was usual with Bennett, he advertised his own innovation:

No one ever attempted till now to bring out the graces, the polish, the elegancies, the bright and airy attributes of social life. We never can be an indepennent [*sic*], a happy, an original people, unless we rely on our resources, either for fashion, gaiety, politics, potatoes, flour, or manufactures. Our purpose has been, and is, to give to the highest society of New York a life, a variety, a piquancy, a brilliancy, an originality that will entirely outstrip the worn out races of Europe, who have been degenerating for the last twenty generations.[35]

Diarist Philip Hone recorded the presence of a *Herald* reporter at a fancy dress ball he attended in 1840. The host consented to the presence of the reporter, Hone wrote, because this imposed on the reporter "a sort of obligation . . . to refrain from abusing the house, the people of the house, and their guests, which would have been done in case of a denial." Hone continued: "But this is a hard alternative; to submit to this kind of surveillance is getting to be intolerable, and nothing but the force of public opinion will correct the insolence. . . ."[36] Public opinion was in no such mood. Bennett devoted most of page one to this ball, suggesting that it "created a greater sensation in the fashionable world than anything of the kind since the creation of the world, or the fall of beauteous woman, or the frolic of old Noah, after he left the ark and took to wine and drinking."[37]

The attention to the everyday, and particularly the focus on the social life of the rich, helped obscure the division of public and private life. For an editor like Bennett, little was privileged, personal, or private—though he was cautious enough in his reports on high society to use initials rather than names. Penny papers introduced news of family squabbles and scandals. While notices of marriages and deaths were familiar in newspapers, printing birth announcements was not. When the *Pittsburgh Daily Express* advocated the propriety of recording births in the papers, Bennett's sarcastic comment in the *Herald* indicated his approval, while protecting his flank of propriety: "Why, the practice would rouse up all the Miss Squeamishes in the country. It is no argument that they do such things in England; they do a great many things in England that would not suit here!"[38]

In February, 1848, a Washington correspondent for the *New York Tribune,* writing under the name "Persimmon," sketched the luncheon habits of Representative William Sawyer of Ohio. His article detailed how each day at two o'clock Sawyer moved from his seat in the House to a place behind and to the left of the Speaker's chair, near the window, and proceeded to take out his lunch. He would unfold a greasy paper and eat the bread and sausage it contained, wipe his hands on the paper, and throw the paper out the window. He used his jackknife for a toothpick and his pantaloons and coatsleeves for a napkin. Sawyer objected to this coverage and his friends succeeded in passing a resolution (119 to 46) ousting all *Tribune* reporters from their seats or desks on the House floor. "What was the offense of the 'Tribune,' after all?" asked the *Tribune* correspondent in a later article. "Nothing in the world but stating a few facts, not against the moral character of anybody, but about the personal habits of a member of the House."[39]

Shortly before this incident, the House had failed to censure the organ of the Democratic administration for calling a member of the House a liar. That was a kind of journalism they were used to. The new journalism of the penny press, on the other hand, ushered in a new order, a shared social universe in which "public" and "private" would be redefined. It is no wonder that this should have appalled those who believed the early days of the American Republic had re-established the elevated public realm of the Greek city-states and the Roman Forum. Something new was threatening this idyll, something Hannah Arendt refers to as the creation of *society*, "that curiously hybrid realm where private interests assume public significance."[40] Both meanings of interest—self-aggrandizement and curiosity—seem fitting here. With the growth of cities and of commerce, everyday life acquired a density and a fascination quite new, "society" was palpable as never before, and the newspapers—especially the penny papers—were both agent and expression of this change.

Granting that this fairly describes the changes in American journalism in the 1830s, what can account for it? Why did it happen? More precisely, why did it happen when and where it did? Recapitulating, what took place is that a cheap press originated in the 1830s in New York, a city which was already the national hub of interurban trade, transportation, and communication.[41] It quickly spread to the other leading urban centers—Boston, Philadelphia, and Baltimore. The new press was distinctive economically—in selling cheaply, in its distribution by newsboys, and in its reliance on advertising; politically—in its claims to independence from party; and substantively—in its focus on news, a genre it invented. What accounts for all this?

These changes in journalism were closely connected to broad social, economic, and political change which I shall refer to as the rise of a "democratic market society." This meant the expansion of a market economy and political democracy or, put another way, the democratization of business and politics sponsored by an urban middle class which trumpeted "equality" in social life. To show that this is what was happening in the 1830s and to relate it to journalism is to do more than conclusive and compact evidence will allow. But there is much to make the case persuasive. It becomes all the more appealing when the inadequacies of likely alternative explanations are made plain. The two that require most attention are the technological argument and the literacy argument.

Explanations of the Revolution in Journalism

The Technological Argument

The technological argument is the powerful idea that technological advances in printing and related industries and the development of railroad transportation and later telegraphic communications were the necessary preconditions for a cheap, mass-circulation, news-hungry, and independent press. This idea is more a reflex in commentary on American journalism than a well-considered theory, but it is a common and fundamental reflex and bears examination.[42]

The pertinence of a technological explanation to radical changes in journalism in the 1830s is beyond question. The wooden, hand-powered press, practically unchanged since Gutenberg, was transformed in the early nineteenth century. The first iron presses came into use at the turn of the century. While no faster than the wooden presses, they were easier to operate and the quality of their impressions was higher. A series of mechanical innovations in the next two decades improved these flatbed hand presses, but the manually powered presses began to give way to steam and the flatbed design to a cylinder press. The first book in America printed by a steam-driven press was published in 1823. By the 1840s the steam press dominated the American market. The change from the flatbed to the cylinder press was just as important. Frederick Koenig pioneered in both developments, inventing a steam-powered cylinder press which was first used to print the *London Times* of November 29, 1814. It produced one thousand sheets per hour per side, roughly ten times faster than the best flatbed hand press. Still, it was not instantly accepted. The cylinder press required greater skill to use than the flatbed press, and the quality of the work it produced was not great. Further, its productivity far outstripped the needs of most printers, so its use was confined to newspapers and magazines. The first two-cylinder press was the "Hoe Type Revolving Machine," first operated for the *Philadelphia Public Ledger* in 1847. The Hoe machine, and its improvements, became standard equipment for the world's newspapers in the nineteenth century. The speed and convenience of the cylinder press were increased in the 1850s and 1860s when "stereotyping" (casting plates for printing from molds) was perfected for curved plates.

What may have been the most important technical development of the early nineteenth century came in paper manufacture. During the eighteenth century, scarcity of paper was the greatest problem for printers. Paper was made primarily from rags. In an early effort in consumer ecology, popular education stressed the preservation of rags which were then picked up by carts to be taken to the paper mills. In 1799, N. L. Robert patented the Fourdrinier paper-making machine, still using rags for raw material. (Not until 1844 would a process be developed to make ground wood pulp available for paper, and it was not introduced to the United States until 1866.) By the late eighteenth century, processes for reducing rags to pulp had developed faster than processes for transforming the pulp to paper. The Fourdrinier process changed this and, after 1827, when it was first imported, was widely used in America.[43]

None of these improvements were unrelated to changes in transportation. The development of railroads and canals in the early nineteenth century made it possible for the best equipment in manufacturing to reach a wider market. In 1810 the two-hundred-odd American papermills furnished newsprint only to nearby localities, but, during the 1830s, railroad transportation began to carry the best products of the best machinery to more distant places. In 1830 the United States had only twenty-three miles of railroad. In 1840 it had three thousand and would have thirty thousand by the Civil War.[44]

Needless to say, these developments were crucial to the rise of high circulation newspapers and helped make it possible to sell newspapers cheaply. (At the same time, one might add, they made starting a newspaper a more weighty capital investment.) But the causal relationship did not go only one way. Most of the early nineteenth century developments were merely mechanical—few could not have been developed, in terms of the world's supply of knowledge, decades, or even centuries, before. Invention in printing and paper manufacture was not autonomous but was stimulated by other factors. The increasing demand for books and newspapers was what one historian of printing called a "permanent incentive to invention." [45] A far from negligible factor was that newspapers themselves supported inventors. Koenig's work was subsidized by John Walter, proprietor of the *Times*. In America, the penny papers were consistently the first to install the latest machinery in printing. Indeed, it may be more accurate to say that the penny press introduced steam power to American journalism than to say that steam brought forth the penny press. The *New York Sun* printed its first edition on a flatbed hand-run press making two hundred impressions an hour. Within a few months editor Benjamin Day announced the purchase of a cylinder press making one thousand impressions an hour. By that time the *Sun* was already a spectacular success, rivaling the largest six-penny papers in the city with a circulation of four thousand. By 1835, when the *Sun* became the first newspaper in the country to purchase a steam-driven press, its circulation was already approaching twenty thousand.[46]

The development of the telegraph illustrates a similar interaction between technological change and business enterprise in journalism. The telegraph came into use in the 1840s, after the penny press had proved itself. The newspapers encouraged the development of the telegraph, and this was especially true of a penny paper, the *Baltimore Sun*. The first telegraph line in the United States was an experimental line between Washington and Baltimore. The *Sun*'s early use of it encouraged wider acceptance of telegraphic communication, although most of the press, like most of the public, was at first unwilling to believe, or unable to comprehend, its promise.[47] The *Sun*'s printing of the telegraphically communicated news of President Polk's war message in 1846 was reprinted in Paris by the French Academy of Sciences alongside an authenticated copy of the original address; this demonstration of the accuracy of the telegraph helped persuade the French government to make appropriations for a Paris-Brussels telegraph line.[48] While Robert Luther Thompson, in his history of the American telegraph industry, argues that the outbreak of the war with Mexico in 1846 "virtually forced" newspapers to use the telegraph, the evidence he cites suggests something different. He indicates that James Gordon Bennett of the *New York Herald,* Horace Greeley of the *New York Tribune,* Moses Beach, the new editor of the *New York Sun,* and William Swain of the *Philadelphia Public Ledger* made the first and fullest use of telegraph services.[49] Only the penny press, then, exploited the telegraph, just as the penny papers had been first to use new machinery in printing. Penny papers specifically, not newspapers generally, made use of the telegraph; the peculiar disposition of the penny press to seek timely news, not an irresistible attraction of fast news service in wartime, is important here.

The modern mass-circulation newspaper would be unimaginable without the technical developments of the early nineteenth century. They obviously facilitated the rise of the penny press. But they do not explain it. Technological change was not autonomous and itself begs explanation. And while it made mass circulation newspapers possible, it did not make them necessary or inevitable. Further, while the technological argument relates to the low cost and high circulation of the penny papers, it says nothing at all about their distinctive content.

The Literacy Argument

A second hypothesis is worth considering. We could say that schooling and widespread literacy developed in the nineteenth century and stimulated the demand for newspapers. Because new readers were unsophisticated, their tastes tended to be simple, concrete, particular, and local. Not only would this explain the growth of newspaper circulation, but it would explain the emphasis in the penny press on local news and human interest.

This hypothesis, which, like the technological argument, appears as a kind of reflex in histories of journalism, is difficult to investigate.[50] While it is hard to trace the effects of technology, it is at least easy to know when technology is introduced or altered. It is hard to know anything at all about literacy in the early nineteenth century. Most historical studies of literacy are, at best, studies of illiteracy. That is, we can know what percentage of married men in a particular village were so illiterate that they could not sign their own marriage certificates. But we do not know whether or not they could read.[51] Nor do we know what we can assume of those who did sign their own names. Could they have read a broadside? a newspaper? the Bible? Blackstone? Did they? Would they have wanted to or needed to?

Without literacy, large-circulation newspapers are impossible. But is an increase in literacy in itself a stimulus to newspaper circulation? There are good reasons to doubt it. In general, we make too much of a fetish of the term "literacy." The difference between not being able to read at all and being able to read a bit may not be socially or psychologically significant; it may not represent much of a leap in mental powers or capacities for abstraction. It may be simply a marginal increase in receptivity to an environment which includes some print. Becoming literate is not primarily a question of the intelligence of the learner and the availability of formal instruction; it has more to do with the nature of the environment and the character of instruction.

This condenses two points. The first point is that the nature of the environment constrains the development of literacy. "The most pervasive factor of all in restricting literacy," Ian Watt writes of eighteenth-century England, "was probably the lack of positive inducement to learn." He goes on:

Being able to read was a necessary accomplishment only for those destined to the middle-class occupations—commerce, administration and the professions; and since reading is inherently a difficult psychological process and one which requires continual practice, it is likely that only a small proportion of the labouring classes who were technically literate developed into active members of the reading public, and further, that the majority of these were concentrated in those employments where reading and writing was a vocational necessity.[52]

If Watt is right that people learn to read when reading becomes important, then the literacy argument should be inverted. Rather than looking for direct evidence of literacy,

we might instead seek reasons why literacy would be necessary or encouraged and *presume* from that a growth in
literacy. Rather than reading through the marriage records,
we should look for the use of the written word in advertising
posters and shop signs; we should look for the growth of
coffeehouses, artificial lighting, and newspapers.[53] The appeal
in the history of newspapers, the history of books and
printing, and the history of literature and culture to the
changing "demands" of a growing literate public very nearly
puts the cart before the horse. No doubt it is true that a
literate society is radically different from a nonliterate society,
and the invention of writing was surely a sea change in
human consciousness.[54] But the spread of literacy to the
illiterate portion of a literate society is quite another matter—
more subtle, more complex, and, very likely, as much a result
of increased printing as a cause of it.

But even this formulation—that literacy follows inducements to it—is too narrowly conceived. This is the second
point: learning to read is a social process dependent for its
success on who is teaching, what kind of reading materials are
being used, and how the students feel about themselves. The
Brazilian educator, Paulo Freire, has written of the larger
human context of literacy:

Learning to read and write ought to be an opportunity for men to
know what *speaking the word* really means: a human act implying
reflection and action. As such it is a primordial human right and not
the privilege of a few. Speaking the word is not a true act if it is not
at the same time associated with the right of self-expression and
world-expression, of creating and re-creating, of deciding and
choosing and ultimately participating in society's historical
process.[55]

What would explain a rise in literacy, then, in a literate
society, would be an extension of political and economic rights
or, more generally, an extension to more persons of the sense
that they are actors in history. That Americans were more

likely than Europeans to have this sense in the eighteenth and nineteenth centuries may help account for the country's reputation as unusually literate and attached to reading.[56]

What would account for an absence of widespread literacy in a literate society would be any conditions preventing the participation of people in the society's decision making. There is evidence for nineteenth century England which supports this. It appears that the rudiments of literacy were available in England before literature developed to improve or exploit it. There apparently was a literate working-class public able to read newspapers before 1820. The circulation of several of the radical papers ran far ahead of that of the leading daily, the *Times,* or the leading weekly, the *Observer.* These latter papers had circulations only slightly larger than their six-penny American counterparts. But Cobbett's two-penny *Register* ran forty to sixty thousand copies a week in 1816–1817. The *Northern Star* sold ten thousand papers a week within its first four months during the Chartist movement. At its height in 1839, it sold forty to sixty thousand copies a week.[57]

Was this a "demand" for newspapers? Or was it a result of "inducements" to a reading public? If a demand, why was the demand so fitful, rising and falling with the availability of radical political papers and radical political hopes? If a demand, why so specific, failing to increase the circulation of the major dailies? If a general "demand" for newspapers in a competitive market, why did it fail to force the major dailies to lower their prices and seek a wider readership? The notion of "demand" explains nothing by itself. As for "inducements," there are different kinds, and the strictly occupational inducements that Watt writes about, important as they may appear, may be less vital than the whole range of social changes, many of them political, that enable persons to emerge from what Freire calls the "culture of silence."[58]

To state the case more modestly, literacy is a necessary, but not sufficient, condition for a growth in newspaper circulation. Kenneth Lockridge's study of literacy in colonial New England is relevant here. Lockridge found that, in 1660, 60 percent of New England males signed their wills; it was 70 percent in 1710, 85 percent in 1760, and 90 percent by 1790. He estimates that half of those unable to sign wills could read. Thus, there was practically universal adult male literacy in New England by 1790. Lockridge links this to a Protestant educational impulse and strengthens his case by showing that literacy elsewhere in the colonies was lower than in New England, while literacy in other devoutly Protestant countries—Scotland and Sweden—was remarkably high.[59]

But what did the literacy of New England and Scotland and Sweden do for advances in printing technology? What did it do for newspaper circulation? It did nothing at all. The main reading material remained religious books. The extraordinary literacy rate did not produce a secular press, and when the cheap, high-circulation press appeared, it did not appear in these areas of highest literacy but in urban commercial centers and, most of all, in New York.

The Natural History Argument

The literacy argument begs important questions, but it has the merit of being a genuine explanation—a statement of a cause and its consequences and an effort to trace a reasonable connection between them. Most histories of American newspapers have sought only to describe, not to explain, the changes in American journalism. They take a Whiggish tone, intimating a natural progress toward the "modern" newspaper, though they never bother to define what "modern" means. The progress they see is from a captive press to a free, independent press. Walter Lippmann, in an essay written in 1931, provides a statement of this position more elegant than most but still representative of many of the works of historians and journalists-turned-historians. Lippmann suggests that any nation's press will naturally pass through stages of development. In the first stage, the press is a monopoly controlled by government. The press then passes to a stage where political parties, not government, control publication. In the third stage, the press breaks from both government and party "by enlisting the commercially profitable support of a large body of readers." In the United States, of course, this stage begins with the penny papers. Lippmann sights a fourth, or "professional," era in journalism emerging after World War I. When this stage should reach full flower, he writes, newspapers would institutionalize the use of "trained intelligence." They would be so attached to the conscientious pursuit of an "approximation to objective fact" that they would be free even of the changing tastes and prejudices of the public itself.[60]

Lippmann intended to help usher in this final stage, but his essay suggests that it will evolve of its own accord. The view that the development of the press is governed by a self-explanatory evolutionary dynamic is made explicit in one of the few significant sociological comments on the press, Robert Park's 1925 essay, "The Natural History of the Newspaper":

The newspaper, like the modern city, is not wholly a rational product. No one sought to make it just what it is. In spite of all the efforts of individual men and generations of men to control it and to make it something after their own heart, it has continued to grow and change in its own incalculable ways.[61]

The history of a newspaper, then, is a *natural* history, the story of the unfolding evolution of a social form. The modern newspaper is "the type that has survived under the conditions of modern life," and so the natural history of the press is the history of this "surviving species." It is, Park writes, "an account of the conditions under which the existing newspaper has grown up and taken form."

Park then makes a further specification: the struggle for existence, for a newspaper, is the struggle for circulation.

This is right, on the whole, for the period since the 1830s, wrong for any time before that. Part of the significance of the penny papers is precisely that they created a struggle for circulation. This is not the only instance where Park read a modern assumption of journalism back into the past. He argued that the first newspapers were "simply devices for organizing gossip." In fact, the first newspapers were more attuned to business and political news than anything resembling local "gossip." Park emphasized gossip, incorrectly, because he was trying to establish that the newspaper was an important institution in the transition of social life from tradition to modernity, from village to city, from "community" to "society." Thus he argued that "the work of the newspaper, as a gatherer and interpreter of the news, was but an extension of the function which was otherwise performed spontaneously by the community itself through the medium of personal contact and gossip." According to Park, the newspaper has the same function in modern society that gossip took in the traditional village. How well does it serve its function? Park's answer was foreordained by his governing Darwinian assumptions: "Humanly speaking, the present newspapers are about as good as they can be."

Park's essay is important because his self-consciousness about "natural history" makes explicit what would most probably be the standard explanation of the history of American journalism, if standard histories of journalism sought self-consciously to be explanatory. It is a "natural history" Lippmann offers in his stages of the growing independence of newspapers (or, as it might be better put, the changing character of the dependence of newspapers, which bowed first to government, then to parties, then to the public, and finally to the professionals). It is a natural history, often self-congratulatory or self-serving, seldom self-evident, that most histories of newspapers provide. The basic reference work is

Frank Luther Mott's *American Journalism,* an invaluable chronicle—but only a chronicle, characterized by what Mott calls his "sympathetic admiration" for American journalism and his conviction that "no generalization about it is safe."[62] (No generalization *is* safe, but we live by them and with them.)

Mott offers no overarching explanation of changes in American journalism. Where he does seek to explain pieces of the puzzle, he is brief and unconvincing. He lists four factors to account for the growth of newspaper circulation between 1833 and 1860. First, the population grew. Second, public education and increased literacy created "a nation of readers." Third, more democratic forms of government increased popular interest in public affairs. Finally, the reduction in newspaper prices made the press available to poorer people. But why, for instance, were newspaper prices reduced? Mott acknowledges only the technological improvements in presses and paper-making which made cheaper papers possible. Why did only the penny papers lower prices? Mott does not say. He identifies the penny press with the industrial revolution, but he is most laconic in defining what this means. He tells us only that "behind it all was the machine."[63]

In one respect, I will emulate Park's advice, if not his example. Park called for an account of the "conditions" that brought into being the newspaper as we know it. I will try to provide such an accounting. But to do so is not to write a natural history nor to write a history without explanation. The endeavor does not take inevitability for granted, nor does it assume that the important factors are unconnected to conscious human activity. On the contrary, the inadequacies of the arguments about technology and about literacy stem from their eagerness for technical solutions which bypass considerations of how individual and collective human choices are made. Constrained by social circumstances, people make their own history and, sometimes, even unmake the conditions and conventions that guided them.

The Age of Egalitarianism and the Press

The 1830s are commonly known as the "Jacksonian era" or the age of "Jacksonian Democracy." A standard pocket history of the United States by Allen Nevins and Henry Steele Commager titles the chapter on this period "Jacksonian Democracy Sweeps In." The authors summarize Jackson's creed as "faith in the common man; belief in political equality; belief in equal economic opportunity; hatred of monopoly, special privilege, and the intricacies of capitalistic finance." They argue that Jackson's policies implemented this creed and that a democratic wave swept the country in the form of manhood suffrage, informal manners, a cheap press, public schooling, and the advance of the religious sects most democratic in their governance.[64]

For all the abuse this view has taken in the past decade or two, it does not seem to me to have been seriously tarnished. Rather than destroying the view of the 1830s as a democratic era, revisionist historians have just located the egalitarianism more precisely, not in the person or party of Jackson, but in a sharp democratization of both business and politics that transcended party. Revisionists have shown that long before Jackson, as Tocqueville and other European visitors observed, the United States was more democratic in politics and manners than European nations. They have shown, sometimes in excruciating detail, that wealth was not more evenly distributed in the 1830s than before—indeed, it appears that the contrary may be true.[65] Douglas Miller has even argued that

America had become progressively more democratic from 1789 to the 1820s and that the Jacksonian period reversed this development; the gentry declined, but a wealthy capitalist class replaced it so that visions of a classless society were belied in the very years in which they were most fervently discussed.[66]

But all this, it seems to me, far from being an attack on the idea that the 1830s were an egalitarian age, confirms just that hypothesis. Equality in the 1830s and 1840s meant the opening of careers to talent, the opening of opportunity to persons regardless of birth or breeding. *That* is what the age of Jackson celebrated. An even distribution of income had nothing to do with it. But more people acquired wealth and political power and brought with them a zeal for equal opportunity that led to the expansion of public education, the denial of government-granted monopolies to corporations and more flexible procedures for incorporating, the abolition of licensing regulations for doctors and lawyers, and other reforms we identify as "Jacksonian." It seems clear that in the United States, not unlike France and England in the same era, the angry shouts of "aristocracy" and "monopoly" came primarily from a growing urban middle class, while the epithets "anarchy" and "democracy" were hurled at this bourgeoisie by established mercantile elites. Contrary to Tocqueville and contrary to the implications of the revisionists, America did have to suffer a democratic revolution. It did so beginning in the years after 1815 and reaching a height in the 1830s and 1840s. In those decades the country was transformed from a liberal mercantilist republic, still cradled in aristocratic values, family, and deference, to an egalitarian market democracy, where money had new power, the individual new standing, and the pursuit of self-interest new honor. This is what Fenimore Cooper, on his return from Europe, had sensed and feared.

In the 1830s, established mercantile and financial leaders

in the cities were jostled by a newer, more numerous group of enterprising capitalists whose advance culminated symbolically, if not practically, in the assault on the United States Bank. There was not a sharp division between the old gentry and the new wealth; in New York, the center of the nation's economy, all came to meet at the common forum of the New York Stock Exchange. But the Exchange itself, founded in 1817 and not of much significance until the late 1820s, symbolized the new economic order.[67] A democratization of economic life was in progress.[68] By this I mean simply that more people were entering into a cash (and credit) nexus by becoming investors and by consuming goods produced outside the household and that their attitudes and ambitions were increasingly conditioned by this fact.

Economic development was promoted and shared by many rather than few. This is well illustrated in the financing of the railroads. Between 1830 and 1850, the miles of track rose from less than one hundred to nearly nine thousand. The rails were promoted by the large and small merchants of the chief seaport cities. When the Western Railroad in Massachusetts was financed in 1835, it had 2,800 individual stockholders, most of them owning from one to four hundred-dollar shares. The largest stockholder had just 200 shares and the 100 largest stockholders together held less than 40 percent of the stock.[69] What private capital came to the railroads before 1860, historian George Taylor observes, came from "a multitude of private savers, both large and small."[70]

After the War of 1812 and especially after the depression of 1818, investment shifted from shipping to manufacturing and transportation. Booming economic conditions in the South and West in the 1820s led to increased demand in those regions for the manufactured goods of the Northeast—textiles, leather products, clothes, shoes, and farm machinery. More and more products were included in the market; fewer things were made at home for home use. By 1830, the radical shift from homemade to shop- and factory-made goods was well along, especially in the Northeast. Not only goods, like textiles, but also services were sold in the market. For instance, people turned from home care and home remedies to doctors and patent medicines for their health needs. Doctors could compete favorably with family care because the improvement of roads and the concentration of population in cities dramatically cut the cost of a physician's home visit.[71]

The penny papers themselves contributed directly to the extension of the market in two ways. First, they made advertisements more available to more people and so enlarged the potential market for manufactured goods. Second, they transformed the newspaper from something to be borrowed or read at a club or library to a product one bought for home consumption. Isaac Clark Pray observed that matches, which replaced the tin box and flint and steel, became popular about the same time as the penny press and had this same effect:

The cheap matches and the cheap newspapers were sold in every street. Families before this, had borrowed coals of fire and newspapers of their richer neighbors. With the reduced prices, each family had a pride in keeping its own match-box, and in taking its favorite daily journal.[72]

The democratization of economic life brought with it attitudes that stressed economic gain to the exclusion of social aims; business practice more regularly began to reward strictly economic ties over broader ones. A poor boy from Connecticut who became a successful New York businessman, recalling this period, observed that New England boys did better than native New Yorkers in store, counting room, and office work. He gave two explanations:

One is, they are not afraid to work, or to run errands, or do cheerfully what they are told to do. A second reason, they do their work quickly. A New York boy has many acquaintances—a New England boy has none, and is not called upon to stop and talk, when sent out by the merchant.[73]

The comment is instructive: socializing was coming to be seen as, and perhaps to some extent coming to be, a barrier to economic success, not its prerequisite.

The bourgeois revolution of the Jacksonian period was as visible in politics as in business. By the 1820s the party system of the early years of the Republic had collapsed. Though fourteen states had had relatively well-established two-party systems, by 1824 only five states still had elections contested in terms of the old party designations of Federalist and Republican. But a "second American party system" emerged between 1828 and 1840. It was not a continuation or revival of the earlier system. It was something quite new. For one thing, electoral regulations changed what politics meant. In 1800 only two states chose presidential electors by popular vote, but after 1832 only South Carolina did not. The property qualification for voting, boldly advocated by the likes of John Adams as late as 1820, died out. By 1840, in most states, universal white manhood suffrage was so widely supported that it was a political liability to have *ever* advocated anything else.[74]

Probably more important, party organization changed. Party machinery replaced the legislative caucus; formal organization supplanted the informality and avocational character of the old politics. This meant, among other things, that there was simply more political work to be done, and patronage and prestige attracted men from different social strata to do it. "For increasing numbers of men," Richard McCormick writes, "politics, or more specifically the operation of party machinery, was to become a vocation."[75] Indeed, Richard Hofstadter has for this reason offered Martin Van Buren, rather than Andrew Jackson, as the representative figure of Jacksonian Democracy. Van Buren was one of the "new breed" of political leaders. He and other members of New York's "Albany Regency" were prototypes of the new class of professional politicians. Van Buren, like two other members of the Regency, was the son of a tavernkeeper; others in the group had grown up on farms, and few had formal education. Hofstadter describes them:

They were, in short, modern political professionals who love the bonhomie of political gatherings, a coterie of more-or-less equals who relied for success not on the authority of a brilliant charismatic leader but on their solidarity, patience, and discipline. Their party gave them a creed, a vocation and a congenial social world all in one. It is hardly surprising that they should have developed a firm and self-conscious awareness of the imperatives of party organization, and have laid down a comprehensive set of canons for its management.[76]

These new professionals did not re-establish old parties run by personal cliques but invented new organizations, popularly based and democratically run.

The new parties were doctrinally, as well as institutionally, new. They shared more with one another than with either the Federalists or the Republicans of an earlier day.[77] In the 1830s both Whigs and Democrats subscribed to principles of political democracy that neither Federalists nor Republicans would have recognized. The meaning of politics, as well as the nature of politicians, had changed. Leadership in the past had been defined by "the problems and responsibilities of *general* development" in society, but leadership became "a task of representing a particular element of the system and attempting to secure its objectives through conflict and compromise with the other elements."[78] In other words, the old politics had focused on *what* was *right;* the new politics centered on *who* was *rightful,* who could amass the most units of private interest, rather than who could define the general interest.

In the old politics, the very idea of party was suspect. Party had been associated with everything particular, artificial, and selfish. Antiparty sentiment was identified with community, tradition, and deference in politics. Antiparty feelings persisted into the 1830s, especially among the Whigs, but it was dying, and what Richard Hofstadter calls "the idea of a party system" was born. In the 1830s people began to identify—deeply—with political parties. Historian Ronald Formisano writes that it was in this period that "mass party loyalty as a stable basis came into being for the first time in American history."[79]

The democratization of business and politics in the 1830s suggests a framework for understanding the revolution in journalism in the same period. The social upheaval in America, like that in England in the same years, was characterized by a lot of rhetoric about "democracy," some working class agitation, and some socialist and unionizing efforts, but primarily it was a middle-class revolution. This is not to diminish it but to identify it. England's celebrated Reform Bill of 1832, both promoted and feared at the time as the ultimate democratization of the body politic, only modestly enlarged the voting population. But at the same time, the Reform Bill was the beginning of changes reaching far beyond the relative insignificance of its immediate practical achievement. The same was true in the United States. The Age of Egalitarianism in America was no special friend to the common person, the laborer, the immigrant. It was more the day of the skilled craftsmen, the small and large merchants, the small and large tradesmen who were able to move up in the worlds of politics and business and transform those worlds. Here, too, the entering wedge of a commercial middle class brought with it new institutions and a new consciousness that would radically affect every stratum of society.

This framework for understanding the 1830s helps explain and is itself illuminated by the penny press. The founding of the penny papers is evidence of the new kind of entrepreneur and the new type of enterprise the 1830s encouraged. The qualities contemporaries admired or detested in these papers—relative independence from party, low price, high circulation, emphasis on news, timeliness, sensation—have to do with the rise of an urban middle class. The nature of the connection between the middle class and the new journalism can be appreciated by looking more closely at the most important of the penny papers, the *New York Herald*.

The Social Standing of the Penny Press

James Gordon Bennett was born in Scotland in 1795, a Catholic on Calvinist soil. At the age of twenty-four he emigrated to Halifax. After teaching school, clerking, and proofreading in Halifax, in Addison, Maine, in Boston, and in New York, he got his first serious newspaper experience on the *Charleston Courier* in 1822. A year later he was back in New York, writing for various journals. In 1827 and 1828 he served James Watson Webb's *New York Enquirer* as a Washington correspondent, during which time he enlivened Washington reporting, making newspaper discourse less a simple record of events and more a news "story." Bennett worked for Webb until 1832, after which he tried to set up a paper of his own. In 1835, with five hundred dollars, a few months shy of his fortieth birthday, he began the *New York Herald*. He remained its editor until his death in 1872.

There is no question that Bennett was the most original figure in American journalism, at least until Joseph Pulitzer. Nor is there any doubt that the *Herald* was the most important and widely read American newspaper in the decades before the Civil War. When Bennett died, Samuel Bowles, editor of the *Springfield Republican,* wrote an appraisal of Bennett and the *Herald* which judiciously sums up the consensus:

He was a coarse and vigorous writer, but excelled more in organization and enterprise. He was never troubled with principles, or accustomed to espouse and defend a cause from any far-sighted conviction, or faith in the nobler springs of human action.

The character of the man has been reflected by his works. Under him, the Herald was the first of American papers, indeed, the first journal in the world, to apprehend the truth that the collection of news at any price was the first duty of journalism. This was the conviction and the faith which served Mr. Bennett in place of every other. The Herald, though fickle in politics and worthless in editorial judgment, thus became the symbol of newspaper enterprise all over the world. . . . we must not deny to Mr. Bennett his place in journalism, as the great teacher and enforcer of the principle that in devotion to news-gathering lies at once the first duty and chief profit of a newspaper. Though other papers have in more recent years excelled the Herald in this respect, the first enunciation and demonstration of the principle will be yielded by history and popular tradition to Mr. Bennett.[80]

What made the *Herald* so successful? Why was it the American paper most widely read in Europe? Who were the people who read it and why?

While we can safely assume from the low price of the penny papers and their large circulation that many more low- and middle-income persons bought the penny papers than purchased the six-penny sheets, we cannot assume that wealthy people did *not* read the penny papers. In fact, it may be that "new money"—the people investing in stocks and yearning for respectability—was very attracted to the penny papers, especially to the *Herald*. Like other penny editors, Bennett sought a wide readership for his paper, but he repeatedly tried to distinguish its editorial course, not only from the six-penny papers, but from the other penny sheets, as in this comment on May 20, 1835:

The small daily papers around us were solely directed to mere police reports, melancholy accidents, or curious extracts. They indicated no mind, no intelligence, no knowledge of society at large. The larger [papers] were many of them without talent and without interest. There was plenty of room, therefore, for a cheap paper managed on our plan, calculated to circulate among all ranks and conditions; to interest the merchant and man of learning, as well as the mechanic and the man of labor.[81]

A year later Bennett distinguished the *Herald* from the six-penny papers, arguing that this "Wall Street press" was at the mercy of powerful interests: "The banks and corrupt *cliques* of men control them altogether."[82] On the other hand, he distinguished the *Herald* from his penny brethren. In boasting of the *Herald's* circulation—10,000 at the time—he compared it only to the Wall Street press, the largest representative of which was the *Courier and Enquirer* with a circulation of 6,400. He justified excluding the penny papers from tabulation with disparaging remarks about the fluctuations in their circulation:

For instance, the Sun publishes, probably, about 15,000, but great quantities are never read, and indeed the proprietors find it as profitable to sell their paper for wrapping up tea and enveloping hog's lard, as for any other purpose.[83]

The penny press, he wrote, loses half its circulation in winter when the loafers who make up such a large part of its readership are not on the street. He criticized the penny papers for having no talent, no knowledge of business, and no acquaintance with society.[84]

Bennett sought a middle road for the *Herald*—more serious and responsible than the penny press, more lively and enterprising than the Wall Street papers. The middle road was marked when Bennett raised the price of the *Herald* to two cents on August 19, 1836. Nine months later Bennett indicated the direction he hoped the *Herald* would take when he announced the publication of the *Evening Chronicle,* an evening version of the *Herald:*

The extraordinary increase in popularity of the Herald as a commercial, business, and general newspaper of the highest rank, have necessarily crowded out of its columns a great deal of local and amusing matter which is interesting to the public at large.[85]

For this reason, he went on, the *Chronicle* would be published to take up the slack.[86] This tends to indicate that the *Herald* itself was appealing to the practical needs and somewhat refined tastes of a well-to-do segment of the city's population. In the same issue that published a rather scholarly "History of Banking" over the first three columns of page one, Bennett editorialized on his own independence and intelligence, again distinguishing himself from the six-pennies, while courting the readership of those with money to invest. Bennett was proud that the *Herald* appealed to the wealthy classes:

No newspaper establishment, in this or any other country, has ever attained so extensive a circulation, or is read by so many of the business, educated, and intelligent classes.[87]

The readership Bennett sought, his contemporary biographer claims he attained. Isaac Pray wrote that by 1839 the *Herald,* with a circulation equal to the *London Times,* was "respected for its valuable statistics and thoughts by commercial men and statesmen, while its idiosyncrasies in literature and in social life kept it, in spite of the most determined opposition, under the eye of the fashionable and of the middling classes." He also observed that the money article, Bennett's innovation and special pet, "is the most important department of a public press, but only one journal in ten seems to be aware of the importance of making it independent, searching, and impartial."[88]

The "money article" deserves special attention. In the money article, a daily feature of the *Herald* from its inception, Bennett did for financial reporting what he had done years before for the coverage of Washington politics—he turned the recording of facts into the analysis of the shape of events. As Bennett put it:

The spirit, pith, and philosophy of commercial affairs is what men of business want. Dull records of facts, without condensation, analysis, or deduction, are utterly useless. The philosophy of commerce is what we aim at, combined with accuracy, brevity, and spirit.[89]

Reporting the "mere details" of the markets was not enough, Bennett wrote on another occasion; only an account of "broad leading features" is of general interest to merchants.[90]

Bennett missed no opportunity to crow about the popularity of his money article: "I have struck out the true Baconian path in commercial science, and it must succeed."[91] In January, 1837, he quoted the *New Orleans American* as saying that the money reports of the *Herald* were "comprehensive" and would be published for *American* readers. Other commercial papers in almost every large city, Bennett claimed, felt the same way. "We have every reason to believe that the Wall Street Reports of the Herald are beginning a new era of commercial intelligence and commercial science."[92] When Bennett announced circulation gains, he frequently would attribute them to the quality of his commercial reporting and the attraction of his paper for the business classes.[93]

There is good reason to believe that Bennett's boasts were well-founded. Even Bennett's enemies acknowledged the popularity of the money article. In 1840 the *Commercial Advertiser* attacked the *Albany Argus* for defending the reputation of the *Herald,* and it reprinted the *Argus* piece it criticized. The *Argus* wrote that it would not defend nine-tenths of the content of the *Herald,* but it felt otherwise about the money article:

We are aware that a thousand motives operate on those who buy the Herald to read, but we venture to say that nearly all its regular subscribers take the paper for these articles.[94]

The money articles, the *Argus* said, had given the *Herald* influence with American property holders and capitalists at home and abroad. The *Commercial Advertiser* did not deny it.

There is another kind of evidence to indicate that Bennett gained the new middle-class readership he was seeking. This lies in the fact that the Wall Street papers singled out Bennett for attack rather than assaulting all of the cheap papers. Further, their attacks apparently had some success in reducing the *Herald's* circulation. Whatever may have been the case with the other penny papers, the *Herald* appealed to an expanded and expanding class of people who emulated the respectability the Wall Street papers stood for and were influenced by their claims of the disrepute of the *Herald*. By Bennett's own report, his daily circulation, two years after the Wall Street papers began their "Moral War" in 1840, was just 14,460, down from 17,000. Not until 1844 did the *Herald* recover its earlier popularity.

The "Moral War" was a campaign of the six-penny papers to put the *Herald* out of business. Supported by some papers in Boston and Philadelphia, New York's leading six-penny papers charged Bennett with indecency, blasphemy, blackmail, lying, and libel. The *Journal of Commerce,* the *Commercial Advertiser,* and the *Courier and Enquirer* all proclaimed that they were abandoning the policy of not mentioning the *Herald* in their columns and began to attack Bennett directly, either in their own editorials or in reprinting anti-*Herald* pieces from other papers. Advertisers in the *Herald* were threatened. The *Courier and Enquirer* said that New York editors had made an agreement not to take ads for places of public amusement which continued to advertise in the *Herald.*[95] It wrote that gentlemen would not buy newspapers from newsboys who also sold the *Herald*—this apparently was both a report and a recommendation.[96] The *Herald* was declared off-limits to self-respecting men and women, which suggests that the self-respecting men and women the established papers courted had been reading the *Herald.* Hotels, reading rooms, and clubs were cajoled into excluding Bennett's "dirty sheet," thereby indicating that the *Herald* had found its way into hotels, reading rooms, and clubs patronized by the well-to-do.[97]

The "Moral War" of New York journalism has the earmarks of other moral wars of the same period. These crusades were the shields of an old elite jousting with a rising middle class. The temperance movement in the 1820s, for instance, has been described as "the reaction of the old Federalist aristocracy to loss of political, social, and religious dominance in American society."[98] Something similar could be said of the early abolitionist movement. Of 106 leaders in the movement who had become abolitionists before 1840, *all* came from Federalist families, according to David Donald's research. Their fathers had been preachers, doctors, or teachers, a few merchants, a few manufacturers. All but one of the sons were anti-Jacksonians. The abolitionists were men displaced in a new world. They were not hostile to labor but indifferent to it; what they objected to was a society increasingly dependent on trade and manufacturing and the ethics of the marketplace. They did not question capitalism or private property, but they objected to "the transfer of leadership to the wrong groups in society," and they took to abolitionism to assert some moral authority over the commercial middle class. "Basically," Donald concludes, "abolitionism should be considered the anguished protest of an aggrieved class against a world they never made."[99]

William Charvat makes a similar argument about the romantic movement in American literature in the 1830s and 1840s. Hawthorne, Emerson, and Thoreau paid almost no attention to the depression that lasted from 1837 to 1842, closing nine-tenths of American factories in its first six months. Of course, New England was the area of the country least affected by the depression, and these were New England writers. But probably more important, the income of these writers was relatively steady. They believed the reckless speculation of the commercial middle class brought on the bad times. They loathed and feared the bourgeoisie, not the poor: "The whole romantic movement in America," Charvat concludes, "may be considered in part as a protest against the new bourgeoisie."[100]

In this context, it is clear that the "Moral War" on the *New York Herald,* while a matter of business competition, was not simply that. Why should competition take this peculiar form? Why didn't the six-penny papers lower their prices, increase their reporting of news, expand their coverage of the stock market, make their writing more lively, change their mode of distribution, and take advantage of their ties to the business community to increase advertising revenue? Some of them, in time, did do many of these things. But their first response came not as a matter of shrewd calculation in a competitive market. The six-penny editors did not understand their roles or responsibilities in narrowly economic terms. Their moral wars were not so much business competition as deadly serious social conflict, a class conflict in which they were on the defensive against a new way of being in the world which we awkwardly summarize as "middle class" and which was symbolized and strengthened by the rise of the penny press.

Conclusion

Modern journalism, which is customarily and appropriately traced to the penny papers, had its origins in the emergence of a democratic market society. What "democratic market society" means has already been indicated, but needs to be restated and amplified. By "democratic," I refer to the replacement of a political culture of gentry rule by the ideal and the institutional fact of mass democracy. After the 1830s, the assumption that one had to have a propertied stake in society to be a reliable voter and that an elect, rather than an electorate, should govern could no longer be maintained. Indeed, it could not even be voiced with impunity. As I have indicated, the beginnings of the modern American system of bureaucratic, non-ideological parties can be traced to the Jacksonian democratization of politics.

But "democratization" was not solely political either in its causes or consequences. The growth of a market economy in the 1820s and 1830s integrated and rationalized American economic life—but it did more than this. Not only did more people and a greater range of goods participate in the marketplace, but a culture of the market became a more pervasive feature of human consciousness. And this culture, it is fair to say, was democratic. In the market there were no special categories and privileges. Land could be bought and sold, and even human labor had a price set by supply and demand, not by custom. In the market, one individual was as good as the next; in the ideology of the marketplace, all individuals acting separately to promote their own advantage would produce the greatest possible aggregate wealth for society as a whole. It became more acceptable to think of "self-interest" as the mainspring of human behavior and, indeed, in the theory of the market, as a motive to be admired, not distrusted.

The word "society" in the phrase "democratic market society" is probably the most difficult to pin down. "Society" is not only a general term referring to any human social organization but an historical ideal type characterizing the modern social order. It is distinguished from "community." Only in the nineteenth century did this distinction become a prominent theme in politics and in social thought.[101] And no wonder: there was little we could identify as "society" before then. "Community" in the nineteenth century came to mean the old world of face-to-face human ties—of family, kinship, neighborhood, and social circle. As the nineteenth century viewed it, "community" was the world of the Brueghel paintings of peasants—a group of people which, at work or at play, was at one with itself. In contrast, "society" was the rather grim world of the city, the stranger, and the individual. As sociologist Louis Wirth described it in a classic essay on "Urbanism as a Way of Life," urban living involved "the substitution of secondary for primary contacts, the weakening of bonds of kinship, and the declining social significance of the family, the disappearance of the neighborhood, and the undermining of the traditional basis of social solidarity." [102]

The differences between community and society, rural life and urban, tradition and modernity, agricultural and industrial worlds have been exaggerated, and dependence on these terms as theoretical constructs has sometimes been misleading.[103] Nevertheless, with the movement from country to city, from self-sufficent family economies to market-based commercial and manufacturing economies, people came unstuck from the cake of custom, found chances to form individual personalities, and faced new possibilities of impersonality in the social relations of modern life. Human ties, once conferred by family and residence, became more subject to choice. Nowhere was this more true than in the United States, which all of Europe recognized in the 1830s as the leading experiment in untraditional social organization, politics, and culture. And nowhere was the American world more novel than in the cities of the Eastern seaboard—Boston, Baltimore, Philadelphia, and, most of all, New York. A city, as Richard Sennett has concisely defined it, is "a human settlement in which strangers are likely to meet." [104] This was the problem and the hope of the cities; this was the meaning of the "society" coming into being. At the same time that people became free to feel themselves as new and important beings, they also came to feel the weight of social relationships and social institutions—society took on an existence objectified itside the person. On the one hand, living became more of a spectacle of watching strangers in the streets, reading about them in the newspapers, dealing with them in shops and factories and offices. On the other hand, as people understood their own ordinary lives to be of value and of possible interest to others, they both sought strangers as audiences or publics and avoided them to protect a private space for the self.[105]

This was the world in which modern journalism took root. There were rural papers, hundreds of them, but the papers which set the standard for journalism then and passed on their legacy to the present were urban. There were party papers, there were socialist papers and labor papers, there were business papers, but, again, the papers to which modern journalism clearly traces its roots were the middle-class penny papers. These papers, whatever their political preferences, were spokesmen for egalitarian ideals in politics, economic life, and social life through their organization of sales, their solicitation of advertising, their emphasis on news, their catering to large audiences, their decreasing concern with the editorial.

The penny papers expressed and built the culture of a democratic market society, a culture which had no place for social or intellectual deference. This was the groundwork on which a belief in facts and a distrust of the reality, or objectivity, of "values" could thrive. But in 1840 or 1850 or 1860, American journalism did not yet have clearly articulated common ideas and ideals. American journalism had not yet become an occuptional group or an industry. It would be both by the end of the nineteenth century, by which time one can identify the emergence and differentiation of professional ideals in journalism.

CHAPTER 2

TELLING STORIES:
JOURNALISM AS
A VOCATION AFTER 1880

IN DECEMBER, 1896, William Randolph Hearst, a newcomer to New York journalism who had recently become owner and editor of the *New York Journal*, sent Richard Harding Davis and Frederic Remington to Havana to cover the conflict there between Spanish authorities and Cuban insurgents. Remington was a thirty-five-year-old artist whose drawings appeared frequently in newspapers and popular magazines. Davis, at thirty-two, was already a popular culture hero through his reporting, his fiction, and his stylish manner. Hearst offered him $3,000 for a month of reporting from Cuba; Davis counted as well on $600 from *Harper's* for an article on his travels, and he had promises that his dispatches would be collected with Remington's drawings and published in book form.

Like other reporters in Cuba, Davis and Remington were barred from the "war zone" by Spanish military authorities. News was hard to get. Rumors and minor incidents were generally the best the correspondents had to offer. This so discouraged Remington that he wired Hearst: "Everything is quiet. There is no trouble here. There will be no war. Wish to return." Hearst is supposed to have responded, "Please remain. You furnish the pictures and I'll furnish the war." Despite such encouragement, Remington left Cuba after a week.

Davis stayed in Cuba. On February 10, 1897, he wired a story to New York that Hearst splashed over the first and second pages on February 12. Davis described how Spanish police boarded an American ship bound for Key West to search three Cuban women passengers. The police claimed that the women were carrying messages to insurgent leaders in New York. The ship's captain protested, but the women were stripped in a search for the documents. The *Journal* paraded the story on page one under the headline: "Does Our Flag Protect Women? Indignities Practised By Spanish Officials on Board American Vessels. Richard Harding Davis Describes Some Startling Phases of Cuban Situation. Refined Young Women Stripped and Searched by Brutal Spaniards While Under Our Flag on the Olivette." The story was accompanied on page two by a half-page drawing by Remington, imagining the scene from New York, showing one of the women naked and surrounded by Spanish officers going through her clothing.

It was good stuff for Hearst's purpose—building circulation. Nearly a million copies of the paper were sold. But the story was not quite true. The drawing, in particular, was not accurate. The leading paper in New York in 1897, Joseph Pulitzer's *New York World,* interviewed the Cuban women when they arrived in Tampa and discovered they had been searched by matrons, not by the Spanish officers. The *World,* whose leadership of New York journalism was threatened by the popular antics of Hearst, was delighted. It ran a front-page story headlined: " 'Tale of a Fair Exile.' Senorita Arango's Own Story of the Olivette 'Search Outrage.' A Statement to the World. She Loved Cuba for Whose Freedom All Her Brothers Are Now Fighting. Visited Them in Camp;

JOURNALISM AS A VOCATION AFTER 1880

Banished, She Denies Richard Harding Davis' Story That
Men Saw Her Stripped and Searched. . . ."

The headline summarizes the story well. The important
point was that Clemencia Arango denied being searched by
Spanish officers. This popped the *Journal's* balloon of scandal
and outrage. Richard Harding Davis considered the revelation a reflection on his integrity, and so he wrote to the *World*
to defend himself. On February 17 the *World* featured on
page two a story headlined, "Mr. Davis Explains." Davis
argued that not he but Remington was responsible for any
misrepresentations:

I never wrote that she was searched by men . . . Mr. Frederic
Remington, who was not present, and who drew an imaginary
picture of the scene, is responsible for the idea that the search was
conducted by men. Had I seen the picture before it appeared, I
should never have allowed it to accompany my article . . .

Davis broke with Hearst over this incident and never again
wrote for a Hearst paper.

This was an important moment in journalism, but its
importance needs to be carefully defined. On the surface, it
appears that the significance of the incident is that a reporter,
proud of his professional standing and faithful to the norms of
factual reporting, stood up to the evil influences of a circulation-building editor-publisher. Here, fidelity to facts is identified with reporters and threats to accuracy, with publishers,
their eyes on the cash box. But this is not a fair picture of
American journalism in the 1890s. For one thing, Hearst was
the least scrupulous of all New York editors at the time, the
most determined to build circulation, at any cost (and, indeed,
he operated the *Journal* at huge losses for its first years).
Other editors, even Pulitzer who vied with Hearst in the war
for readership, were more concerned that their newspapers
picture the world fairly.

If editors were not generally indifferent to accuracy in the
news, neither were reporters generally devoted to it, and that

led Richard Harding Davis. Davis wrote fiction as a
of documentary journalism; his journalism was frequently a documentary fiction—the facts would be there, but their
point was as often to entertain as to inform. Even in the
incident in question, Davis cannot be absolved from blame for
the misrepresentation. His report was ambigous, as he admitted. He did not say that men searched the women, but he
did not say that women had conducted the search. Given
earlier reports in the *Journal* and other New York papers
regarding Spanish mistreatment of Cuban women, it was
possible, even likely, that any artist or headline writer would
have made the interpretation the *Journal* made. True, Davis
did feel an obligation to get the facts right and a willingness,
at least in theory, to leave editorial judgment to the editors.
He wrote in his report from Cuba on January 31, "I was
taught in the days of 'old journalism' that reporters were
meant to describe things they saw, and not to write editorials
but to leave the drawing of conclusions to others. . ." But in
the story on the Olivette search, Davis clearly expressed his
shock at the actions of the Spanish authorities and suggested
that American intervention in Cuba would be justified. If
Remington's drawing got the details of Davis' story wrong, it
nonetheless caught the tone Davis expressed.

The incident, then, does not locate a devotion to facts in a
particular echelon of the newspaper staff. It does not picture a
typical editor. It does not feature a typical reporter. Nonetheless, it reveals one of the most important aspects of journalism
in the 1890s: reporters were, for the first time, actors in the
drama of the newspaper world. Davis felt himself independent of his employer, knew himself to have an authority with
the reading public more valuable than his salary, and could
with equanimity stand against his editor. Of course, Davis'
fame was unusual, and it is perhaps unique in the history of
journalism that an editor and a reporter should play out their
feud in the pages of a rival newspaper, but nothing could

better indicate that this was, as one newspaperman remembered it, the "Age of the Reporter."[1]

As news was more or less "invented" in the 1830s, the reporter was a social invention of the 1880s and 1890s. Early newspapers had been one-man bands: one man acted as printer, advertising agent, editor, and reporter. "Correspondents" for eighteenth-century and early nineteenth-century newspapers were generally travelers or friends of the editor in foreign ports who wrote letters back to their hometown newspapers. In the course of the nineteenth century, editors came to rely less on these informal sources of news and more on free-lance writers and hired reporters who wrote for pay. The penny papers were the first to employ reporters for local news. James Gordon Bennett pioneered once again in making the "foreign correspondent" a paid staff member.

In the 1840s and 1850s, American journalism continued in the direction set by the penny papers. Political independence of newspapers, for instance, became a common feature of journalism. In 1847, the new *Boston Herald*, a penny paper, had its morning edition edited by George Tyler, a Whig, and its afternoon edition managed by William Eaton, a Democrat. The arrangement did not last, but it is notable that the paper's proprietors could have supposed, as the *Herald*'s historian wrote in 1878, that "a double-jointed paper like this ought to suit everybody."[2] When Lincoln broke from the policy of maintaining a semiofficial organ among the Washington newspapers, the traditional link between paper and party, at least on the national level, was conclusively broken.[3]

If New York was the hub of journalistic enterprise in the 1830s, it was no less so by the time of the Civil War. By 1860, the *Tribune* and the *Herald* both had daily home delivery in Washington. In newspapers around the country the designation "From the HERALD" or "From the TRIBUNE" told all: everyone knew the reference was to the New York papers. The *Tribune*, the *Herald*, and the *Times*, a penny paper begun in 1851 by Henry J. Raymond, formerly managing editor at the *Tribune,* had grown from four pages to eight. Their competition for news continued, and they frequently emphasized the news-gathering process itself in headlines. The lead stories in one typical issue of the *Herald,* for instance, were headlined "News by Telegraph" and "Arrival of the Asia"; the former article included news from Washington, Albany, Buffalo, and elsewhere, while the latter included all the overseas news brought by the most recent steamer.[4] A *New York Times* story which featured the texts of speeches by Victor Emmanuel and Count Cavour of Italy began: "The steamship *Fulton,* whose arrival off Cape Cod has been already announced, reached her dock at this port last evening." [5]

In the *New York Herald* of the 1850s, one still can find several columns of advertising on page one—not every day, but not infrequently—and there sometimes was a serialized romance on the front page. Occasionally, there were "hoaxes"—stories of pure fiction presented as news—as there had been in the 1830s. Still, part of the delight of the hoax was its revelation as a literary invention. "Making news"—promoting or producing events one could then legitimately claim to report as news—was still unheard of. The most common and modest form of making news—interviewing a public figure—was a practice which did not make even its first tentative appearance in journalism until the 1860s.[6] While the pursuit of news had grown more vigorous by the Civil War, the idea of news had not changed significantly since the first days of the penny press.

As for the Civil War itself, it is often taken to be a turning point in the history of the American press.[7] It was not. It did not "turn" the direction of journalism; its impact was to intensify the direction in which journalism had been turning since the 1830s. As before, the leaders in this were the New York papers and, most of all, the *Herald.* Most striking was the sheer size of the news-gathering efforts of the leading papers. In the first years of the war, New York papers spent from $60,000 to $100,000 a year reporting the war, while papers in Boston, Philadelphia, and chief cities in the West spent between $10,000 and $30,000. In New York, only the *Herald* kept up its investment in news gathering throughout the conflict, although the *Times* and the *Tribune* maintained extensive reporting services, too. The number of reporters grew enormously; the *Herald* had more than forty correspondents covering the war at any one time. Newspaper circulation rose; extras appeared more often; newspapers printed more pages; and Bennett's Sunday *Herald,* published since the 1830s, found competition in the new Sunday papers published by the *Times* and the *Tribune.* Just days before the war began, the *Tribune* became the first paper to introduce "stereotyping," a process in which the paper is printed from curved stereotype plates cast from a mold taken from the original plates of type. This was a major step forward in printing technology; within four months the *Herald* and then the *Times* adopted stereotyping. The familiar pattern of the 1830s and 1840s was repeated: the penny papers set the pace of American journalism.[8]

Journalism in the Civil War, then, was not so much different as bigger, more prominent, and, as people anxiously followed campaigns that involved their husbands and brothers and sons, more important to ordinary people. The war pushed the newspaper closer to the center of the national consciousness. Frederic Hudson, in his 1872 history of journalism, paid tribute to the newspapers' coverage of the Civil War and the European wars of the next few years:

No record of previous wars can surpass those of the years between 1861 and '71. Anterior to these events we spoke of Napier, Thiers, Gibbon, Bancroft. They were compilers from old documents. Now we speak of the TRIBUNE, TIMES, WORLD, HERALD. They have been eye-witnesses.[9]

Indeed they were. But Hudson's language is good indication that, despite the courage of some Civil War reporters and the color of war correspondence, despite the temporary introduction of by-lines in 1863 (stipulated by General Joseph Hooker as a means of attributing responsibility and blame for the publication of material he found inaccurate or dangerous to the Army of the Potomac), and despite the great numbers of correspondents, the age of the reporter had not yet arrived. In the Spanish-American War, the names of Sylvester Scovel and Richard Harding Davis were as familiar as the names of the papers for which they wrote. This was not the case for correspondents in the Civil War.

It was only in the decades after the Civil War that reporting became a more highly esteemed and more highly rewarded occupation. The growing marketability of a college degree in journalism was an indicator of the reporter's new status. Horace Greeley, in the 1860s, would not hire a college graduate who did not show he could overcome the "handicap" of a college education. But times were already changing when Julius Chambers sought a job on the *Tribune* around 1870. Chambers told Greeley that he had just graduated from Cornell. Greeley replied, "I'd a damned sight rather you had graduated at a printer's case!" But Chambers got his *Tribune* job anyway by talking to managing editor Whitelaw Reid, who hired him when he discovered that they were both members of the same college fraternity.[10] Charles Dana favored college graduates on the *New York Sun* in the 1880s, and Lincoln Steffens, in his brief stint as editor of the *Commercial Advertiser* at the turn of the century, hired college graduates almost exclusively. *The Journalist*, a trade publication for journalism begun in 1883, declared in an editorial in 1900, "Today the college bred men are the rule." With more gentlemen and fewer Bohemians in the profession, *The Journalist* observed, newspaper writing improved, and the ethics and status of newspapermen rose.[11]

Stereotypes of the old-time reporter and the new reporter quickly developed and pervade memoirs of editors and reporters, just as they do the pages of *The Journalist.* The "old reporter," according to the standard mythology, was a hack who wrote for his paycheck and no more. He was uneducated and proud of his ignorance; he was regularly drunk and proud of his alcoholism. Journalism, to him, was just a job. The "new reporter" was younger, more naïve, more energetic and ambitious, college-educated, and usually sober. He was passionately attached to his job and to the novels he felt his experience as a reporter would prepare him to write. David Graham Phillips exemplified the new spirit in saying, "I would rather be a reporter than President."[12]

The reporter's rising status was marked and promoted by steadily rising income in the 1880s and 1890s.[13] At the same time, reporting was becoming a more steady sort of employment. *The Journalist* repeatedly urged that newspapers give up the habit of relying on free-lance reporters who were paid "on space"—according to the number of column-inches their stories occupied in the paper.[14] By 1898 *The Journalist* noted that not only did each of the large New York newspapers have at least ten college graduates on their staffs, but that the reporter working "on space," rather than on salary, was practically extinct.[15]

Reporters in the 1880s and 1890s received popular acclaim. The popular appeal of Nelly Bly going around the world in eighty days, Henry Morton Stanley finding Livingston in Africa, or the war correspondence of Richard Harding Davis added greatly to the esprit that attracted young men and more and more young women to the world of journalism and kept them there happily. Reporters were as eager to mythologize their work as the public was to read of their adventures. The Whitechapel Club in Chicago, founded in 1889 and named after the London site of some of the crimes of Jack the Ripper, was a gathering place for reporters. The club was decorated with mementos of crime—murder weapons, human skulls, and a coffin-shaped table; the reporters glamorized their familiarity with the rawness of city life while also creating the atmosphere of a college fraternity. But the Club had an important practical function, too, for reporters criticized one another's work there. Reporters became as sensitive to the reception of their stories at the Club as to the judgments of their city editors. In New York, the nightly gatherings of the newspaper fraternity for drink and talk at "Doc" Perry's Park Row pharmacy provided a similar forum for mutual criticism and collegiality.[16] Formally organized press clubs had begun with the New York Press Club in 1873. In the 1880s, clubs were organized in Chicago, Minneapolis, Milwaukee, Boston, St. Paul, and San Francisco. In Washington, a socially exclusive Washington Correspondents' Club was organized in 1867, but most journalists shared a social and professional life simply because, in the late 1860s and 1870s, they almost all took offices in "Newspaper Row" on Fourteenth Street, between Pennsylvania and F Streets. Another exclusive club—the Gridiron Club—was established in 1885; the National Capital Press Club began in 1891 but folded within a few years on the bad credit of its members. The National Press Club we know today dates from 1908.[17]

Whether the collegiality of journalism was formally organized or not, reporting in the 1880s and 1890s became a self-conscious and increasingly esteemed occupation in American cities. By 1890 E. L. Godkin could confidently write that news gathering had become "a new and important calling."[18] There were even guides for aspiring young men and women on how to become a reporter;[19] reporting was less strictly a job one drifted into, more and more a career one chose.

Reporters came to share a common world of work; they also shared common ideas about how to conduct their work. Competing with one another for circulation, newspapers tried to satisfy public standards of truth, public ideals of decency, and public taste in entertainment. That meant, on the one hand, that newspapers had to be lively, colorful, and entertaining. It meant, on the other hand, that they had to be factual. Reporters believed strongly that it was their job both to get the facts and to be colorful. In their allegiance to facts, reporters of the late nineteenth century breathed the same air that conditioned the rise of the expert in politics, the development of scientific management in industry, the triumph of realism in literature, and the "revolt against formalism" in philosophy, the social sciences, history, and law.[20] But in their desire to tell stories, reporters were less interested in facts than in creating personally distinctive and popular styles of writing. This seems—and sometimes seemed to the reporters—to run counter to the zeal for facts. But they experienced the contradiction as conflict with their editors, not as ideological disharmony. It would be a mistake to read contemporary views of objectivity into the fact-mindedness of the 1890s. Objectivity is an ideology of the distrust of the self, something Richard Harding Davis and his colleagues did not feel. The Progressives' belief in facts was different from a modern conviction of objectivity; just what it was we shall now examine.

Science and Literary Realism

Reporters in the 1890s saw themselves, in part, as scientists uncovering the economic and political facts of industrial life more boldly, more clearly, and more "realistically" than anyone had done before. This was part of the broader Progressive drive to found political reform on "facts." At the turn of the century, state and federal labor bureaus began to gather better information on economic and social issues, as did private agencies like the Charity Organization Society of New York in its tenement house investigation of 1900. In the first decade of the twentieth century, systematic social investigation practically became a craze; it was a favorite project of the new Russell Sage Foundation, which sponsored social surveys in Pittsburgh, St. Paul, Scranton, Topeka, Ithaca, Atlanta, and Springfield, Illinois. There was a "public demand for facts," writes historian Robert Bremner, intentionally echoing the recollections of reporter and writer Ray Stannard Baker: "Facts, facts piled up to the point of dry certitude, was what the American people really wanted." [21]

Many of the journalists of the 1890s and after were either trained in a scientific discipline or shared in the popular admiration for science. Ray Stannard Baker took special interest in his science courses at Michigan Agricultural College; Lincoln Steffens did graduate work in Wilhelm Wundt's world-famous psychological laboratory. The appeal of Herbert Spencer was strong among reporters, as it was among other educated Americans. Baker studied and imbibed Spencer's views on economy in literary style under Fred Newton Scott at Michigan Agricultural College; Theodore Dreiser read Spencer, as well as Darwin, Tyndall, and Huxley. Jack London, who, like Dreiser, began his literary career as a reporter, was influenced by Spencer. Abraham Cahan, a reporter who founded the *Jewish Daily Forward* in New York in 1897 and served as its editor for half a century, read Spencer avidly, especially his writings on art.[22]

Whether reporters thought of themselves as scientists or as artists, they believed always that they should be realistic. Their ideal of literature, as of reporting, stressed factuality. Abraham Cahan championed realism in art in an essay printed in 1889; he argued that "the power of realistic art arises from the pleasure we derive from recognizing the truth as it is mirrored by art." [23] Clarence Darrow, himself the author of one novel, expressed the dominant view of the time in an essay on realism in *The Arena* in 1893: "The world has grown tired of preachers and sermons; to-day it asks for facts. It has grown tired of fairies and angels, and asks for flesh and blood." [24] The dean of American letters in the 1880s and 1890s, William Dean Howells, argued that a philosophy of art should be based on the laws of natural science; his own work, according to Everett Carter, was "dominated by the positivistic concern with the objective observation, analysis, and classification of human life." [25] Reporters who turned to fiction followed him in this. Most of the turn-of-the-century writers whose novels we still read, wrote in a self-consciously realistic vein growing out of their experience as newspaper reporters—Theodore Dreiser, Jack London, Stephen Crane, Frank Norris, and Willa Cather, for instance. Other writers of fiction, enormously popular at the time, began as newspapermen—Richard Harding Davis, Lafcadio Hearn, David Graham Phillips, Ray Stannard Baker, Joel Chandler Harris, Harold Frederic, Ambrose Bierce, and George Ade. Ade, a Chicago reporter, wrote, in both his journalism and his fiction, a blend of sentiment and realistic detail which he generally subordinated to humor and to what Larzer Ziff terms "false geniality." [26] Still, Ade shared in the literary ideology of his times and spoke for many others when he wrote that his ambition was to be known as a "realist" and a man with "the courage to observe human virtues and frailties as they showed on the lens." [27]

The word "observe" was all-important to the reporters and realistic novelists of the 1890s; George Becker aptly notes that romantics praised a writer's powers of invention, while realists praised powers of observation.[28] And Ade's word "lens," too, is well-chosen: it conveys the realists' sense that the newspaper story, the magazine article, and the novel could be, and should be, photographically true to life. What is important, however, is not that realists believed art to have a mimetic function—there was nothing new in that, and the term "realism," in the 1890s, was more a boast and an advertisement than a descriptive label. What is important is that realists identified "reality" with external phenomena which, they believed, were subject to laws of physical causality as natural science revealed them and as social science might reveal them. This *was* new. The world was disenchanted as never before, and the realists, embracing disenchantment to distinguish themselves from their literary fathers, were delighted.[29]

Why this realism developed as and when it did is not easy to say. William Dean Howells wrote that nothing caused realism: it just "came" and it seemed "to have come everywhere at once." [30] We can at least say a few things about what did not cause it. Autonomous developments in the arts did not cause it. Frank Norris followed the growth of a theory of realism in France, but most American realists were without knowledge of French intellectual life and came to their realism on their own.[31] Nor did "the pervasive materialism of industrial capitalism," contrary to Alfred Kazin, cause it.[32] Writers in ante-bellum America also responded to what they experienced as "pervasive materialism," but they did so in a style called "romantic."

Nor was realism simply the inevitable consequence of the growing popularity of science. "Science" had long been a magical word in America. For instance, lawyers on both sides of the codification controversy in the 1830s defended themselves in terms of a "science of the law."[33] There was, however, an important difference between the conservative tradition of "science" as the personal acquirement of learnedness and the idea of science invoked by middle-class reformers favoring codification of the law. The codifiers took science to be a body of knowledge necessarily clear, written, and public; in the law this meant that they favored legal rules legislatively enacted rather than judicially interpreted. They *externalized* the idea of science, making what conservative thinkers took to be a subtle and mysterious faculty of mind into an institution of democratic political life. This notion of science as only that body of knowledge constructed by the public and available to public view was especially congenial to a democratic market society. The idea of science as a process of data collecting open to all expressed a democratic epistemology and helped make the collecting and classifying activities of botany, zoology, and geology the models of natural science in Jacksonian America. By the late nineteenth century, under the influence of Darwin and Spencer, the meaning of science to the popular mind shifted. Evolutionary theory had become the model of science; it emphasized not just the collection, but the historical connections, of facts. Still more important, it included human beings as objects about which facts could be gathered and studied. The human mind externalized or objectified the human body, and, as psychologists and other social scientists worked out the implications of Darwinian theory, human beings objectified themselves.

This changing concept of what science is, rather than simply the growing popularity of science, contributed to the rise of realism. But this begs a question: while science surely has some internal logic, it is also clearly shaped by social circumstances. What social circumstances promoted a fact-gathering and fact-connecting science which took human society as its subject?

My inclination is to argue that this idea of a science of human society would not have gained support without the advance of a market economy, the ideal and institutions of political democracy, and the emergence of an urban habitat. Such is the general theme of this study. But can it be stretched to cover the phenomenon I am now describing? The problem is not a simple one. Any explanation of the idea of science in the late nineteenth century as an expression of the culture of a democratic market society must handle the following puzzle. In the early nineteenth century, science was the darling of democrats, the open book of progress which anyone could write in and anyone could read. Empirical inquiry was a weapon of the middle class against the received wisdom of an established order. By the end of the nineteenth century, however, science was becoming an established institution in its own right, connected to the universities and professional associations and standing *against* popular democracy both in principle ("reason" and expert judgment versus the mob) and in actual class antagonism (the educated middle class against immigrants and workers). Science, at one time consonant with the culture of a democratic market society, seems, in retrospect, to have opposed it as the society matured.

While I feel tentative about this statement and uncertain about its implications, I believe that this general sociological approach to understanding the idea of science is sound. The history of science is not an autonomous intellectual history. It is, instead, a history of the interaction of a way of seeing the world, a set of ideas and institutions which promote the way of seeing, and the social conditions conducive or constraining to the way of seeing. In many areas of American life in the nineteenth century, people were ready to accept empirical sciences before science as an institution, or a set of workable ideas, appeared. Religion and religious explanations were not destroyed by science; they were in decline already. For instance, Charles Rosenberg shows, in his study of the American response to the cholera epidemics of 1832, 1849, and 1866, that by 1866 Americans, including religious leaders, were much more likely than they had been to think of cholera as a medical, rather than a moral, problem, even though the identification of the cholera vibrio was nearly two decades in the future. But by 1866 there was an "unashamed empiricism, not only in medical writings, but in sermons and editorials as well."[34] A democratic age wanted a democratic vision, and empirical inquiry, not religion, fit most comfortably.[35]

In journalism from the 1830s on, there was a growing emphasis on getting the facts. Still, in journalism, as in other fields, the idea of an empirical inquiry concerning human society did not triumph all at once. It is important to ask, in the case of journalism, not only why the journalists' belief in facts was so strong by the end of the nineteenth century, but why it was no stronger.

Occupational Ideals of Journalists

Reporters of the 1890s who later wrote memoirs recall, with grudging fondness, their first city editors. Julius Chambers, who served as managing editor of the *New York Herald* and the *New York World,* remembered his own apprenticeship in the 1870s under the *New York Tribune's* W. F. G. Shanks. Shanks forced Chambers to acquire "a form of composition very difficult to overcome in after years—a style accurately described by John Hay, then a paragraph writer on the *Tribune,* as 'The Grocer's Bill.'" That meant, Chambers recalled:

> Facts; facts; nothing but facts. So many peas at so much a peck; so much molasses at so much a quart. The index of forbidden words was very lengthy, and misuse of them, when they escaped the keen eye of a copyreader and got into print, was punishable by suspension without pay for a week, or immediate discharge. It was a rigid system, rigidly enforced.[36]

Lincoln Steffens made a similar complaint about the training he received on E. L. Godkin's *Evening Post:*

> Reporters were to report the news as it happened, like machines, without prejudice, color, and without style; all alike. Humor or any sign of personality in our reports was caught, rebuked, and, in time, suppressed. As a writer, I was permanently hurt by my years on the *Post.*[37]

Joseph Appel, later to be John Wanamaker's advertising manager and a pioneer in "journalizing" advertising copy, got his first job with Colonel McClure's *Philadelphia Times* in the 1890s. As he recalled, his first meeting with McClure was not auspicious. McClure waved a newspaper column at Appel and asked, "Young man, young man, did you write this?" Appel replied that he had. McClure then said: "Well, I want you to know and I don't want you ever to forget it, that when the *Times* expresses an editorial opinion I will express it and not you—go back to your work."[38]

Young reporters were impressionable, and these sorts of encounters must have influenced them. Theodore Dreiser remembered Maxwell of the *Chicago Globe,* his editor when he first entered journalism in 1892. Maxwell told him that the first paragraph of a news story had to inform the reader of "who, what, how, when, and where." Maxwell noted, for emphasis, that there was a sign in the office of the *Chicago Tribune* which read, "WHO OR WHAT? HOW? WHEN? WHERE?" When Dreiser would bring in a story, Maxwell would go at it with a blue pencil, advising as he went: "News is information. People want it quick, sharp, clear—do you hear?"[39]

Dreiser was not surprised, then, when he moved to New York and walked into the city room of the *New York World:*

I looked about the great room, as I waited patiently and delightedly, and saw pasted on the walls at intervals printed cards which read: Accuracy, Accuracy, Accuracy! Who? What? Where? When? How? The Facts—The Color—The Facts! I knew what those signs meant: the proper order for beginning a newspaper story. Another sign insisted upon Promptness, Courtesy, Geniality! Most excellent traits, I thought, but not as easy to put into execution as comfortable publishers and managing editors might suppose.[40]

The *World's* exhortation to accuracy took it for granted that there was no contradiction between "the facts" and "the color"—the good reporter should be alert to both. Edwin L. Shuman, in his handbook for aspiring journalists, *Steps into Journalism* (1894), wrote that a reporter with sparkle would be forgiven inaccuracy, just as a reliable reporter would be forgiven "a moderate degree of dullness" in style, but that the combination of "reliability and sparkle" was the recipe for professional success.[41] This was the spirit of the times and it is remarkable how far even texts for journalists would go in promoting color, as well as facts. Shuman advocated the reporter's using his imagination to create images he had not witnessed and had no direct testimony about. This is, he wrote, "perhaps excusable as long as the imaginative writing is confined to non-essentials and is done by one who has in him at least the desire to represent the truth." Shuman cautioned that even this mild form of fakery is dangerous, but he acknowledged that it was practiced by all newspapers. Indeed, he went further:

In spite of the fact that editors come to grief once in a while by its use, this trick of drawing upon the imagination for the non-essential parts of an article is certainly one of the most valuable secrets of the profession at its present stage of development. Truth in essentials, imagination in non-essentials, is considered a legitimate rule of action in every office. The paramount object is to make an interesting story.[42]

If facts could not be championed to the exclusion of imaginative embellishment, neither could they be supported wholeheartedly to the exclusion of opinion. Here, of course, as is evident in the advice of editors to their young reporters, there was in principle a more rigid distinction: news and opinion should be kept apart. But even this distinction was not absolute. Shuman advised his readers:

Opinions are the peculiar province of the editorial writer. The spirit of modern journalism demands that the news and the editorials be kept distinctly separate. The one deals with facts, the other with theoretical interpretations, and it is as harmful to mix the two in journalism as it is to combine church and state in government. *This, at least, is the only safe theory for the beginner.*[43]

The last line is significant. It suggests that the separation of facts from opinion was more a principle of tutelage than an absolute ideal in journalism. Indeed, as Shuman would point out in a later edition of his book, it was customary for Washington and foreign correspondents to blend fact and opinion at will.[44]

This, too, is a theme in the memoirs of reporters: that the rules one learned as a beginner one had to unlearn to stand out as a journalist. H. L. Mencken, as a young reporter in Baltimore in the 1890s, found himself confronted, like Dreiser in New York at the same time, with the demands of editors for accuracy. He recalled later that there was "immense stress upon accuracy" at the *Baltimore Sun*. The *Sun* "fostered a sober, matter-of-fact style in its men." The *Herald,* where Mencken began in 1899, was looser. Mencken preferred it to the *Sun* where, he felt, reporters "were hobbled by their paper's craze for mathematical accuracy. . . ." The best *Sun* reporters overcame their paper's policies, "but the rank and file tended to write like bookkeepers." Much as Mencken tries in his recollections to distinguish his own early newspaper experience from that of the rival *Sun,* this must be weighed against his account of the advice the *Herald's* managing editor gave him in his first days as a staff member: never trust a copy; verify reports whenever possible; try to get copy in early; be careful about dates, names, ages, addresses, and figures; keep in mind the dangers of libel; and do not be discouraged by the *Sun's* monopoly on news.[45]

What was true on newspapers was true for magazines as well. *McClure's,* founded in 1894 by Sam McClure, was the first of the new mass-circulation magazines which, as one contemporary regretfully observed, "journalized" magazine literature.[46] While *McClure's* was designed to entertain, to be interesting, the editor and his staff "evinced an unusual preoccupation with facts and possessed a desire to let events and documents speak for themselves."[47] McClure welcomed comparison of the magazine story to the news article of daily journalism: "I wish to go over the Pittsburgh article very carefully before it is published," he wrote to David Graham Phillips regarding an essay by Steffens. "I think that the article to begin with should be free from bias, just the same as a news article or newspaper. . . ."[48] Facts and more facts: "If Turner has any defect in writing it is a defect that almost all writers lean towards," McClure wrote Willa Cather, "that is a certain distaste towards documentation."[49]

These accounts suggest that reporters may have developed their attachment to facts despite themselves, forced into it by the organizational pressures of daily journalism. Young reporters came to the big-city dailies to make their reputations, to launch their literary careers. They had every reason to want to be colorful and enterprising, every reason to resent the dull discipline their editors tried to impose. The city editors, for their part, had to look in two directions: toward grooming reporters to get the news and write it with accuracy and verve; and toward satisfying the editor-publisher, which meant, at a minimum, keeping the paper free of the easily identifiable errors and excesses that would lead to libel, embarrassment, or public criticism for the newspaper. The city editor might well seek color in a news story, but he was likely to require factuality first of all. Besides, if he could hold reporters in conformity with rules and procedures he imposed, he could break them of some of their arrogance, make his own work easier, and make his own mark on the newspaper.

The conflict between editors and reporters is evident again in the recollections of Jacob Riis, a police reporter for the

New York Tribune in the 1880s, who culled from his experience one of the important reform documents of the era, *How the Other Half Lives* (1890). In his autobiography, Riis tried to explain how he took up photography as a tool for reporting. He confessed that he was not a good photographer, though he wanted to be. What kept him from his goal? According to Riis, it was his delight in the miracle, rather than in the technique, of photography:

I do not want my butterfly stuck on a pin and put in a glass case. I want to see the sunlight on its wings as it flits from flower to flower, and I don't care a rap what its Latin name may be. Anyway, it is not its name. The sun and the flower and the butterfly know that. The man who sticks a pin in it does not, and never will, for he knows not its language. Only the poet does among men. So, you see, I am disqualified from being a photographer.[50]

In his search for poetry, Riis felt the eyes of science derisively upon him. This is even more clear in his comments on his writing style. He complains that his editors told him his style was "altogether editorial and presuming, and not to be borne." They told him to give facts, not comments, to which he responded:

By that I suppose they meant that I must write, not what I thought, but what they probably might think of the news. But, good or bad, I could write in no other way, and kept right on. Not that I think, by any manner of means, that it was the best way, but it was mine. And goodness knows I had no desire to be an editor. I have not now. I prefer to be a reporter and deal with the facts to being an editor and lying about them.[51]

There may be some contradiction here in Riis' defending his mixture of facts and comments by appealing to his insistence on "dealing with facts"; it is interesting that his explanation of his own style is so defensive. He relies most of all on claiming his style as a fault of his own nature which he cannot change. Still, there are other passages in the autobiography where he offers a more positive account of the business of reporting as he practiced it. He took pride in reporting what he called the "great human drama." The reporter behind the scenes, he wrote, "sees the tumult of passions, and not rarely a human heroism that redeems all the rest. It is his task so to portray it that we can all see its meaning, or at all events catch the human drift of it, not merely the foulness and the reek of blood." He continued:

If he can do that, he has performed a signal service, and his murder story may easily come to speak more eloquently to the minds of thousands than the sermon preached to a hundred in the church on Sunday.[52]

In this passage, Riis distinguishes his teaching from the minister's, but the very idea of comparing his work to the preacher's and the religious language he uses ("a human heroism that redeems . . .") contrasts sharply with reporters' usual borrowings from the language of science. Not surprisingly, other reporters were sometimes critical of Riis. Steffens criticized him for refusing to believe, or even to hear, some of the awful things going on in the world. Riis did not have the "scientific" interest in reporting Steffens boasted of himself; he cared, in Steffens' words, only for "the stories of people and the conditions in which they lived."[53] Steffens recalled how Riis reacted when his assistant, Max Fischel, told him of a police raid on a party of homosexuals:

"Fairies!" Riis shouted, suspicious. "What are fairies?" And when Max began to define the word Riis rose up in a rage. "Not so," he cried. "There are no such creatures in this world." He threw down his pencil and rushed out of the office. He would not report that raid, and Max had to telephone enough to his paper to protect his chief.[54]

Steffens derided Riis' moralism, but he admired the personal style Riis cultivated. He must have, for that is exactly what he sought in his reporters when, in 1897, he became an editor himself, of the *Commercial Advertiser*. He recalled in his autobiography that he was inspired as an editor by little besides a love of New York. He inherited the politics of the paper from his apprenticeship on the *Evening Post*; he was self-conscious about literary ideals, not politics. He was determined to avoid the old "professional newspapermen" in creating a staff:

> I wanted fresh, young, enthusiastic writers who would see and make others see the life of the city. This meant individual styles, and old newspaper men wrote in the style of their paper, the *Sun* men in the *Sun* style, *Post* men in the Godkin manner.[55]

So Steffens hired young graduates of Harvard, Yale, Princeton, and Columbia, men of literary ambition more hopeful of being writers than reporters. Steffens remembered himself as ruthlessly stressing freshness and individuality in his reporters. As soon as two staff members wrote alike, he would fire one of them.

While there are differences among all these recollections, there are strong similarities, too, almost more than seems reasonable. This may indicate that the occupational world of the big-city newspaper reporters was, indeed, a common one; it may also suggest, however, that the common experience was that of recalling and dramatizing one's past. Not all autobiography is as hearty and uncritical as the reminiscences of journalists; theirs seem to continue in the relatively unreflective, uncomplicated, and untragic sense of life they expressed as reporters. And their autobiographies, like their newspaper articles, seem to aim for an entertaining, lively tone without sacrificing a necessary factuality. The resulting contributions to the collective self-portrait of journalism standardize a mythic pattern. The myth centers on the struggle between a young eager reporter and a wizened, cynical editor. The reporter, a deracinated stranger in the big city, who has chosen not to follow in his father's footsteps, creates a father of the man whose footsteps he does follow. Then the myth is played out between editor and reporter as between father and son: the son dares to express himself and the father punishes; the son conforms to the father's demands and the father comes to trust him; the son rebels to express himself again, with more maturity this time, and triumphs over the father; the father grows old or dies, becomes a memory, and the son forgives, acknowledging that he had, after all, taken his father's admonitions to heart.

Steffens, Chambers, Mencken, Dreiser, Appel, and Riis all recalled the directives of their first editors for factual, impersonal reporting. Most of them remembered this emphasis on facts with some resentment, even though they claimed, after their own fashion, to be scrupulously faithful to reality. At the same time, they were happy to have incorporated into their own outlooks some of their editors' world-weary cynicism. They wanted their reports of the world to be lively, they wanted to speak in personal tones to a world growing impersonal about them, but they believed they could do that without interpretation, with complete mirrorlike accuracy. They had only contempt for the critical, and generally moralistic, efforts of editorial writers. In part, this was a contempt for the person who does not dirty his hands. The ideal of the Chicago journalist in the 1890s, as Hugh Dalziel Duncan puts it, was to dramatize the news, not as an impartial observer, but as "a participant who spits on his hands, rolls up his sleeves, and jumps into the fight."[56] Thus, while turn-of-the-century reporters were unattuned to the ways in which their own values shaped their perception of "the facts," they were eager to accept the position that wishes should submit to facts, soft dreams to hard realities, moralism to practical politics, and religion to common sense. Dreiser was probably typical in being attracted to reporting by what he called its "pagan or unmoral character," which he contrasted to the "religionistic and moralistic point of view" of the editorial offices:

While the editorial office might be preparing the most flowery moralistic or religionistic editorials regarding the worth of man, the value of progress, character, religion, morality, the sanctity of the home, charity and the like, the business office and news rooms were concerned with no such fine theories. The business office was all business, with little or no thought of anything save success, and in the city news room the mask was off and life was handled in a rough-and-ready manner, without gloves and in a catch-as-catch-can fashion. Pretense did not go here. Innate honesty on the part of any one was not probable. Charity was a business with something in it for somebody. Morality was in the main for public consumption only. "Get the news! Get the news!"—that was the great cry in the city editorial room. "Don't worry much over how you get it, but get it, and don't come back without it! Don't fall down! Don't let the other newspapers skin us—that is, if you value your job! And write—and write well. If any other paper writes it better than you do you're beaten and might as well resign." The public must be entertained by the writing of reporters.[57]

Reporters were united in opposing moralism, sham, and hypocrisy. They thought little of clergymen, political orators, reform efforts to close saloons and brothels, and editorial writers.[58] The city editors, with whom they were in constant contention, they felt kin to. Dreiser wrote admiringly that city editors were nearly all distrustful of conventional principles and "misdoubted the motives, professed or secret, of nearly every man."[59] Reporters felt a close emotional bond to their hard-driving editors and, as well, to the tough and gritty men—both police and criminals—they got to know on the police detail. They felt close, too, as Lincoln Steffens made clear in his autobiography, to the cynical and shrewd businessmen and politicians they interviewed and exposed. They struck a pose and saluted an ethic in which nonbelief was their pride. Dreiser summed up this posture of negatives: "One can always talk to a newspaper man, I think, with the full confidence that one is talking to a man who is at least free of moralistic mush."[60]

And yet, the reporters themselves were full of a mush much

the same. Richard Harding Davis was angry when the veracity of his report on the Olivette search was questioned in a *World* editorial. His letter to the *World* stressed the accuracy of his own report and the guilt of his friend Remington for the fabricated drawing. He then added, hoping to fully absolve himself from blame:

My only object in writing the article was to try and show the people in the United States how little protection they may expect on one of their own vessels, under their own flag, in the harbor of Havana, where there should have been an American man-of-war stationed for the last six months.[61]

For a contemporary journalist to make such a confession, and still contend that he or she had been scrupulously faithful to the facts, would be inconceivable; it would be a contradiction in terms. It was not so to Davis. The antagonism of journalists in the Progressive era to moralism may have been more a matter of style than of substance. McClure, for instance, told his writers to concentrate on telling an absorbing story, and the story, he believed, should have a moral— but the moral element was to be present "unconsciously."[62] This was not difficult for writers of the Progressive era to accept, for they understood facts to provide moral direction of themselves and prided themselves that their own moral precepts grew naturally out of their association with the real world. They did not feel the moral declarations of the editorial writers to be subjective but to be dreamy; their own, of course, they took to be as irrefutable as the facts they uncovered. That assurance, already in question in some fields, would not last much longer, even in journalism.

CHAPTER 3

STORIES AND INFORMATION: TWO JOURNALISMS IN THE 1890s

R EPORTING was an invention of the end of the nineteenth century, but it was a two-part invention: the emergence of the new occupation played off against the industrialization of the newspaper. And while there was much that united the ideology of reporters, there was much that divided the identities of the newspapers for which they worked. In New York, most of the major papers were direct descendants of the penny press: the *Sun,* the *Herald,* the *Tribune,* and the *Times.* Of papers that antedated the penny press, only the *Evening Post* still had an important following. The two largest papers were the *World,* begun in 1859 and revived by Joseph Pulitzer in 1883, and the *Journal,* begun in 1882 by Pulitzer's brother but escorted to the stage of history when William Randolph Hearst bought it in 1895. Both of these papers were sharply distinguished from the others; they represented what contemporaries generally referred to as "the new journalism." The established papers found their competition and their manners deeply disturbing and wrote of them with the same moral horror that had greeted their own arrival in New York journalism fifty years before.

While reporters subscribed concurrently to the ideals of factuality and of entertainment in writing the news, some of the papers they worked for chose identities that strongly emphasized one ideal or the other. The *World* and the *Journal* chose to be entertaining; the old penny press, especially the *Times* after Adolph Ochs rejuvenated it in 1896, took the path of factuality. I shall refer to these two models of journalism as the ideal of the "story" and the ideal of "information." When telling stories is taken to be the role of the newspaper, journalism is said to fulfill what George Herbert Mead described as an "aesthetic" function. Mead wrote that some parts of the news—the election results or stock market reports—emphasize exclusively "the truth value of news," but for most of the news in a paper, the "enjoyability" or "consummatory value" is more important. The news serves primarily to create, for readers, satisfying aesthetic experiences which help them to interpret their own lives and to relate them to the nation, town, or class to which they belong. Mead took this to be the actual, and the proper, function of a newspaper and observed that it is manifest in the fact that "the reporter is generally sent out to get a story, not the facts."[1] In this view, the newspaper acts as a guide to living not so much by providing facts as by selecting them and framing them.

An alternative model of the newspaper's role proposes that the newspaper is uniquely defined as a genre of literature precisely to the extent that the facts it provides are unframed, that it purveys pure "information." Walter Benjamin suggested that "information" is a novel form of communication, a product of fully developed capitalism, whose distinguishing characteristic is that it "lays claim to prompt verifiability." Its aim, above all, is to be "understandable in itself." While it may actually be no more exact than varieties of "intelligence" of the past, unlike earlier intelligence, which might be justified by reference to the miraculous, "it is indispensable for information to sound plausible." For this reason, in Benjamin's analysis, information "proves incompatible with the spirit of storytelling."[2] This view of the newspaper is echoed in the recent work of Alvin Gouldner, who refers to news as "decontextualized" communication. It is a form of what Basil Bernstein, on whose work Gouldner relies, calls an "elaborated code," in which all is spelled out, nothing left to implicit or tacit understanding.[3]

Rightly or wrongly, the informational ideal in journalism is associated with fairness, objectivity, scrupulous dispassion. Newspapers which stress information tend to be seen as more reliable than "story" papers. But who makes this judgment and on what grounds? Who regards the information model as more trustworthy than the story ideal, and what is meant, after all, by "reliable" or "trustworthy"? If journalists on the whole give credit to both ideas at once, how is it that different newspaper institutions come to stand for one or the other? And how is it that those which stand for the information model come to be regarded as the more responsible?

It is the unexceptional theme of this chapter that, in the most general terms, there is a connection between the educated middle class and information and a connection between the middle and working classes and the story ideal. The puzzle here, as in most other discussions of popular culture, is why this should be the case. What is it about information that seems to appeal to the educated middle class? What is it about the story that seems to attract the working-class reader? Is it right to associate the information model with the notion of objectivity? Should we regard it as a "higher" form of journalism than the story model? In the critical decades from 1883 to the first years of this century, when at the same moment yellow journalism was at its height and the *New York Times* established itself as the most reliable and respected newspaper in the country, why did wealthier people in

New York read the *Times* and less wealthy people read the *World?* What is the meaning of the two journalisms of the 1890s?

Journalism as Entertainment: Joseph Pulitzer and the *New York World*

Joseph Pulitzer began his newspaper career in St. Louis. Party papers prevailed there until the 1870s when "independent journalism" gained a foothold. A turning point for St. Louis journalism came in 1871 when the *Morning Globe* hired Chicago's Joseph McCullagh as editor. McCullagh stressed news, rather than opinion, and, on what was by then the increasingly familiar model of James Gordon Bennett, concentrated on local police, court, society, and street reporting.

Pulitzer was an Austrian Jewish immigrant who arrived in the United States in 1864, at the age of seventeen, to fight in the Civil War. In St. Louis, after the war, he studied law and was admitted to the bar, but, in part because of his limited facility in English, he did not practice law. Instead, he became a reporter for the city's German-language newspaper, the *Westliche Post.* Active and successful in journalism and in politics—first Republican, then Democratic—Pulitzer was able to buy the *St. Louis Post and Dispatch* in 1878. He served as its publisher, editor, and business manager. Under his guidance, the paper became more audacious in promoting the Democratic Party and turned much brighter in its style. It began to carry statistics of trade from the Merchants' Exchange, the produce markets, and the waterfront. In 1879 it became the first St. Louis paper to publish quotations on stocks issued by local firms. Pulitzer repeatedly appealed to "the people," by which he meant, it seems, "the stable householder, of whatever class."[4] The *Post and Dispatch* was antagonistic to labor, and it held to the high price of five cents an issue. According to Julian Rammelkamp, historian of Pulitzer's years as St. Louis editor, "The fundamental aims of the paper were middle class—to foster the development of St. Louis as a business center and as an attractive place of residence for the average citizen."[5] Pulitzer's great innovation in his years in St. Louis was the development of the newspaper crusade. The crusade was by no means unknown elsewhere, especially in New York, but Pulitzer made startling headlines and political exposés a constant feature of his paper, stimulating circulation and presumably changing the city for the better.

In 1883 Pulitzer plugged his Western voice into the amplifier of the East, New York City. He bought the *New York World,* a paper of some reputation during the 1860s and 1870s which had fallen on hard times. When Pulitzer bought it, its circulation was about fifteen thousand. A year later it was sixty thousand. In another year it was one hundred thousand, and by the fall of 1886 it passed a quarter million. Pulitzer attributed this astonishingly rapid success to his editorial position. "We can conscientiously say," he wrote in an 1884 editorial, "that we believe the success of THE WORLD is largely due to the sound principles of the paper rather than to its news features or its price."[6]

There was a measure of truth in this. It is not an accident that the *World* and Hearst's *Journal,* the city's two most widely read papers at the turn of the century, were both Democratic. But this was not the mainspring, or mainstay, of Pulitzer's (or Hearst's) success. Pulitzer's energy and innovation in business practice played a larger role. Publishing the *World* at a penny a copy, he forced the *Times* to drop its price from four cents to two, the *Herald,* from three to two, and the *Tribune,* from four to three (the two-cent *Sun* stayed the same). He initiated the practice of selling advertising space on the basis of actual circulation and selling it at fixed prices; at the same time, he abandoned the traditional penalties for advertisers who used illustrations or broke column-rules.[7] Pulitzer thus helped rationalize newspaper business practice and the relations between newspapers and advertisers.

This was a significant achievement. Until the 1880s, despite James Gordon Bennett's business enterprise, magazines and newspapers were hostile to advertisers. Most newspapers believed large ads wasted space and were "unfair" to the small advertisers who were the foundation of advertising revenue. Editors felt that advertising should command only so much of the newspaper's space, which, from the expense of paper and from custom, was severely limited. Advertising, then, was confined to agate-size type. James Gordon Bennett, in fact, held that the advertiser should gain advantage from what he said, but not from how the advertisement was printed or displayed.[8]

The relationship between newspapers and advertisers changed dramatically in the 1880s. Thanks in part to the growth of department stores and the development of brand names and trademarks by national manufacturing concerns, business demand for advertising space accelerated.[9] The ratio of editorial matter to advertising in the newspaper changed from about 70-30 to 50-50 or lower.[10] Advertising revenue represented 44 percent of total newspaper income in 1880, 55 percent by 1900.[11] This did not diminish the reliance of newspapers on circulation but, on the contrary, made circulation more firmly the measure of a newspaper's competitive standing. Newspapers became brokers of their own columns, selling their space and the readership it represented to advertisers. Circulation became less a private matter of pride and income, more a public and audited indicator of the newspaper's worth as an advertising medium. Newspapers no longer could judge their advertisers from on high; they were themselves judged by the advertisers. This became especially true as advertising developed as an independent institution apart from the press and separate from businesses themselves. Entrepreneurial advertising agents, in the years after the Civil War, would buy newspaper space and then try to sell it to advertisers; agents would be tempted to exaggerate the circulations of newspapers in which they owned space to increase their chances to resell the space. But, in 1869, George P. Rowell, who later founded *Printer's Ink,* published his first newspaper directory listing all the newspapers in the country and the best available circulation figures for them. This did not win friends among newspapers or among advertising agents, but as Rowell's reliability came to be accepted, advertising agents were forced to find new bases for competition. N. W. Ayer and Son, the first modern advertising agency, inaugurated an "open contract" system in 1875. Under this plan, the agent became the sole advertising representative of the advertiser and offered him expert advice on how and where to advertise in return for a fixed commission. This led newspapers to become more businesslike, as Daniel Boorstin observes:

Advertising space in newspapers and magazines became a commodity in the open market, and publishers were finally under pressure to give full and accurate facts about the circulation and character of their publications.[12]

The new relationship between newspapers and advertisers was marked in 1887 by the establishment of the American Newspaper Publishers Association. The main concern of this trade association in its early years was regulating the newspapers' business with advertising agencies. It regulated commissions paid to agencies, it standardized the means by which advertising rates would be computed, and, as early as 1889, began to publish a list of approved ad agencies.[13]

Pulitzer's rationalization of the *World*'s advertising policies helped the *World* adapt to general changes in the social organization of business, but the innovation most responsible for the paper's rapidly growing circulation was, in a word, sensationalism. The sensationalism Pulitzer brought to New York was not altogether revolutionary. Its attention to local news, especially crime and scandal and high society, continued in the tradition of the penny press. Indeed, this subject-matter focus, which had scandalized the established press of the 1830s, was typical of most major papers by the 1880s in New York—with some variation, of course, and with the lagging and Olympian exception of the *Evening Post*. But what defined sensationalism in the 1880s was less substance than style: how extravagantly should the news be displayed? Sensationalism meant self-advertisement. If, as James Gordon Bennett recognized in the 1840s, everything, including advertising, could and should be news, the sensational papers of the 1880s and 1890s discovered that everything, including news, could and should be advertising for the newspapers. For instance, the *World* in the 1890s regularly took a column or two on the front page to boast of its high circulation. It regularly headlined the fact, in its advertising pages, that it printed more advertisements than any other paper in the country and included the facts and figures to prove it.

Self-advertisement, as I use the term, is anything about newspaper layout and newspaper policy, outside of basic news gathering, which is designed to attract the eye and small change of readers. One of the most important developments of self-advertising in this sense was the use of illustrations. Pulitzer, perhaps feeling that illustrations lowered the dignity of a newspaper, intended at first to eliminate them from the *World*, but he found, as *The Journalist* wrote, that "the circulation of the paper went with the cuts." [14] Pulitzer reversed field and, within the first year of his *World* management, hired Valerian Gribayedoff, a portrait artist, and Walt McDougall, a cartoonist. Their efforts, according to Robert Taft's history of American photography, "mark the beginning of the modern era of newspaper illustration." [15] The *New York Daily Graphic,* in 1873, became the first American daily to regularly use illustrations—and it offered little except illustrations. At first, Pulitzer did not regard the *World* as competing with the *Daily Graphic.* By the summer of 1884, however, Pulitzer classified both papers as "illustrated daily journals"; by 1889, the *World's* extravagant use of both political cartoons and, especially in the Sunday editions, "cuts whose only justification was the fun of looking at pictures" drove the *Daily Graphic* out of business. [16]

Another major development in self-advertisement was larger and darker headlines. Here Pulitzer remained conservative for years. Rather than introduce headlines spanning several columns, he emphasized important stories simply by adding more banks of headlines within the same column. Headlines, like advertisements, abided by column-rules. Not until 1889 did the *World* run a two-column headline, but by the late 1890s, especially through the competition with Hearst, large, screaming headlines were frequently a part of the *World's* make-up. [17]

Newspaper self-advertising also had to do with the newspapers' promotion of their own exclusive features. Comparing the *World,* the *Times,* and the *Evening Post* in the 1890s, sharp differences in the amount of self-advertising become apparent. For the first week of January, 1896, the *Evening Post,* true to its long-standing editorial and stylistic conservatism, was free of overt self-advertisement. The *Times* was different. On January 2, it devoted almost all of its front page to historian John Bach McMaster's essay on the Monroe Doctrine, which was relevant at the time with respect to conflict over Venezuela. The next day, the *Times'* front page featured the remarks of Congressmen who responded (favorably) to McMaster's paper. The *Times'* decision to print the McMaster piece made it news, of a sort, and the follow-up coverage proved the *Times* to be an important paper read by important people. The McMaster essay had no other notable significance. The *World*, meanwhile, was crusading against J. P. Morgan and the financial manipulations of his "bond syndicate." On six of the first seven days of January, the *World*'s lead story was the bond issue. The *Times* featured the bond story just twice the same week, leading with Venezuela three times. Both were important events. But it is clear that the reason the *Times* featured Venezuela, and the *World* the bonds, was linked to the possibilities the stories afforded each of the papers for self-promotion, not to the relative importance of the stories in some abstract scale of significance.

If we can argue that the *World* became the circulation giant of New York journalism in the 1880s because of its vigorous and unembarrassed use of illustrations and other techniques of self-advertisement, we must still ask *why* that helped the *World*'s circulation. The answer to that is complicated and reminds us how closely intertwined are the histories of newspapers and the histories of cities. New York, in the 1880s and 1890s, was a city of immigrants. The first year in which more than half a million immigrants came to America was 1881, and immigration would reach that figure or higher in six more years of the next twelve. Immigrants from southeastern Europe outnumbered those from northwestern Europe for the first time in 1896, which suggests not only that there were more immigrants in these years than ever before but that, especially with respect to language, they were more "foreign" than ever before. By 1900, the United States had 26 million citizens whose parents were immigrants and 10 million who were immigrants themselves—46 percent of the country's population.[18] Most immigrants settled in cities, and many of them settled in New York. New York's foreign-born population rose from 479,000 in 1880 to 640,000 in 1890, by which time it was about 40 percent of the city's total population.[19]

Many immigrants could not read, or could not read English; almost all of them wanted to learn. They could learn something from the foreign-language press that grew rapidly at the end of the nineteenth century. But many of the foreign papers were edited by immigrant intellectuals whose understanding of journalism was modeled on the journals of politics and opinion they were used to in Europe. The foreign-language press that proved most successful benefited from imitating the liveliness and style of mass-circulation papers like the *World*. Abraham Cahan, editor of the *Jewish Daily Forward*, pruned his Yiddish paper of difficult expressions, introduced English words most immigrants would know, and tried to make his paper bright, simple, and interesting, as he had learned to do while working with Lincoln Steffens on the *Commercial Advertiser*.[20] The *World*'s liberal use of cartoons and drawings, liberal use of headline type, and its own emphasis on relatively simple words, content, and sentence structure appealed to people inexperienced in reading English.

Pulitzer intended the *World* to provide both editorial leadership and news. As he wrote, he wanted the *World* to be "both a daily school-house and a daily forum—both a daily teacher and a daily tribune."[21] This equal estimation of the editorial and news functions of the press was unusual in the late nineteenth century. Pulitzer may have created the first modern mass-circulation newspaper, but he did so as the last of the old-fashioned editors. Most leading newspaper proprietors of the late nineteenth century were businessmen rather than political thinkers, managers more than essayists or activists. Pulitzer cared deeply about his editorial page, but Adolph Ochs considered eliminating the *Times'* editorials altogether; Hearst looked upon the editorial page with contempt; James Gordon Bennett, Jr., toyed with dropping the editorial department of the *Herald*.[22] But if the newspaper was losing one function in the eyes of many of the leaders of journalism, it was—for some of them—gaining another: entertainment. Hearst proudly proclaimed: "It is the *Journal*'s policy to engage brains as well as to get the news, for the public is even more fond of entertainment than it is of information." [23] Melville Stone, of the *Chicago Morning News* and *Daily News,* maintained that the newspaper had three functions: to inform, to interpret, and to entertain.[24]

Pulitzer did not talk up the idea of entertainment, but the *World* came to embody it. The importance of the entertaining function of the paper was marked especially by the growth of the Sunday *World* which, like Sunday newspapers still, was as close to an illustrated magazine as to a daily newspaper in style and content. Sunday papers had been rare early in the century. In 1842 only one New Yorker in twenty-six bought a Sunday paper, while one in seven bought a daily. In 1850, after heavy Irish immigration, one in nine New Yorkers bought a Sunday paper. The Irish and other later immigrants came to the country without the American conservatism about Sabbath observance. This, plus the practice newspapers developed during the Civil War of printing special Sunday editions with war news, made it easier for papers to take the plunge into Sunday journalism and to appeal directly to the interests of readers for diversion on the day of rest. By 1889, one New Yorker in two bought a Sunday paper, making more Sunday newspaper readers than daily readers that year.[25] Charles Dana, editor of the *Sun,* estimated in 1894 that a paper with a daily edition of 50,000, at two or three cents, would have a Sunday edition of 100,000 to 150,000, at five cents.[26] What readers found and liked in the Sunday papers, they began to find in the daily press, too. Pulitzer used the Sunday *World* "as a laboratory to test ideas that finally proved to be applicable throughout the week."[27] Illustrations and comic strips (the first color comic strips appeared in the Sunday *World* in 1894) spread from the Sunday paper to the daily editions.

The Sunday papers also led the way in special women's

pages. Romantic fiction, which began in the Sunday *World* in 1883, and poetry tended to be confined to Sundays, but other features for women made their way into the daily *World*. George Juergens explains the *World*'s growing attention to women readers in the 1880s as Pulitzer's response to the rising status of women. He could not ignore feminism, or the "New Woman" movement, but neither could he endorse it if he were to keep expanding his working class readership. The compromise he worked out was to give more space to women's issues, but especially domestic life, fashion, and etiquette, rather than women's suffrage or the question of women working in traditionally male occupations.[28] This suggests that the status of women was changing as much as it was "rising," and that some of the change had little or nothing to do with women's emancipation. What was "rising" in importance was not, in the first instance, women so much as *consumption,* the side of economic life for which women were conventionally more responsible than men.

Not the status of women, then, but the status of consumption and the consumption of status were more important than ever before, and this affected the newspapers. Many goods once produced by women in the home for home use were now manufactured outside the home for women to buy. Moreover, many goods once sold in neighborhood stores were now promoted by department stores which sought city-wide distribution. Advertisers, and especially the department stores, sought a female audience and were surely impressed by newspapers which made conspicuous efforts to attract women readers. While the advertisers had no vested interest in women's suffrage—or its absence—they must have been favorably impressed by the growing coverage of fashion, etiquette, recipes, beauty culture, and interior decorating in Pulitzer's *World*.[29]

Advertisers may also have taken heart from the evidence in the newspapers of women's consciousness of social status. The first women's "advice" column began in the *World* in 1883 as a series of letters from city cousin Edith to country cousin Bessie. Edith agreed to write "about some points of social etiquette in New York, so that when you move to the city next year from your lovely country home you can be *au fait* at once." [30] Edith's concerns—such as the proper way to leave a calling card—had no connection to the daily problems of women in the tenements, but it was closely tied to, and constituent of, their dreams. Part of the experience of the city, even for the poor, was that it nourished dreams. Every day one walked by, or rode by, one's nighttime visions incarnate; the stories of Horatio Alger may not have been true but must have appeared to be true, or at least possible, and people live by their concept of the possible.

Besides, while most of the *World*'s readers did not come from "lovely country homes," they were nonetheless country cousins uncertain about how to behave in the city. The experience of newcomers to the cities may have been like that of the British working-class families, described by Peter Willmott and Michael Young, who moved from a well-established urban neighborhood to a suburban housing development in the 1950s. In the new environment, they did not know where they stood. Outward signs of status, there being no commonly recognized inner ones, became all-important:

"If," says Mrs. Abbot, "you make your garden one way, they'll knock all theirs to pieces to make theirs like it. It's the same with curtains—if you put up new curtains, they have new curtains in a couple of months. And if someone buys a new rug, they have to hang it on the line so you can see it." [31]

In the settled working-class community, the status of job and income and education and home furnishing was largely irrelevant to judgments of personal worth. But in the housing development where all people were strangers, judgments were made "on the trappings of the man rather than on the man himself." Young and Willmott conclude:

Though people stay in their houses, they do in a sense belong to a strong and compelling group. They do not know their judge personally but her influence is continuously felt. One might even suggest, to generalize, that the less the personal respect received in small group relationships, the greater is the striving for the kind of impersonal respect embodied in a status judgment. The lonely man, fearing he is looked down on, becomes the acquisitive man; possession the balm of anxiety; anxiety the spur to unfriendliness.[32]

If this is a fair generalization, it may also be fair to suggest that the United States in the 1880s and 1890s, particularly in its urban centers, was becoming more oriented to consumption, not only because of the expansion of manufacturing capacity and the rise of population—supply and demand in the crudest form—but because of the changing web of social relationships in the cities. The economy was becoming more social: the market tied together people of unconnected occupations, while factories and offices linked people of related occupations in hierarchies. The society was, at the same time, becoming more economic: it bound people together more and more in a system of social status inscribed in consumer goods.[33]

Newspapers, like the *World,* which sought a wide and general readership responded to the changing experience, perceptions, and aspirations of urban dwellers. This meant, indeed, an enlargement of the "entertainment" function of the newspaper, but it also meant the expansion of what has recently been called the "use-paper" rather than the newspaper, the daily journal as a compendium of tips for urban survival. City living, by the 1880s, had become very different from what it had been in the 1830s. It was much more a mosaic of races and social types; it was much more a maelstrom of social and geographic movement. Geographic mobility for a growing middle class was something it had never been before—it was a daily round of movement from home to work and back again. Improved urban transportation and the movement of the middle class into the suburbs meant that this daily movement could be considerable in terms of miles and time consumed. Horse-drawn omnibuses helped urban expansion away from a port-based locus beginning in the 1830s, but the growth of intracity transportation was even more dramatic in the last half of the century. The walking city of 1850 had become a riding city by 1900. The expansion of horse-drawn buses and railways (horse manure and urine had become a serious pollution problem in New York by 1890), and later cable lines and electric surface lines, elevated rapid transit and subways, made mass suburban living possible by 1900 and created a new segregation in the city: the poor lived near the city's center, while the middle class moved farther out.[34]

This had several consequences for the newspaper. Riding an omnibus or street railway was a novel experience. For the first time in human history, people other than the very wealthy could, as a part of their daily life, ride in vehicles they were not responsible for driving. Their eyes and their hands were free; they could read on the bus. George Juergens has suggested that the *World*'s change to a sensational style and layout was adapted to the needs of commuters: reading on the bus was difficult with the small print and large-sized pages of most papers. So the *World* reduced the size of the page, increased the size of headlines and the use of pictures, and developed the "lead" paragraph, in which all of the most vital information of a story would be concentrated.[35] From the 1840s, the "lead" had been pushed by the high cost of telegraphic transmission of news; now it was pulled by the abbreviated moments in which newspapers were being read. It is likely, then, that the growing use of illustration and large headlines in newspapers was as much an adaptation to the new habits of the middle class as to the new character of the immigrant working class.

What the availability of the role of passive passenger on a vehicle moving through city streets meant for people of many classes is that one could take more naturally to the role of onlooker. Charles Dickens, visiting New York in 1842, observed with wonderment the omnibuses on Broadway, though he paid just as much attention to the variety of private carriages.[36] By 1868, when Walt Whitman wrote of his delight with the omnibus, he was looking *from* it, not at it:

Shall I tell you about [my life] just to fill up? I generally spend the forenoon in my room writing, etc., then take a bath, fix up and go out about twelve and loaf somewhere or call on someone down town or on business, or perhaps if it is very pleasant and I feel like it ride a trip with some driver friend on Broadway from 23rd Street to Bowling Green, three miles each way. (Every day I find I have plenty to do, every hour is occupied with something.) You know it is a never-ending amusement and study and recreation for me to ride a couple of hours on a pleasant afternoon on a Broadway stage in this way. You see everything as you pass, a sort of living, endless panorama—shops and splendid buildings and great windows: on the broad sidewalks crowds of women richly dressed continually passing, altogether different, superior in style and looks from any to be seen anywhere else—in fact a perfect stream of people—men too dressed in high style, and plenty of foreigners—and then in the streets the thick crowd of carriages, stages, carts, hotel and private coaches, and in fact all sorts of vehicles and many first-class teams, mile after mile, and the splendor of such a great street and so many tall, ornamental, noble buildings many of them of white marble, and the gayety and motion on every side: you will not wonder how much attraction all this is on a fine day, to a great loafer like me, who enjoys so much seeing the busy world move by him, and exhibiting itself for his amusement while he takes it easy and just looks on and observes.[37]

The country cousin in the city gawks, and most city dwellers, at the end of the nineteenth century, were from the village or farm. But the city cousin looks, too—the cities of the late nineteenth century were spectacles. Social life, in general, was spectacular. Whitman watched women and foreigners on the street; women, going out to work or to shop, watched one another; immigrants watched and learned as much as they could. Theodore Dreiser's *Sister Carrie*, out looking for work on her first day in Chicago, was "delayed at every step by the interest of the unfolding scene." She headed for the department stores, which she knew through their advertisements in the *Chicago Daily News*. Carrie was dazzled by their displays of goods and awe-struck by "the fine ladies who elbowed and ignored her" and the shop girls with their "air of independence and indifference." Dreiser himself, as a reporter in the 1890s, was a spectator, both by occupation and by avocation:

My favorite pastime when I was not out on an assignment or otherwise busy, was to walk the streets and view the lives and activities of others, not thinking so much how I might advantage myself and my affairs as how, for some, the lightning of chance was always striking in somewhere and disrupting plans, leaving destruction and death in its wake, for others luck or fortune.[38]

Chance and disaster interested others as onlookers, too. Local stores in New York sold a pink booklet which was a key to the fire department's bell system. With the booklet, anyone could listen to the fire bells and then find their way to the scene of the fire. Mabel Osgood Wright declared that "going to fires was one of my greatest desires."[39] Robert Park, a quarter century later to be the chief force in building the first important department of sociology in the country at the University of Chicago, was in the 1890s a reporter for the *New York Journal* and wrote of his delight in watching the life of the city: "Walking on upper Broadway or down to the Battery on a bright afternoon, or watching the oncoming and outgoing human tide as it poured morning and evening over Brooklyn Bridge, was always for me an enthralling spectacle."[40]

Newspapers benefited from the experience of city life as a spectacle, and they contributed to it. They provided their readers a running account of the marvels and mysteries of urban life. The "action journalism" of Pulitzer, and later Hearst, created new marvels. In March, 1885, the *World* called on citizens to contribute pennies to build the pedestal for the Statue of Liberty. By August, the *World* had collected $100,000, almost all of it in small contributions. This enabled the *World* to picture itself as the champion of working people, to criticize the "luxurious classes," and to promote simultaneously the city of New York, the mass of ordinary citizens, and, of course, the *New York World*. This was self-advertising with a vengeance.

As late as 1870, church steeples towered over all other buildings in New York. This changed dramatically in the next several decades. By 1890, the *New York World* completed its new building—the tallest and grandest building in the city. The newspapers not only recorded social change; they were part of it.

In some measure, the mass journalism Pulitzer developed merely extended the revolution of the penny press in its attention to everyday life. But everyday life was different than it had been. It was the everyday life of people new to political participation, to reading, to cities, to America, to the kaleidoscope of social and geographic mobility. They wanted the moral counsel of stories as much as any people did, but the tales of the Bible and the lives of the saints were not suited to the new cities. The new journalism was. Pulitzer, an immigrant, a Jew, a self-made man, was, and his *World* set the pace.

Journalism as Information:
The Rise of the *New York Times*

The *World* may have set the pace for modern mass-circulation journalism, but after 1896 the *New York Times* established the standard. *The Journalist,* in a 1902 editorial on "Standards in American Journalism," recalled Charles Dudley Warner's claim in 1881 that the successful newspaper of the future would be the best newspaper: ". . . only that type of newspaper can live which represents something, accurately and sufficiently, to command a growing and attached clientelle." *The Journalist* took this to be a prophecy of the success of the *New York Times:* ". . . there is a clear recognition as the road to substantial success in the newspaper business of the course which the *New York Times* has aimed to follow. . . ."[41] Reporter and newspaper critic Will Irwin wrote in 1911 that the *Times* came "the nearest of any newspaper to presenting a truthful picture of life in New York and the world at large."[42] Melville Stone, writing in the *Times'* seventy-fifth anniversary issue (1926), praised publisher Adolph Ochs for having defied the view that only the sensational newspaper could be a successful newspaper: "He in the end taught them [his competitors] that decency meant dollars."[43] There would probably have been little dissent from Frank Presbrey's estimation of the *Times,* in his 1929 *History and Development of Advertising,* as "the world's most influential newspaper."[44]

Nor did there seem to be much question about the source of the *Times'* influence: wealthy people read the *Times,* attracted by its conservatism, decency, and accuracy. *The Journalist* praised the *Times* in 1897 as follows:

It has lived up to its motto of "All the news that's fit to Print," and the great cultivated, well-to-do class do not want anything beyond that. As an advertising medium for good goods it is steadily growing in value. It may not have so large a number of readers as some of its less conservative contemporaries, but its readers represent more dollars, which, after all, is what the advertiser is after.[45]

Wealthy people found the *Times* of value to them in their business. Chester S. Lord, for three decades managing editor of the *New York Sun,* wrote a guide to aspiring journalists in 1922, in which he approvingly quoted one observer of the journalistic scene as saying:

Probably five hundred men in New York City would pay a thousand dollars a year each for the commercial information alone that they receive from the New York *Times* if they could not obtain it in any other way.[46]

When Ochs took over the *Times* in 1896, he inaugurated the publication each day of a list of out-of-town buyers in the city, he began to report real estate transactions, expanded the financial reporting of the paper, and initiated a weekly review of financial news. The *Times* quickly established itself as the "Business Bible."[47] By the time Elmer Davis published his history of the *Times* in 1921, he felt called upon to defend the paper from charges that it was run by its bondholders and served as an organ for the wealthy classes. His rebuttal is revealing: "*The Times* can be called the organ of the investing class only in the sense that most investors read it because of the volume and reliability of its financial news."[48] It is clear, in comparing the *Times* and the *World* at the turn of the century, that the *Times* not only had more financial news but more financial advertising. Why did wealthy people read the *Times?* Because it was their business to do so.

But this is only the beginning of an explanation. The political tone of the *Times* also made a difference: the *Times* tended to be conservative and expressed its conservatism in both editorials and in presentation of political news. The *Times* characteristically favored the reelection of Republican governor Benjamin Odell in 1902, while the *World* championed the Democrat, Bird Coler. Comparing the front pages of the two papers for the week before the election is instructive. On October 25, both papers featured (by which I mean placed in the right-hand column on page one) the story of a train robbery in Montana. (The *Evening Post,* by the way, did not report this story at all.) On October 26, the lead story in the *Times* covered Odell's speeches upstate in which he defended himself against charges of corruption by the Democratic ex-Senator David Hill. The *World,* typically taking the opportunity to advertise itself, reported that its own canvass showed Odell would win by ten thousand votes, despite the fact that the charges against Odell were "regarded generally as proved." On October 27, the *Times* featured an accident in Yonkers in which twenty persons were injured in a collision of a trolley and an automobile. The *World* took this as its second most important story (reporting twenty-two injured) and featured, instead, a story headlined, "Reports Flying of More Charges Against Odell."

Clearly, it served the *World's* views to play up Hill's charges against Odell; it served the *Times* to play them down. On October 28, both papers featured the Democratic congressional rally in New York. But the *Times* simply headlined the event—Democratic congressional rally—while the *World* announced what it believed happened there: "Hill at Great Meeting Says Odell Confessed." The *Evening Post* showed its colors by failing to find any place on the front page for the Democratic rally and by featuring, instead, a story, "Comment on Hill Charges," in which Republican leaders sought to clear Odell.

This exercise in comparing newspapers is important in two respects. First, it simply helps establish the fact that the *Times* was politically conservative, which no doubt increased its popularity among the rich. Second, it suggests the relative difficulty of establishing, at least in the area of political reporting, that one newspaper is markedly more fair than another. In the emphasis and choice of news, the *Times* and the *World* both were guided by their political biases. That is scarcely a dazzling conclusion, but it is one which asks us to look further to figure out why the *Times* gained the preeminent reputation it did.

Two important aspects of the *Times'* rise after 1896 need to be explained and are not explained by the financial focus or political bent of the paper's contents. First, in advertising itself the *Times* stressed its "decency," not its news coverage or accuracy or politics. Second, the *Times* made its first large leap in circulation two years after Ochs assumed control of the paper, when it lowered its price from three cents to a penny. *The Journalist* spoke for many others in arguing, "Men who want The *Times* would pay 3 cents as soon as 1. The circulation won't increase one little bit."[49] But within a year circulation had grown from twenty-five to seventy-five thousand—not enough to compete with the *World* or the *Journal,* but easily enough to secure a solid place in New York journalism. If we can understand these two aspects of the success of the *Times,* we will be closer to comprehending the "two journalisms" of the 1890s.

Adolph Ochs bought the failing and demoralized *New York Times* in August, 1896. Ochs, at thirty-eight, was a very successful newspaper publisher. The eldest of six children born to German Jewish immigrants in Knoxville, Tennessee, Ochs became a chore boy and printer's devil on the *Knoxville Chronicle* at fourteen, then a printer in Louisville and Knoxville, then a business solicitor for the *Chattanooga Dispatch,* and finally, at age twenty and for $500, publisher of the *Chattanooga Times.* He turned his paper into one of the most lucrative newspapers in the South and hoped, in 1896, to be just as successful with the *New York Times.*[50] He announced his newspaper policies in the *Times* on August 19, 1896:

> To undertake the management of The New York Times, with its great history for right-doing, and to attempt to keep bright the lustre which Henry J. Raymond and George Jones have given it, is an extraordinary task. But if a sincere desire to conduct a high-standard newspaper, clean, dignified and trustworthy, requires honesty, watchfulness, earnestness, industry and practical knowledge applied with common sense, I entertain the hope that I can succeed in maintaining the high estimate that thoughtful, pure-minded people have ever had of The New York Times.
>
> It will be my earnest aim that The New York Times give the news, all the news, in concise and attractive form, in language that is parliamentary in good society, and give it as early, if not earlier,

than it can be learned through any other reliable medium; to give the news impartially, without fear or favor, regardless of any party, sect or interest involved; to make the columns of The New York Times a forum for the consideration of all questions of public importance, and to that end to invite intelligent discussion from all shades of opinion.

There will be no radical changes in the personnel of the present efficient staff. Mr. Charles R. Miller, who has so ably for many years presided over the editorial page, will continue to be the editor; nor will there be a departure from the general tone and character and policies pursued with relation to public questions that have distinguished The New York Times as a nonpartisan newspaper— unless it be, if possible, to intensify its devotion to the cause of sound money and tariff reform, opposition to wastefulness and peculation in administering the public affairs and in its advocacy of the lowest tax consistent with good government, and no more government than is absolutely necessary to protect society, maintain individual vested rights and assure the free exercise of a sound conscience.

It is a remarkable statement. The *World* at the time, in its morning and evening editions, had a circulation of 600,000 and the *Journal,* 430,000. The *Sun's* two editions sold 130,000; the *Herald* sold 140,000; the *Evening Post,* 19,000; and the *Tribune,* 16,000. The *Times'* circulation was just 9,000.[51] And yet, Ochs announced no plan to change the character of the paper. He would not change its staff; he would not alter its politics. And he hoped the paper would continue to address a select readership of "thoughtful, pure-minded people." His words are calm and determined, both high-minded and businesslike.

George Jones, who had edited the *Times* from 1869 until his death in 1891, had boasted that no man had ever been asked to subscribe to, or advertise in the *Times.*[52] Ochs had no such contempt for solicitation. He became the first publisher, in 1898, to solicit circulation by telephone. He offered a bicycle tour of France and England to the one hundred persons bringing in the most new subscribers. The former campaign, of course, reached only the relatively well to do who had telephones. The latter scheme focused on school and college teachers and stressed, in the contest advertising, that "To be seen reading The *New York Times* is a stamp of respectability."[53]

Two months after Ochs took over the paper, the famous motto, "All the News That's Fit to Print," first appeared on the editorial page. At the same time, Ochs started a circulation-building contest offering $100 for a better slogan. The winning entry was "All the World's News, but Not a School for Scandal." Still, the editors preferred their own invention, and by February, 1897, "All the News That's Fit to Print" was moved permanently to the front page.

The *Times'* slogan, like its general statement of policy, emphasized decency as much as accuracy. The *Times* could not, and did not, compete with the *World* and the *Journal* for circulation; advertising in *The Journalist* in 1902, the *Times* claimed the highest circulation of any newspaper in the city— and then, in smaller print, excepted the *World* and the *Journal,* as if they were in another category of publication altogether.[54] In a sense, they were, and the *Times* used them as a foil in promoting itself. The *Times* joined the *Sun* and *Press* and other papers in a new "moral war" in journalism. It pointedly advertised itself with the slogan, "It does not soil the breakfast cloth," as opposed to the "yellow" journals.[55] Some items from the *Times,* in the winter of 1897, are probably representative of its attitude toward the yellow press. In a story headed "The Modern Newspaper" on February 12, the *Times* covered a speech at the Press Club of Colgate University given by the city editor of the *Utica Observer* in which editor W. W. Canfield attacked papers which padded news, printed private matters, spread indecent literature, and proved themselves unreliable. He pleaded for more newspapers like the *Times.* "A newspaper," he said, "was declared to be a companion, and surely the intelligent would not accept as a companion the vicious and the depraved." On the same day, the *Times* editorialized on "Freak Journalism and the Ball." It attacked the *World*'s extravagant coverage of the Bradley Martin ball at the Waldorf, suggesting that the *World*'s artists made their drawings of the festivities before the ball took place. (It should be observed that the *Times* did not skimp on its own coverage of the ball. It reported the gala affair in a page-one, column-one story on February 12 and devoted all of page two to detailing who the guests were, what they wore, and where they dined before the great event.)

A few days later the *World* and the *Journal* were scuffling over Richard Harding Davis' report on the Olivette affair. The *Times* did not discuss the item of news itself but editorialized on the press coverage of it: "We remark with interest the rivalry of our esteemed freak contemporaries, and especially the keen interest they manifest in exposing each other's 'beats'." The *Times* took a bemused tone but it had a certain bite:

The fact that the picture from the point of view of the Cuban young lady was a greater horror and indignity than any to which the detectives could have subjected her was a detail not worth the consideration of an enterprising artist or a freak journal.[56]

Unlike other papers in New York, the *Times* apparently had a good memory. Two weeks after the Olivette affair was first reported, when the exiled Cuban women to whom Davis had talked arrived in New York, the *Times*—and it seems only the *Times*—was at the dock to interview them. On March 2 the *Times* printed a page one story, "Cuban Women Ill Treated." Characteristically, the story made no reference to the earlier news reports in the *Journal* and the *World*. The *Times* account confirmed the *World* story that the women were searched by a matron. But, in spirit, it confirmed the imagination of Remington and the outrage of Davis. The Cuban woman the *Times* interviewed complained that while she was being searched, the Spanish inspector of police looked through the porthole into the cabin and laughed at the humiliation of the women. The *Times* asked her if she had really helped the insurgents as the Spanish claimed. She smiled "significantly" and said: "Well, I am a Cuban, and my father died fighting for Cuba Libre ten years ago."

The next day the *Times* returned to its indirect assault on the yellow journals by running a page-two story on "New Journalism and Vice" which covered the speech of the Reverend Dr. W.H.P. Faunce at the twenty-fifth anniversary of the New York Society for the Suppression of Vice. Faunce said:

The press of this country to-day is engaged in a fearful struggle, one class against another. On one side stand the reputable papers which represent decency and truth, and on the other, is what calls itself the new journalism, but which is in reality as old as sin itself.

On March 4 a *Times* editorial headed "A Work of Moral Sanitation" praised Faunce. It also drew attention to the decision of the public library in Newark to exclude the sensational papers, but offered its own alternate method of reform: "To make the reading of the new journals, except behind a screen, a social offense punishable with scorn and contempt would be a salutary and sufficient measure of reform."[57]

In October, 1898, the *Times* lowered its price from three cents to a penny. Within a year its circulation jumped from 25,000 to 75,000, and after that continued to rise steadily: 82,000 in 1900; 121,000 in 1905; 192,000 in 1910; and 343,000 by 1920. While some critics suggested that the drop in price would reduce the value of the *Times* to advertisers seeking an exclusive readership, it seems only to have enhanced the *Times'* reputation with advertisers. The *Times* had 2.4 million agate lines of advertising in 1897, 2.4 million again in 1898, but then 3.4 million in 1899 and 4.0 million in 1900, 6.0 million in 1905, 7.6 million in 1910, and 23.4 million in 1920.[58] The price cut, it appears, making a high-toned, conservative paper available to more readers, assured the *Times* of success. In the very years that yellow journalism was at its most manic, the *Times* was thriving.

Ochs' own explanation of this was simple: many people bought the *World* or the *Journal* because they were cheap, not because they were sensational. Many people, if they could afford it, would choose "a clean newspaper of high and honorable aims, which prints all the news that is fit to print, and expresses its editorial opinions with sincere conviction and independence."[59] But this blithe confidence was not widely shared and, even for some editors at the *Times,* Ochs himself was the mystery to be explained. In 1915 and 1916, editorial page editor Garet Garrett kept a diary and, in a number of entries, tried to fathom Ochs' power and success. He found Ochs a crude sort of man in some respects. He was too interested in money—he "higgles terrifically over pay" and "is always impressed by large figures of wealth or income." True, Ochs found the suggestion that the *Times* was a commercial success "the unpardonable insult," but Garrett had an explanation for this, too: "His ambition (and it is not strange, seeing how all men long for that which in themselves is unattainable), his ambition is to produce a highbrow newspaper for intellectuals."

Garrett ridiculed Ochs' attention to money and his apparently meager intellectual equipment—"Intellectually he is the inferior of any man at the [editorial] council table"—but Garrett was nonetheless fascinated by Ochs' unquestioned success. He criticized Ochs for choosing words badly and for expressing himself ungrammatically, but he also wrote:

I am aware, however, that the presence of Mr. O. gives our thoughts and expressions an elasticity that they did not have in his absence. None of us values his mental processes highly, and yet, he has a way of seeing always the other side that stimulates discussion, statement and restatement, and leaves a better product altogether than is approached in his absence.

How could this be? It was, Garrett felt, that Ochs, "for his lack of reasoned conviction, is all the more seeing." At another time he wrote that Ochs had "a kind of emotional tolerance of humanity, bordering on sheer sentimentality, which continually expresses itself in the other point of view, whatever that happens to be. Without fixed convictions on anything, he can let his feelings run." And then he came to this judgment of the enigma of Ochs:

The secret—the secret of the man himself and of his success with the *Times* as well—is that Mr. O. has crowd-consciousness. He, with a newspaper, is like the orator. Both of them address a crowd, with an understanding of its emotions, or rather, with a likeness of emotions, and as the orator and the crowd react on each other, so Mr. O. and the *Times* readers react on each other.

"Mr. Ochs," he concluded, "is a crowd."[60]

In an essay on Ochs in the *Atlantic* in 1926, Benjamin Stolberg echoed Garrett's assessment in a more catty tone. Ochs, he wrote, "is not merely an honest, but a congenital conformist. He is the living norm of the median culture of American life." The *Times* succeeded because it appeared on the scene at a time of widespread emulation and conspicuous consumption. Most people read the *Times* because the elite read it. Ochs himself had noted that "no one needs to be ashamed to be seen reading" the *Times*. This, according to Stolberg, not any intrinsic excellence, accounted for the paper's success: "It is in the *Times* that we can all worship the Idols of the Cave without being caught in our idolatry."[61]

Stolberg's gibes are suggestive. The reading public may well be divided morally in ways that are related to class but do not reflect it in any simple way. If Stolberg is right, less educated or less wealthy people read the *Times* to emulate those above them in social standing, and so they read with pride. More educated and more wealthy people read not only the *Times* but the "story" newspapers and magazines, though they do so with a feeling of shame. Today, studies of television viewing indicate that highly educated people do not watch significantly less television, or even "better" television, than the less educated—they simply *feel* differently about it.[62] This repeats what observers at the end of the nineteenth century already saw in the case of newspaper reading. Pulitzer, in 1884, mocked Matthew Arnold's criticism of sensational papers, noting, "Like everybody else, Matthew buys and reads the newspapers that are racy."[63] E. L. Godkin, complaining in *The Nation* in 1895 that sensational papers were getting too much attention, nonetheless observed that they drew their readership from all social strata: ". . . this stuff is greedily read by all classes." He noted that "the grumblers over the wicked journals are often their most diligent readers."[64]

There is, then, a moral dimension to the reading of different kinds of newspapers; there is pride and shame in reading. This helps establish the plausibility of the hypothesis that the *Times'* readership was not won simply by the utility of the articles it printed for businessmen and lawyers or the resonance of its political outlook with the politics of affluent readers. The *Times* attracted readers among the wealthy and among those aspiring to wealth and status, in part, because it was socially approved. It was itself a badge of respectability.

But this only poses the question in a different way: what made the *Times* respectable? What made it seem morally superior? Was it deemed respectable because it appealed to the affluent? Or did it appeal to the affluent because it was respectable? And if the latter, is "respectability" to be understood as a moral ideal emerging from the life experience of a particular social group at a particular time or as a moral ideal with legitimate claims to wider allegiance or, perhaps, both?

This repeats, within the field of journalism, perennial questions about high culture and popular culture. What distinguishes them? Can we find any grounds for asserting that "art" is superior to popular culture? The question is of sociological interest because the taste for high culture is so regularly associated with educated and wealthy classes, the taste for popular culture, with lower classes. And yet, while the tastes of different classes remain different from one another in a given period, they change over time. Up until about the Civil War in the United States, the most sophisticated elements in the population preferred their literature, and even their journalism, flowery rather than plain, magniloquent rather than straightforward.[65] By 1900, when "information" journalism was sponsored by an economic and social elite, it was prized, but in 1835, when the first steps toward an information model were taken by the penny press in challenge of the elite of the day, it was reviled. The moral war between information journalism and story journalism in New York in the 1890s was, like the moral wars of the 1830s, a cover for class conflict.

But it was not *merely* a cover. The *Times* believed what it said about the disreputability of the new journalism. And the new journalisms of the 1830s and the 1890s did have important features in common. Both were great self-advertisers, and self-advertising is a moral stance as well as a journalistic style or commercial strategy. Among professionals like lawyers and physicians, advertising is generally prohibited or regulated by professional associations. The greater a newspaper's self-advertising, the less it appears to maintain a "professional" standing. One who advertises in professional relations, like one who boasts in personal relations, tends to be distrusted, even if there are no other evident reasons for distrust.

Were there other good reasons for the *Times* and its readers to distrust or look down on the *World* and its following? It may be that the *Times* was more faithful to facts, for instance, than the *World*. It may have reined in its own biases, when it knew them, though it did not, of course, always know them. But we cannot infer fairness or accuracy from the fact that the *Times* held to an informational model of journalism. Information journalism is not necessarily more accurate than story journalism. The two journalisms differ intrinsically, to borrow a metaphor from music, not according to what physical tones they include, but according to the dynamic quality of the tones. "Information" aspires to the position of twelve-tone music—music without an inherent, psychologically significant order to it. The "story," on the other hand, plays intentionally on connections to human experience, just as seven-tone music counts on the states of tension, unrest, and resolution it excites in listeners.

The moral division of labor between newspapers, then, may parallel the moral division of the human faculties between the more respectable faculties of abstraction and the less respectable feelings. People control themselves to read of politics in fine print; they let themselves go to read of murders or to look at drawings of celebrities. Information is a genre of self-denial, the story one of self-indulgence.

As one grows older and gains experience, one is supposed to be better able to anticipate life, to order it, to control it. One grows more rational. The *Times* wrote for the rational person or the person whose life was orderly. It presented articles as useful knowledge, not as revelation. The *World* had a different feel to it; in tone and display it created the sense that everything was new, unusual, and unpredictable. There is every reason to believe that this accurately reflected the life experience of many people in the cities, the newly literate and the newly urban, members of the working class and middle class. Life was a spectacle as never before for many, and the *World* spoke faithfully to that experience of the many, as the *Times* did for the more ordered experience of a smaller group.[66]

Perhaps, then, the *Times* established itself as the "higher journalism" because it adapted to the life experience of persons whose position in the social structure gave them the most control over their own lives. Its readers were relatively independent and participant. The readers of the *World* were relatively dependent and nonparticipant. The experience engendered by affluence and education makes one comfortable with a certain journalistic orientation, one which may indeed be, in some respects, more mature, more encompassing, more differentiated, more integrated. It may also be, in its own ways, more limited; refinement in newspapers, people, and sugar, is bleaching. If the *World*'s readers might have longed for more control of their lives, the readers of the *Times* may have wished for more nutrients in theirs.

At the turn of the century and even as late as the 1920s, "objectivity" was not a term journalists or critics of journalism used. Newspapers were criticized for failing to stick to the facts, and the *Times* boasted that it printed "all the news"— by which it meant information. But this was not objectivity; the attachment to information did not betray much anxiety about the subjectivity of personal perspective. The *Times* in 1900 trusted to information, that body of knowledge understandable in itself without context (or with a context taken for granted). That was not to last. By the 1920s, journalists no longer believed that facts could be understood in themselves; they no longer held to the sufficiency of information; they no longer shared in the vanity of neutrality that had characterized the educated middle class of the Progressive era. In the twentieth century, the skepticism and suspicion which thinkers of the late nineteenth century, like Nietzsche, taught, became part of general education. People came to see even the findings of facts as interested, even memory and dreams as selective, even rationality itself a front for interest or will or prejudice. This influenced journalism in the 1920s and 1930s and gave rise to the ideal of objectivity as we know it.

CHAPTER 4

Objectivity Becomes Ideology: Journalism After World War I

NOTHING thus far explains the twentieth century's passion for "objectivity." The rise of a democratic market society helped extinguish faith in traditional authorities, but this did not in itself provide new authority. In a democracy, the people governed, not the "best people," and one vote was as good as another. In the market, things did not contain value in themselves; value was an arithmetic outcome of a collection of suppliers and demanders seeking their own interests. In an urban and mobile society, a sense of community or of the public had no transcendent significance, and, indeed, one responded to other people as objects, rather than as kindred, and trusted to impersonal processes and institutions—advertising, department stores, formal schooling, hospitals, mass-produced goods, at-large elections—rather than rely on personal relations. All of this focused attention on "facts." All of it contributed to what Alvin Gouldner has called "utilitarian culture," in which the normative order moved from a set of commandments to do what is right to a set of prudential warnings to adapt realistically to what *is*. Just when Freud was diagnosing the pathologies of the domineering superego, the superego and moral exhortation were in retreat before the ego and the cognitive dimension of experience. Realism, not religion, became a guiding light. Even so, despite what appears to be the relativistic logic of a democratic market society and a utilitarian culture, not many people were led to distrust the objectivity or reality of their own values. The Progressive era, we might say, wanted to embrace science but did not know how to.[1]

The last decades of the nineteenth century and the first years of this century saw the emergence of the American university, the proliferation of professional associations, and the beginnings of "scientific management" in industry and in city government, but this was not the same as, nor did it produce, a belief in objectivity. Not until after World War I, when the worth of the democratic market society was itself radically questioned and its internal logic laid bare, did leaders in journalism and other fields, like the social sciences, fully experience the doubting and skepticism democracy and the market encouraged. Only then did the ideal of objectivity as consensually validated statements about the world, predicated on a radical separation of facts and values, arise. It arose, however, not so much as an extension of naive empiricism and the belief in facts but as a reaction against skepticism; it was not a straight-line extrapolation but a dialectical response to the culture of a democratic market society. It was not the final expression of a belief in facts but the assertion of a method designed for a world in which even facts could not be trusted.

Losing Faith in the Democratic Market Society

Editor James A. Wechsler recalled the early 1930s as a time of "democratic despair" and "querulous pessimism about the democratic future." He remembered being addressed as a freshman at Columbia in 1931 by President Nicholas Murray Butler. Butler said that only two methods for selecting leaders existed in the twentieth century: election and dictatorship. As between these systems, Butler went on, dictatorship "appears to bring into authority and power men of far greater intelligence, far stronger character and far more courage than does the system of election." [2]

This was not just the cynicism of an isolated antidemocrat. Mussolini was a popular figure in America in the twenties and early thirties, his "pragmatism" appealing to both conservatives and liberals disillusioned with democracy and capitalism.[3] Nor was it simply the despair of a depression year. Even at the height of prosperity in the twenties and even, or especially, among liberal intellectuals, there was deep pessimism about political democracy. Walter Lippmann, in *Public Opinion* (1922), had begun to knock the "public" off the perch that the rhetoric of democracy had built for it. In *The Phantom Public* (1925), he was still more severe and critical of democratic ideals. "The private citizen today," he wrote in the book's opening sentence, "has come to feel rather like a deaf spectator in the back row, who ought to keep his mind on the mystery off there, but cannot quite manage to keep awake." Public affairs are not the private citizen's affairs: "They are for the most part invisible. They are managed, if they are managed at all, at distant centers, from behind the scenes, by unnamed powers." This did not preface a call to arms, or a plea for Progressive politics. Lippmann observed that scholars used to write books about voting, but "They are now beginning to write books about nonvoting." This was not the fault of the citizen, not even the fault of a decent political system rightly conceived. It was, instead, Lippmann argued, the fault of the "unattainable ideal" of citizenship. There is no special wisdom in the will of the majority. On the contrary, wisdom is more likely to lie with insiders, experts in the practice of governing. Voting is an exceptional procedure which enables the public to act only when a problem arises. A problem arises only if someone objects to current policy—insofar as there is general agreement, the public *has no interest* in politics and should have no interest. The people do not govern and should not govern; at most, they support or oppose the individuals who do rule. Voting, Lippmann wrote, is:

... an act of enlistment, an alignment for or against, a mobilization. These are military metaphors, and rightly so, I think, for an election based on the principle of majority rule is historically and practically a sublimated and denatured civil war, a paper mobilization without physical violence.[4]

The Phantom Public directed its rhetoric against "democratic reformers" who placed too much hope in the public—a body, Lippmann argued, they never adequately defined or understood. Secondarily, the book attacked those cynics who pointed all too easily to "what a hash democracy was making of its pretensions to government." According to Lippmann, these critics conclude that the public is uninformed and meddlesome, probably by nature; they fail to see that the main difference between the rulers and the ruled is that between insiders and outsiders, that education for citizenship and education for public office must be, and should be, different. So Lippmann tried to reserve a place in his analysis for public opinion; he tried to cut a pragmatic middle road between a democratic fantasy and a democratic despair. This expressed some hope for the future. Even so, in the wake of a century of optimism about democracy, Lippmann's formulation of the problem of the public was dour; he had tempered his own confidence by cutting it down to a size which would not excite passion or promise.

This is all the more striking when one compares Lippmann's writings of the twenties to his prewar *Drift and Mastery* (1914). There, like many others in the next decades, he diagnosed the problem of modern life as a loss of authority. The world was adrift, no one was in command. Yet, there was a solution. In a sense, it is the same solution Lippmann would offer later—science, but with a difference. In *Drift and Mastery* scientific thinking is "the twin-brother" of democracy in politics. "As absolutism falls," Lippmann wrote, "science rises. It *is* self-government." Lippmann ended the book in an almost millenarian tone: "The scientific spirit is the discipline of democracy, an escape from drift, the outlook of a free man." [5] Indeed, in *Drift and Mastery* Lippmann expressed his faith that ordinary citizens would make great changes: the consumer was to be a center of power in politics; the labor movement and the women's movement were to effect a transvaluation of values. Nothing could be more remote from the Lippmann of *Public Opinion* and *The Phantom Public*. When Lippmann appealed to the idea of science in the 1920s, he took science to be the governor or throttle on popular will, not the democratic engine itself.

Despair about democracy deepened in the 1930s with the growing strength of dictatorships in Germany and Italy and the apparent helplessness of American government in the early thirties to deal with the depression. "Epitaphs for democracy are the fashion of the day," Felix Frankfurter wrote in 1930, although he was more hopeful himself.[6] "Representative democracy seems to have ended in a *cul-de-sac*," Harold Laski told readers of the *American Political Science Review* in 1932; the complacent optimism of just fifty years before had been eclipsed by an "institutional *malaise*."[7] It was a far cry from the Progressive Era when, in 1937, the editors of *The New Republic* introduced a series of articles on "the future of democracy" with the words: "At no time since the rise of political democracy have its tenets been so seriously challenged as they are today." [8] Old Progressives found themselves baffled by the complexity of economic and political

125

problems of the 1930s. William Allen White admitted in 1938, "I don't know what is right. . . . I'm not as smart as I used to think I was." And Ray Stannard Baker, in 1936, said: "Of this I am sure. I cannot settle . . . the tremendous problems now plaguing the world. Most often I cannot fully understand. The factors are too complex."[9]

The pessimism about the institutions of democracy and capitalism in the 1930s had roots in the doubts of the 1920s about the public and human nature, traditional values and received knowledge. The spirit of business in the twenties was buoyant, and there was a feeling of liberation in social science, the arts, and the social life of the urban Bohemians. But the liberation into a new culture marked the rapid disintegration of the old, and many serious thinkers began to fear that the new edifices of the arts and sciences were being raised without foundations.[10] Roscoe Pound, dean of American legal philosophers, felt the uneasiness affecting social thought and social life when he addressed Wellesley's graduating class in 1929. From the Reformation until the twentieth century, he said, the dominant note in Western culture was "confidence." But lack of confidence had overwhelmed the twentieth century. Psychology led us to distrust reason; the distrust of reason led us to doubt our political institutions. Science, once the mainstay of confidence, "has been teaching distrust of itself." Students today, Pound observed, speak proudly of their disillusionment. No illusions take them in, and "frankness" is one of their favorite words. Physics, biology, and economics all find complexity and randomness, rather than the simplicity and order they had once believed present in the world. History no longer believes in facts but only in the subjective judgments of historians. Most devastating of all was the distrust of reason psychology had established:

In place of reason we have subconscious wishes, repressed desires, rooted behavior tendencies, habitual predispositions which are different for each individual economic unit. In place of enlightenment we have—well, perhaps glands.[11]

Pound's answer to the growing consciousness of the irrational was to caution against idolatry: "The irrational is a fact, not an ideal. We must reckon with it, but we are not bound to exalt it." Still, his own affirmation was modest. He retained confidence in a world which generally lacked it because, he said, he was raised in the nineteenth century, before reason had come into doubt. No explanation of his own position could better indicate that Pound wrote in a disillusioned time and was himself deeply affected by its habit of reducing ideas to their biographies.

The distrust of reason Pound spoke of took different forms. Politically it meant a distrust of the public and a doubt that representative institutions could ever act wisely. We have seen this already, in modest expression, in Lippmann. Lippmann spoke for a wider and deeper current of thought that began at the end of the nineteenth century with a rash of writing on "crowds" and the behavior of crowds. Many of these works were antiliberal, attacking the lower orders and even attacking the middle class from an aristocratic point of view: in some of the European literature, electoral crowds, juries, and parliaments were linked to crowds and riots as instances of mass subjection to prejudice and primitive instinct. Leon Bramson, in his study of the political context of sociological thought, argues that American writings on crowds were not antiliberal. American sociologists took the crowd to be a seedbed of new institutions serving the needs an earlier social order had not met.[12] While this may be true for academic sociology as it developed in America, the European antiliberals directly influenced American thinking outside sociology. Everett Dean Martin's *The Behavior of Crowds* (1921)— which lies outside Bramson's study because it was not written by a professional sociologist—was antiliberal, widely read, and cited approvingly by Lippmann in *Public Opinion* (1922). Lippmann observed that Gustave LeBon, one of the leading French antiliberal writers, had been taken up as a "prophet" by those who were most skeptical in America about the rational operation of popular will. Edward L. Bernays, one of the leading figures in the development of public relations in the 1920s, was influenced by Martin's book, by LeBon, and, of course, by Lippmann himself.[13]

While Bramson is right to point out different emphases in American and European thought, Europeans focusing on "the crowd" and Americans on "the public," what seems more important here is that in both Europe and America the meaning of "public" and "public opinion" changed in the same direction in the early twentieth century. Public opinion, as W. H. Mackinnon defined it in 1828, was "that sentiment on any given subject which is entertained by the best informed, most intelligent and most moral persons in the community, which is gradually spread and adopted by nearly all persons of any education or proper feeling in a civilized state."[14] In England, this "public opinion" served as a weapon of the middle class in rising against the aristocracy.[15] Something similar was true in the United States where "the people," in the early nineteenth century, was a term used to refer to the middle class.[16] If, however, public opinion was the voice of the middle class against an aristocracy in the early nineteenth century, by the early twentieth century, it was regarded by the middle class as the voice of some other, large mass of persons having no claims to the middle-class perquisite of education and middle-class virtue of rationality. Public opinion was no longer the readership James Gordon Bennett or Horace Greeley or Samuel Bowles addressed in small, dense type and long-winded editorials; the public was now the urban masses who liked banner headlines, large drawings and photographs, snappy and spicy writing. True, the older journalism had scarcely been as dignified or reasoned as some liked to remember it, and the educated middle class itself liked banners and spice more than it cared to admit. But at the same time it felt a great need to distinguish itself from the rest of the reading public, for it no longer recognized in "public opinion" what it took to be its own voice, the voice of reason. The professional classes now took public opinion to be irrational and therefore something to study, direct, manipulate, and control. The professions developed a proprietary attitude toward "reason" and a paternalistic attitude toward the public.

The distrust, not so much of reason as of the public's capacity for exercising it, had to do with the sense of the middle class that it was surrounded by urban masses and the uneasiness of the white Anglo-Saxon male at the discovery that his was no longer so clearly the loudest voice in the world. In a remarkable monograph on the history of the concept "attitude," Donald Fleming observes that the present usage of the word is relatively new. He argues that "attitude" came into general use, as well as scientific use, at the end of the nineteenth century and the beginning of the twentieth century, when societies were faced with the task of redefining the human condition to include infants, children, adolescents, mental patients, primitive people, peasants, immigrants, Negroes, slum dwellers, urban masses, crowds, and, most of all, women. Once political society expanded to include more than native white males, elites began to modify their sense of what human nature is. Most of the new categories of persons the elites had to reckon with had "often been conceived of as passional beings, incapable of sustained rationality." Rather than attribute rationality to them, social scientists and others began to reconceive human nature generally, replacing a term like "conviction," which stressed human rationality, with terms like "attitude" and "opinion," which indicated that human thought and expression mix reason and passion.[17]

This was a response to the heterogeneous social world of

the cities. In urbanization, historians H. J. Dyos and Michael Wolff write, "a dominant culture is always faced by new groups of people previously thought of as beneath consideration." Speaking of cities in Victorian England, they argue that there was a mutual recognition and distancing of the middle class and the working class. This was something distinctively modern, "the capacity for sustained awareness" of other cultures:

> What the Victorian city began to do . . . was to permit this sustained awareness of differences in social conditions to take place. Here, almost for the first time, was some visible prospect of the advancement of whole classes but, more than that, a stirring consciousness among the lower ranks of society of the removable differences in the quality of human life. It was the city which enabled such things to be seen.[18]

Of course, the American situation was not identical, but the American city enabled such things to be seen, too. The American middle class, at the end of the nineteenth century and increasingly thereafter, began to move from cities to suburbs, creating a residential segregation by class which metropolitan areas had never before known. The efforts of the affluent to insulate themselves shaped the political geography of the country in new ways in the 1920s. In 1916 there were zoning laws in only sixteen American municipalities; by the end of the twenties, eight hundred were zoned, and 60 percent of the country's urban population lived under zoning regulations.[19] Judge David C. Westenhaver found no ambiguity in the aims of zoning ordinances when he decided against zoning (his decision was overturned) in the landmark case of *Village of Euclid* v. *Ambler Realty:* "In the last analysis, the result to be accomplished is to classify the population and segregate them according to their income and situation in life."[20] In the same period, Congress approved restrictions on immigration. While representatives from the South, the West, and rural sections of the country led the fight to restrict immigration, they found support from centers of power in the Eastern cities, too. In 1916 *The New Republic* suggested that modern democracy "cannot permit . . . social ills to be aggravated by excessive immigration." The *New York Times,* as well as the *Saturday Evening Post,* praised Madison Grant's influential racist tract, *Passing of the Great Race,* in editorials. Colleges and universities, including Columbia and Harvard, instituted or tightened quotas on Jews.[21]

Faith in democracy was losing out to fears of unreason—and of the presumably unreasoning, the urban masses, the immigrants, the Jews. Of course, there was new hope, the hope of efficiently controlling irrationality. But if some reformers believed that modeling government and social organizations after the efficient business enterprise was a solution, others were beginning to regard it as part of the problem. "The invasion of the community by the new and relatively impersonal and mechanical modes of combined human behavior," John Dewey wrote, "is the outstanding fact of modern life." Impersonal organizations, not face-to-face relations, dominated the age, Dewey observed in *The Public and Its Problems.* Individuals were counting for less, impersonal organizations for more. The very expansion and intensification of social interaction which had created a "public" led also to impersonal controls which made the public's exercise of its own reason impossible.[22] Democracy was still formally growing; the Progressive movement had introduced initiative, referendum, and recall, direct election of Senators, and popular primaries. The nineteenth amendment to the Constitution finally gave women the vote in 1920. But somehow the popular control of government seemed farther away than ever.

In economic as well as in political life, the public appeared more removed from decision making at exactly the time that, formally, it was more involved. In *The Modern Corporation and Private Property* (1932), Adolf A. Berle and Gardiner C.

Means observed that the transfer of the industrial wealth of the nation from individual ownership to ownership by large corporations meant the divorce of business ownership from business control. With information on 144 of the 200 largest corporations in 1930, Berle and Means found 3 had over 200,000 stockholders, 71 had 20,000 or more, and 124 had 5000 or more. In most cases the stock owned by management came to just a few percent of the total. *The Modern Corporation and Private Property* is a requiem for the small, independent capitalist whose ownership of property involved active control and who derived "spiritual values" from ownership. Berle and Means pictured the old-time capitalist extending his personality through ownership. When wealth was in land, the owner might use it directly and it would take on a subjective value it could not have in the form of stocks. In stock ownership, the capitalist could make use of his property only through sales in the market. Actual control of property had shifted from owners to the "economic autocrats" who managed the corporations.[23]

In formal terms, traditional ideals were being enacted: more and more persons entered the market as small, independent "capitalists," just as more and more people were formally able to participate in politics at the polls. The market, like democracy, was enlarging. Yet, as formal participation expanded, substantial control evaporated, and the voice of the small investor could no more be heard above the clatter of corporate managers than the mutterings of the voting citizen could be heard above the din of administrative imperialism— the mayor or city manager taking power from the alderman, the president taking control from the Congress.

As in politics and social life, so in economic affairs, institutions and individuals in positions of influence reconsidered and reconceived the "public." In business, corporations began to *recognize* a public for the first time: businesses moved from ignoring the public, or damning it, in the nineteenth century, to advising and accommodating it through public relations, in the twentieth century. The "public" that emerged was one of both investors and consumers. In the first decade of the twentieth century, light industry, retail merchants, and other businesses increasingly chose to offer public stock issues to meet their capital needs. At the same time, savings increased, and the consequent availability of funds for investment stimulated a general interest in buying securities. Investment bankers courted the person with just a thousand dollars or so to invest. The firm of Lee, Higginson hired the first securities salesman in 1906 and quickly shifted the bulk of its business from railroad securities to utilities and industrials whose higher interest rates appealed to the small investor seeking a quick return. World War I stimulated small investment again as people got used to buying Liberty bonds. Some firms initially organized to sell war bonds, like Federal Securities Corporation in Chicago, continued their wartime sales techniques to sell other securities after the war. Federal Securities followed its practice with special departments catering to women and to foreign-born investors.[24]

There was not only a growing public of investors but a vast public of consumers. National corporations, at the end of the nineteenth century, used newspapers and magazines to advertise directly to consumers. In the 1920s, installment buying, particularly of automobiles, became an important aspect of family spending, leading John Dewey to observe that buying had become as much a duty in the corporate society of the twentieth century as thrift had been in the individualistic society of the nineteenth.[25] Personal finance companies multiplied. Familiar elements of the world were redefined in terms of consumption. Children, for instance, once regarded as modest economic assets, came to be seen as a source of major expenses.[26] The increasing recognition by many people that America was becoming a "consumer society"[27] led some liberal thinkers to urge the reconstruction of American politics on the ground of a consumers' movement.[28] They were too optimistic, but they were on target in recognizing the growing importance in the economy of consumption and its management. Even the rise of the small investor may not have indicated the enlargement of the field of active ownership so much as the consumerization of owning, a pacification of property.

Public relations developed in the early part of the twentieth century as a profession which responded to, and helped shape, the public, newly defined as irrational, not reasoning; spectatorial, not participant; consuming, not productive. This had a far-reaching impact on the ideology and daily social relations of American journalism.

The Decline of "Facts" in Journalism

There is such distaste in intellectual circles for the very notion of public relations that it is difficult to believe that the public relations of Ivy Lee, Edward L. Bernays, and others pioneered in the first three decades of this century was, in many respects, progressive. An incident which symbolized the new public relations occurred in 1906 soon after Ivy Lee had been hired as public relations counsel to the Pennsylvania Railroad. An accident took place on the main railroad line near Gap, Pennsylvania. Railroads had traditionally tried to suppress news of accidents.[29] Lee, in contrast, invited reporters to the scene of the accident at the railroad's expense. An accident on the New York Central soon thereafter was hushed up, as usual. But, in light of the new Pennsylvania policy, reporters got angry and gave the New York Central a bad press.[30] This was the beginning of a new relationship between the railroads, then the largest and most powerful corporations in the country, and the press and reading public: Lee's insistence on "absolute frankness" for the Pennsylvania Railroad forced other railroads to follow suit.

Ivy Lee was the son of a Methodist minister. He grew up in the South, was educated at Princeton, and in 1899 began work as a reporter in New York, first for the *Journal,* then the *Times,* and finally the *World.* He then moved into publicity work, establishing the firm of Parker and Lee. "Accuracy, Authenticity, Interest" was the motto which the partners apparently took seriously. *Editor and Publisher,* generally hostile to public relations, admitted that Parker and Lee never tried to deceive but sent copy to the press "with the frank statement that it is in behalf of the client, and that no money will be paid for its insertion in the columns of any newspaper."[31]

Lee, generally regarded as the "first" public relations agent, was surely one of the most self-conscious. He was a determined publicist for public relations itself. In 1924 and 1925 he expressed his views in addresses to the American Association of Teachers of Journalism and also to the Advertising Club of New York. He argued that propaganda, which he defined simply as "the effort to propagate ideas," was acceptable as long as the public knew who was responsible for it. Lee based this relatively cavalier attitude toward propaganda on a disillusioned, distinctively modern attitude toward "facts." No one, he said, quoting Walter Lippmann approvingly, can present the whole of the facts on any subject. The very notion of a "fact" he regarded as suspect: "The effort to state an absolute fact is simply an attempt to achieve what is humanly impossible; all I can do is to give you *my interpretation of the facts.*"[32] Lee implicitly denied that disinterestedness was possible for an individual or institution. "All of us," he said, "are apt to try to think that what serves our own interests is also in the general interest. We are very prone to look at everything through glasses colored by our own interests and prejudices."[33] While this perception in some hands was a sociology of knowledge used as criticism, for Lee it was a cynical epistemology used to defend business's use of public relations. Since all opinions are suspect, all are equally entitled to a place in the democratic forum.

Edward L. Bernays, who, along with Lee, was the most prominent publicist for public relations, took a similar line. Like Lee, he denied that there was anything wrong with propaganda. "Propaganda," he wrote in 1923, "is a purposeful, directed effort to overcome censorship—the censorship of the group mind and the herd reaction."[34] Bernays, Sigmund Freud's nephew and a man sensitive to the irrational sources of human thought, relied on the works of Everett Dean Martin and William Trotter in his *Crystallizing Public Opinion* to argue that political, economic, and moral judgments are "more often expressions of crowd psychology and herd reaction than the result of the calm exercise of judgment."[35] Where Lee stressed that opinion was self-interested, Bernays argued that it was irrational. Either way, opinion was not true or trustworthy. This led Bernays, like Lee, to a libertarian rationale for public relations:

In the struggle among ideas, the only test is the one which Justice Holmes of the Supreme Court pointed out—the power of thought to get itself accepted in the open competition of the market.[36]

Public relations was much in need of a rationale. Trade journals in publishing frequently attacked public relations during the twenties and into the thirties. *Editor and Publisher* feared that public relations agents helped businesses to promote as news what otherwise would have been purchased in advertising. It decried publicity agents in general as "space grabbers" and Bernays in particular as a "menace."[37] Bernays coined the term "counsel on public relations" in the early twenties to insist that he was a new professional in a new role, not the old "press agent" of the nineteenth century. "This was no mere difference in nomenclature, no euphemistic change-over," Bernays recalled in his memoirs, but euphemism was precisely what others took it to be. Mencken's *American Language* (1936) dismissed it as a euphemism, while Stanley Walker, city editor of the *New York Herald Tribune,* irreverently lumped it with a mixed bag of other terms in a 1932 essay in *Harper's:*

> . . . public relations counsel, publicity adviser, advocates at the court of public opinion, good-will ambassadors, mass-mind molders, fronts, mouthpieces, chiselers, moochers, and special assistants to the president.[38]

Walker's essay captures the uneasy response of editors and reporters to public relations. The response of newspaper business managers was unambiguous: they opposed public relations. The editorial staff was more ambivalent. Walker's essay is full of a breezy humor which smooths over an awkward mix of distaste, disgust, rivalry, and grim affection for the public relations agent. Walker observed with mock despondency that the 5,000 public relations agents in New York outnumbered the journalists, that schools of journalism produced more public relations agents than newspapermen, and that half or more of the news items in the daily press originated in public relations work. But the mocking died when Walker concluded that the publicity agent and the newspaper are inevitable enemies and will always be so, despite the yearning of some public relations agents for a code of ethics and professional status, "anything to take them out of the red light district of human relations."[39]

The press itself was partly responsible for the growth of publicity or propaganda. (Today publicity or public relations would be called "propaganda" only as an epithet, but in the twenties both "publicity" and "propaganda" were rather new terms; both had unsavory connotations—though "propaganda" more so—and they were used to some extent interchangeably.) Nelson Crawford, in his well-regarded text, *The Ethics*

137

of Journalism (1924), held that newspaper inaccuracies and the habit of reporters of giving most space to those who furnished them with "typed copies of speeches, ready-prepared interviews, and similar material" encouraged the use of public relations by individuals and organizations.[40] Still, journalists scorned the "handouts" they took and resented the press agents with whom they worked. "Why is it then that this amiable gentleman," a *New York World* reporter asked about Ivy Lee, "who provides so many good stories, is so generally disliked by newspaper men?"[41] The answer is not hard to imagine. Public relations threatened the very idea of reporting. News appeared to become less the reporting of events in the world than the *reprinting* of those facts in the universe of facts which appealed to special interests who could afford to hire public relations counsel. It was just as Ivy Lee said it was: there are no facts, everything is interpretation. Reflective reporters did not like relying on the publicity agents, but the facility with which the agents were able to use the newspapers for their own purposes surprised even the agents themselves. After a publicity campaign that won considerable newspaper space for a Rockefeller gift to Johns Hopkins University, Ivy Lee wrote to his most famous and most faithful employer, John D. Rockefeller, as follows:

In view of the fact that this was not really news, and that the newspapers gave so much attention to it, it would seem that this was wholly due to the manner in which the material was "dressed up" for newspaper consumption. It seems to suggest very considerable possibilities along this line.[42]

The public relations counsel, Bernays boasted, "is not merely the purveyor of news; he is more logically the *creator* of news."[43] That was exactly what journalists feared.

There was another reason for journalists to dislike public relations: it undermined the traditional social relations of the newspaper fraternity. Reporters who delighted in going backstage for news were now stopped at the stage door; public relations men seemed to be everywhere. "The problem of propaganda," Nelson Crawford told students of journalism, "is serious." He estimated that a large newspaper received 150,000 words of public relations material daily.[44] Frank Cobb, of the New York *World,* observed in 1919 that there had been about twelve hundred employed press agents in New York before the war, but that their numbers had rapidly increased since:

How many there are now I do not pretend to know, but what I do know is that many of the direct channels to news have been closed and the information for the public is first filtered through publicity agents. The great corporations have them, the banks have them, the railroads have them, all the organizations of business and of social and political activity have them, and they are the media through which the news comes. Even statesmen have them.[45]

This was so. Government agencies and public officials, as well as businesses, increasingly made use of public relations. As a self-conscious activity of government, this was a development new and startling enough to excite some controversy. The Congress insisted in 1908 on amending the Agricultural Appropriations bill to read that "no part of this appropriation shall be paid ... for ... the preparation of any newspaper or magazine articles." In 1910 the Congress questioned, but did not act against, the Census Bureau's maintenance of a "press bureau." In 1913, after further congressional investigation of the publicity work of federal agencies, a law was passed denying the use of any appropriations for payment of "publicity experts," unless specifically designated by the Congress. But the law was a dead letter; government public relations proliferated in and after World War I.[46]

Theodore Roosevelt was the first president to set up a room for the press in the White House; Woodrow Wilson initiated the regular press conference; Warren Harding originated the use of the term "White House spokesman" to refer to statements he made at press conferences. Reporters thus gained a more secure relationship to White House news, but one more formal than it had been, and more easily organized and manipulated by the president or his secretaries. The newspaper fraternity turned into a press corps. What had been the primary basis for competition among journalists—the exclusive, the inside story, the tip, the scoop—was whisked away by press releases and press conferences. Newspapers that had once fought "the interests" now depended on them for handouts. Just as public relations, in general, was "progressive" in rationalizing the relationship of business and the public, so the press release was progressive in rationalizing the reporting of news.[47] The publicity agents played no favorites, protected their employers from direct contact with reporters, and turned news into a policy rather than an event, a constant stream rather than eddies, rapids, and whirlpools.

There was, perhaps, another reason reporters disliked the public relations agents: the agents doubted their own worth. They had much in which they took pride: Eric Goldman, who wrote a brief history of public relations, suggests that public relations changed from a nineteenth-century "public be damned" or "public be fooled" attitude to a "public be informed" attitude at the turn of the century, and then to a "public be understood" stance after World War I, in which the public relations counsel interpreted and adjusted his client and the public to each other. The public relations counsel, equipped with modern psychology's understanding of the irrational roots of human opinion, tried to understand the public as "an expert with the technical equipment, the ethics, and the social view associated with the lawyer, doctor, or teacher."[48] But this did not keep Ivy Lee, at least, from wondering about the value of his work. He wrote, in 1929:

A good many years ago I started on the work I am doing, feeling that there was a real field in it for usefulness. I know now that there is a great deal to be done that is useful. But of course a great many people feel that it is an undignified work that I am doing and not worthy of great intellectual effort. There is a great deal to be said on both sides.[49]

Still more brooding and doubtful, Lee told a friend:

Sometimes in my low moments I have thought of throwing the whole thing overboard and taking a minor job as a newspaper editor. Even then I wonder if I would not still be suspect; whether I have not been so thoroughly tainted as a propagandist that people would always suspect that there was an angel in the closet telling me what to say and think.[50]

The publicity agent, John Dewey wrote in 1929, "is perhaps the most significant symbol of our present social life."[51] Public relations spoke—created—the language of twentieth century business and politics. It exemplified and encouraged the self-interested sensitivity to social nuance and psychological fine points characteristic of an age of organizations. It managed or manipulated the public in the name of public service. Yet it never established itself as the "profession" it hoped to be, and its leaders, at least in occasional pensive moments, could not come to terms with their work.[52]

Public relations was one of two key developments which made journalists suspicious of facts and ready to doubt the naive empiricism of the 1890s. The other development was wartime propaganda. "It was the astounding success of propaganda during the war," Edward Bernays wrote, "which opened the eyes of the intelligent few in all departments of life to the possibilities of regimenting the public mind."[53] Many journalists were directly involved in World War I propaganda. On the one hand, American journalists found themselves the victims of military censorship as war correspondents in Europe. On the other hand, they themselves served as agents of the American propaganda machine at home or abroad. James Keeley, managing editor of the *Chicago Tribune* and publisher of the *Chicago Herald,* represented the United

States on the Inter-Allied Board for propaganda; Walter Lippmann for a time served as a captain of military intelligence and directed the editorial side of American propaganda in Paris; Charles Merz, later to be editorial-page editor at the *New York Times,* was a first lieutenant intelligence officer with Lippmann.[54] On the domestic scene, President Wilson created the Committee on Public Information in 1917 and appointed George Creel, a muckraking editor, to run it. The Committee, which employed many journalists, wrote, collected, and distributed information favorable to the American war effort. It churned out 6,000 press releases, enlisted 75,000 "Four Minute Men" to deliver short speeches in movie theaters and other public places, and even enrolled the Boy Scouts to deliver copies of Wilson's addresses door to door.[55]

The *New York Times* described the European conflict as "the first press agents' war," and historian Jack Roth has called the war "the first modern effort at systematic, nationwide manipulation of collective passions."[56] Nothing could have been more persuasive than the war experience in convincing American newspapermen that facts themselves are not to be trusted. Reporters had long taken pride in their own cynicism, but this expressed itself in a love of being close to, and conversant with, the "inside story" of political and economic life. Their cynicism had sneered at popular illusions while relishing hard, stubborn, and secret facts. But in the war and after, journalists began to see *everything* as illusion, since it was so evidently the product of self-conscious artists of illusion.

War propaganda directly influenced the wider growth of public relations in the twenties. The war stimulated popularly approved public relations campaigns for war bonds, the Red Cross, the Salvation Army, and the Y.M.C.A. Community Chests developed publicity campaigns based on wartime models. By 1920, according to the contemporary newspaper critic Will Irwin, there were nearly a thousand "bureaus of propaganda" in Washington modeled on experience during the war.[57] In the business world, the case of Samuel Insull is especially instructive. Insull, Chicago's electric power baron, had begun advising the American branch of the British propaganda office in 1914. Insull was instrumental in encouraging the British to allow newspaper interviews with cabinet ministers, something unheard of before the war. This increased the interest of American newspapers in the British cause. Insull contributed a quarter million dollars of his own to help distribute highly colored war information to American newspapers which had no wire service affiliations. After the United States entered the war, Insull became chief of the State Council of Defense in Illinois; out of this committee came the idea for "broadcasting without radio"—the "Four Minute Men." After the war, in 1919, Insull organized the Illinois Public Utility Information Committee, borrowing the propaganda machinery he had used during the war. Insull's biographer writes that by 1923 the utilities in many other states had followed suit and "were turning out a stream of utility publicity that almost matched the volume of patriotic publicity during the war. . . ."[58]

The public relations of the public utilities in the twenties was the most prominent campaign of any industry. It prompted a thorough Federal Trade Commission investigation of the utilities and a carefully documented, angry volume by Ernest Gruening in 1931, *The Public Pays*. Gruening described the campaign as "the most far-reaching, most elaborate, most protean propaganda in the peace-time history of the United States."[59] But while the public utilities' campaign may have been the biggest use of public relations, it was by no means singular, and everywhere in American life there was growing interest in, and concern about, propaganda and public relations.[60] A Belgian reporter in 1921 referred to an "American Obsession" with propaganda.[61] Harold Lasswell, in *Propaganda Technique in the World War* (1927), noted the great interest in propaganda and in ways of controlling public opinion and wrote that it "testifies to the collapse of the traditional species of democratic romanticism and to the rise of a dictatorial habit of mind."[62]

That this posed a special problem to the newspaper reporter was clear. Propaganda and public relations undermined the old faith in facts. Lippmann put this well in *Public Opinion:*

> The development of the publicity man is a clear sign that the facts of modern life do not spontaneously take a shape in which they can be known. They must be given a shape by somebody, and since in the daily routine reporters cannot give a shape to facts, and since there is little disinterested organization of intelligence, the need for some formulation is being met by the interested parties.[63]

Silas Bent determined that at least 147 of 255 stories in the *New York Times* of December 29, 1926, originated in the work of press agents, as did 75 of 162 stories in the *New York Sun* of January 14, 1926.[64] John Jessup, long an editor at *Fortune* and *Life,* recalls that when he worked for the J. Walter Thompson agency in the early thirties, he was shocked at being told that about 60 percent of the stories in the *New York Times* were inspired by press agents.[65] In 1930, political scientist Peter Odegard estimated that 50 percent of news items originated in public relations work, and he concluded what some journalists themselves feared: "Many reporters today are little more than intellectual mendicants who go from one publicity agent or press bureau to another seeking 'handouts.' "[66]

Subjectivity and Objectivity in the Press

The press responded to the apparent subjectivization of facts in a variety of ways. One response was to openly acknowledge subjectivity as a factor in reporting. The signed news story appeared more frequently. A look at front pages of the *New York Times* indicates that in the early 1920s by-lines were used sparingly. They generally appeared only for foreign correspondence and, even then, with consistency only when the correspondent wrote in the first person. By the 1930s, by-lines were used liberally for domestic as well as foreign correspondence.[67] The first by-lined Associated Press story appeared in 1925. It was explained away as a special case, but within a few years the by-line was common in AP stories.[68]

Specialization was another response. If the by-line gave the reporter greater authority in relation to the copy desk, specialization could provide the reporter greater capacity to be critical of his sources. "Truly the age of specialization is at hand," the *Journalism Bulletin* wrote in 1924. This was premature, but there was at least a beginning to specialization in the twenties. The *Bulletin* noted proposals for special reporters on medicine, surgery, sanitation, and health, and "a demand for automobile critics who would throw the press agent news of the latest models into the wastebasket and write critical articles on the new makes as they appear."[69] Specialists in reporting on labor, science, and agriculture emerge by the late twenties.[70]

An important change was the development of "interpretative reporting." Two works of the 1930s charted its growth. In *The Changing American Newspaper*, Herbert Brucker pointed approvingly to a series of innovations in newspapers around the country which he believed would change the face of American journalism. One kind of change he felt to be significant was the introduction of weekend news summaries. The *New York Sun* began a Saturday review of the news in 1931; the *Richmond News Leader* replaced its Saturday editorial page with an interpretive summary of the news; the *New York Times*, in 1935, began its Sunday news summary as, in a more interpretive vein, did the *Washington Post;* and the Associated Press began distribution of a one-page week-end review of the news. These developments, according to Brucker, increased the interpretive function of the newspaper; they were responses to "the increasing complexity of the world" in the face of which readers clamored for more "background" and more "interpretation." Brucker felt that the "traditional prejudice" of newspapermen against inter-pretation arose in a simpler world:

Did Tippecanoe and Tyler too get the nomination? Did Chicago burn? Did the banker's son seduce a village maiden? To report these things meant simply to recite the facts. Anyone could under-stand them without help from Walter Lippmann.

In contrast, Brucker claimed, "life is now more complex, more highly integrated with other lives out of sight and even out of ken, than ever before," and this was a view widely shared.[71]

The best document of the change toward interpretive reporting was the successful journalism textbook (its recent editions are still in use) by Curtis MacDougall. It was first published in 1932 as *Reporting for Beginners;* when revised and republished in 1938, its title was *Interpretative Report-ing.* In the 1938 edition's "note to teachers," MacDougall explained the changes he had made:

The principal difference between *Reporting for Beginners* and *Interpretative Reporting* is one of point of view toward the task the news gatherers of the immediate future will be asked to perform. A clue to the writer's present attitude is in the present volume's title; it is his belief that changing social conditions, of which students of the principal media of public opinion have become increasingly aware during the past six years, are causing news gathering and dissemi-nating agencies to change their methods of reporting and interpret-ing the news. The trend is unmistakably in the direction of combining the function of interpreter with that of reporter after about a half century during which journalistic ethics called for a strict differentiation between narrator and commenter.[72]

In the text itself, MacDougall stated his position in a chapter on "giving substance" to the news. He argued that the United States had been unprepared to understand World War I because the wire services and newspapers had reported only what happened, not an interpretation of why it was happening. In 1929, the beginning of the depression also found journalism unprepared and newspaper writers "utterly unqualified to cope with a major news event in anything but a factual manner." Interpretive reporting, he held, was a major change in American journalism, but it was not at all inconsistent with the aim of what, by the mid-thirties, was called "objectivity":

... the most successful newspaper men and women of the future will be those with wide educational backgrounds, a specialist's knowledge in one or more fields, the ability to avoid emotionalism and to remain objective, descriptive styles, the power of observation, and, above all, the ability to comprehend the meaning of immediate news events in relation to broader social, economic, and political trends.[73]

The challenge of interpretive reporting to conventional journalism could be stated more boldly and was, particularly by foreign correspondents who felt the need for it most deeply and had the occupational autonomy to try it out. Raymond Gram Swing, for twenty years a foreign correspondent for the *Chicago Daily News,* told the American Society of Newspaper Editors in 1935:

If European news is to be comprehensible at all it has to be explained. If it is explained it has to be explained subjectively. There is no getting around it, the man in Europe who is of most value to his newspaper is the man who expresses opinions in his writings. That goes against the ethics of the profession, but it is absolutely essential to understand that.[74]

Against the ethics of the profession it might be, but the American Society of Newspaper Editors had already, in 1933, supported interpretive reporting in principle by passing this resolution:

> Whereas, The procession of national and international events, significant, complex and colorful, is moving more rapidly than at any other period in the recent history of the world; and
> Whereas, There is new evidence that men and women in every walk of life are taking a deeper interest in public affairs,
> RESOLVED, That it be the consensus of this Society that editors should devote a larger amount of attention and space to explanatory and interpretative news and to presenting a background of information which will enable the average reader more adequately to understand the movement and the significance of events.[75]

The Newspaper Editors advocated interpretation, and later observers explain its rise, as a response to a world grown suddenly very complex. The idea is that the war, the depression, and then the New Deal made political, economic, and social affairs so complicated that they forced journalism to emphasize "the meaning" of the news and the context of events. This assumes that people will naturally recognize complex happenings to be complex. It may be a safer first approximation to say that people will generally take complex happenings to be simple. An explanation of the rise of interpretive reporting will have to focus on how reporters came to believe the world was complicated.

It is fashionable in the social sciences, and has been since the 1930s, to view a society, or even the world of nations, as constituting a "system" in which the various parts are functionally related so that an event in one place or arena will have consequences in every other. However useful this may be heuristically, one can still distinguish some periods as being more "systemic" or more integrated than others. Until World War I, and to some extent until World War II, it was possible for Americans to think of their affairs as distinct from European and world politics, and it was even possible for Americans to be relatively uninterested in national politics, for the federal government had only remote connections to the daily lives of most citizens. Reporter Walter Trohan recalls that in the 1920s Washington was not the Mecca for journalism it would very soon thereafter become:

In those days Washington was not the goal of reporters that it has become today. Nor had Washington become everyone's city hall as it is today. I can remember men being elected to Congress, mostly as a reward for faithful party service. They would be given a farewell banquet and forgotten.[76]

But as the United States became integrated into a world system, particularly through the war, and as the depression focused national attention on policy makers in Washington, the world was not only more "complex," but more *visibly* complex because centralized in Washington.[77]

Still, the perception of complexity would not necessarily lead to an interest in interpretive journalism, unless there is an assumption at hand that complexity is more than an accumulation of facts. That assumption, of course, was growing in journalism. Journalists could no longer believe that facts speak for themselves. The new view of facts was institutionalized in an extreme form in *Time* magazine, founded in 1923 by Henry Luce and Briton Hadden. *Time*'s saucy prose inscribed in every sentence a jaunty attitude toward facts. Luce was forthright in advocating a blend of fact and opinion in a news magazine. "Show me a man who thinks he's objective," Luce said, "and I'll show you a man who's deceiving himself." Luce recommended that newspapers drop their division of the editorial page from the news and put on the front page "intelligent criticism, representation and evaluation of the men who hold offices of public trust."[78] *Time* did not please everyone, but it became a significant influence on the newspapers; MacDougall recognized it as "a worthy competitor of the daily press" and saw it as an indicator that the public was no longer satisfied with straight news.[79]

What was probably the most important sign of journalism's adaptation to the sense of the subjectivity of facts and the centralization of a complex world in Washington was the invention of the syndicated political columnist. Signed columns appeared as early as the 1890s in Chicago papers, but they tended to focus on humor, literature, or local color reporting. Even as late as the mid-twenties, general guides to writing a newspaper column, like C. L. Edson's *The Gentle Art of Columning* (1920) and Hallam W. Davis' *The Column* (1926), dealt exclusively with humorous writing.[80] Columns primarily devoted to appraising political and economic affairs did not appear until the twenties with the work of David Lawrence, Mark Sullivan, and Frank Kent.[81] Heywood Hale Broun's column in the *World* began in 1921, while Lippmann's "Today and Tomorrow" first appeared in the *Herald Tribune* in 1931. When, in 1934, Raymond Clapper, who had served as Washington bureau chief for the United Press and who went on to work for the *Washington Post*, was asked to write a daily column for the *Post*, his wife opposed the move. She later wrote:

I was opposed to it because in 1934 the place of the columnist in journalism was uncertain. It seemed to me that editorial comment was more potent from the mouths of editors; I doubted Ray's appeal to the reader who wanted a glamorous personality.[82]

But Clapper took the job and, it turned out, the political column was the newspaper sensation of the thirties. By 1937, Walter Lippmann's column was syndicated in 155 papers, Arthur Brisbane's in 180, David Lawrence in 150, Frank Kent in 125.[83] When sociologists Robert and Helen Lynd returned to "Middletown" (Muncie, Indiana) in 1935, ten years after their original study, the major change in the newspapers was clear: "The outstanding innovation in Middletown's newspapers is the increased share of signed syndicated features from Washington and New York in the news columns."[84] In 1925, only Brisbane and Lawrence had appeared; in 1935, the morning paper had five political syndicated columnists, the afternoon paper four others. *The New Republic* observed in 1937 that "much of the influence once attached to the editorial page has passed over to the columnists."[85] The political column was, among other things, journalism's most important institutional acknowledgment that there were no longer facts, only individually constructed interpretations.

Not all journalists could be columnists, nor were all free to write interpretively. Daily reporters still needed to believe in the value of their own best work in the gathering and presentation of facts. They needed a framework within which they could take their own work seriously and persuade their readers and their critics to take it seriously, too. This is what the notion of "objectivity," as it was elaborated in the twenties and thirties, tried to provide.

Walter Lippmann was the most wise and forceful spokesman for the ideal of objectivity. In *Public Opinion* he explained the emotional impulse behind the quest for objectivity: "As our minds become more deeply aware of their own subjectivism, we find a zest in objective method that is not otherwise there."[86] Lippmann had been concerned about the subjectivity of facts and, at the same time, hopeful about the professionalization of journalism as early as 1919. In an essay in the *Atlantic Monthly* later reprinted as *Liberty and the News* (1920), Lippmann warned that "the present crisis of western democracy is a crisis in journalism." Could democracy survive in a world where "the manufacture of consent is an unregulated private enterprise"? The problem of the press went to the heart of democratic government:

... men who have lost their grip upon the relevant facts of their environment are the inevitable victims of agitation and propaganda. The quack, the charlatan, the jingo, and the terrorist can flourish only where the audience is deprived of independent access to

151

information. But where all news comes at second-hand, where all the testimony is uncertain, men cease to respond to truths, and respond simply to opinions. The environment in which they act is not the realities themselves, but the pseudo-environment of reports, rumors, and guesses. The whole reference of thought comes to be what somebody asserts, not what actually is.[87]

Lippmann believed that "science" might hold a solution: "There is but one kind of unity possible in a world as diverse as ours. It is unity of method, rather than of aim; the unity of the disciplined experiment."[88] In practical terms, Lippmann suggested that this might mean legislation to make false documentation illegal, identification of news sources in news stories, the creation of nonpartisan research institutes, the establishment of an international nonpartisan news agency, and the professionalization of journalism—somehow it would be necessary to upgrade the dignity of the profession and design a training for journalists "in which the ideal of objective testimony is cardinal."[89]

The urge for professionalization in journalism did not begin with Lippmann. For several decades journalists had sought institutional means to make their occupation more respectable. Joseph Pulitzer, for instance, endowed the Columbia School of Journalism in 1904 (although it did not open its doors until 1913). Critics within the profession charged that a college of journalism would establish class distinctions in the newspaper world. Pulitzer answered that this was exactly what it should do—establish a distinction between the fit and the unfit: "We need a class feeling among journalists—one based not upon money, but upon morals, education and character." The journalists should emulate the lawyers and doctors and find in the solidarity of the profession independence of moneyed interests. If there is a modestly antipopular tone to Pulitzer's sense of a profession, it is more forthrightly anticommercial. The school of journalism, Pulitzer wrote, "is to be, in my conception, not only not commercial, but anticommercial." Journalism should have all the laurels of professionalism:

I wish to begin a movement that will raise journalism to the rank of a learned profession, growing in the respect of the community as other professions far less important to the public interest have grown.[90]

What was original with Lippmann, then, was not the interest in professionalization, but the reasons for advocating it. Some critics, notably Upton Sinclair in *The Brass Check* (1919), still saw the primary threat to honest journalism in the vested interests of publishers and advertisers. The problem Lippmann identified was perhaps more severe. For Lippmann, journalism did not have to be rescued from capitalists but from itself. With Charles Merz, an associate editor of the New York *World,* Lippmann wrote a celebrated critique of the *New York Times'* coverage of the Russian Revolution. After demonstrating the antibolshevik bias of the *Times'* coverage, Lippmann and Merz concluded:

The news as a whole is dominated by the hopes of the men who composed the news organization. . . . In the large, the news about Russia is a case of seeing not what was, but what men wished to see. . . . The chief censor and the chief propagandist were hope and fear in the minds of reporters and editors.[91]

Lippmann and Merz proposed that reporters be equipped with a more serious education and more expert knowledge. The reason they called for a new professionalism was that they were aware of the subjectivity of reporting—and its consequences.[92]

Lippmann and Merz made the philosophical ground of their critique explicit in a reply to critics. They observed that they had been criticized for simply having shown that human nature is frail and that newspaper reporters and editors, like the rest of us, make mistakes. They responded:

But admitting the whole indictment against human nature, what is the moral? Is it that all is for the best in the best of all possible worlds, or is it that the frailty of human nature requires honest and persistent attention? Since human beings are poor witnesses, easily thrown off the scent, easily misled by a personal bias, profoundly influenced by their social environment, does it not follow that a constant testing of the news and a growing self-consciousness about the main sources of error is a necessary part of the democratic philosophy?[93]

They concluded that "the greater the indictment against the reliability of human witnesses, the more urgent is a constant testing, as objectively as possible, of these results. When you consider how profoundly dependent the modern world is upon its news, the frailty of human nature becomes an argument not for complacency and apology, but for eternal vigilance."[94]

Lippmann's prescription for the ills of journalism was science. He believed that the pursuit of scientific method in journalism would make the press not only more professional, but more liberal and more heroic. Liberalism meant openness, he wrote—remaining free in mind and action before changing circumstances without being paralyzed by skepticism. The person taking on the liberal spirit makes an effort "to remain clear and free of his irrational, his unexamined, his unacknowledged prejudgments."[95] For Lippmann, this was a kind of heroism. Heroes, conventionally, impress their personalities upon the world; the heroism of Lippmann's idols lies in their refusal to do so. In a dialogue Lippmann wrote in 1928, he has "Socrates" say:

Have you ever stopped to think what it means when a man acquires the scientific spirit? It means that he is ready to let things be what they may be, whether or not he wants them to be that way. It means that he has conquered his desire to have the world justify his prejudices. It means that he has learned to live without the support of any creed. . . . There are not many men of this sort in any age.[96]

The "acids of modernity" had worn away the rock of religion, Lippmann wrote in *A Preface to Morals* (1929). But pure science was the modern incarnation of higher religion's best teachings. Virtue, as Lippmann defined it, is the capacity to respond to larger situations and longer stretches of time regardless of immediate pleasure or displeasure; it is the refusal to credit one's own tastes and desires as the basis for understanding the world. Detachment, disinterestedness, maturity: these are the marks of morality, and they are best exemplified in "the habit of disinterested realism" of the scientist.[97]

Lippmann's writings provide the most sophisticated rationale for objectivity as an ideal in journalism. One cannot infer from his work that daily reporters, even if they express allegiance to the ideal of objectivity, meant by it what Lippmann meant. It is quite likely that often their concept of "objectivity" was simply the application of a new label to the naive empiricism which reporters of the 1890s had called "realism." Still, even with journalists less philosophical than Lippmann, there was an important change. In the 1890s reporters rarely doubted the possibility of writing realistically; in the 1930s even journalists committed to objectivity acknowledged that objective reporting was ultimately a goal beyond reach—the perils of subjectivity were well recognized. When Leo C. Rosten interviewed Washington correspondents for a doctoral dissertation in 1935–1936, he took "objectivity" to be a familiar term, and he used it in his schedule of questions. For instance, he asked reporters to respond to the following statement:

It is almost impossible to be objective. You read your paper, notice its editorials, get praised for some stories and criticized for others. You "sense policy" and are psychologically driven to slant your stories accordingly.

Forty-two reporters agreed with that statement, twenty-four disagreed, and four felt uncertain.[98] Both Rosten's question and the response are of interest. The question indicates that objectivity was understood as an ideal counter to the reality of the reporter's own subjectivity, although here that subjectivity is taken to be most influenced by editorial suggestion, not personal predisposition. The response is evidence that, at least among the journalistic elite of Washington correspondents, there was great skepticism that the ideal of objectivity was, or perhaps even could be, realized. Rosten himself argued that " 'Objectivity' in journalism is no more possible than objectivity in dreams." He wrote:

Since absolute objectivity in journalism is an impossibility, the social heritage, the "professional reflexes," the individual temperament, and the economic status of reporters assume a fundamental significance.[99]

By the mid-thirties, the term "objectivity," unknown in journalism before World War I, appears to have been common parlance. It was a term hurled back and forth in staff debates at *Time* and *Fortune* in the thirties.[100] It made a significant appearance before the United States Supreme Court in 1937, when Morris Ernst represented the American Newspaper Guild as a friend of the court in the *Associated Press* v. *National Labor Relations Board*. The N.L.R.B. determined that the Associated Press had fired a reporter for his loyalty to the Newspaper Guild, while the AP claimed that it dismissed him for writing biased prolabor news. Ernst commented:

. . . the Constitution does not guarantee objectivity of the press, nor is objectivity obtainable in a subjective world; and that the question . . . really raised is not whether news shall be unprejudiced but rather whose prejudices shall color the news.[101]

The Guild had been organized in 1933 as a union for the editorial personnel on newspapers and other publications. When, in 1937, the Guild endorsed a series of political resolutions, it encountered substantial dissent in its own membership, and Guild member Walter Lippmann resigned over the issue. But it was the existence of the Guild as a militant union, not its political stands, which impelled publishers to oppose it and to use the cry of "objectivity" as a weapon. In 1937, the American Newspaper Publishers Association, the American Society of Newspaper Editors, and nine other publishers' groups jointly met "to discuss the closed shop as a matter of journalistic and public principle, not as an economic issue." Yet their concern seemed clearly to be thwarting union power:

This vital service of the press ["uncolored presentation of the news"] to the public can be performed properly only when those who are responsible for the publication are free to choose the persons whom they deem best qualified to report and edit the news.[102]

The Guild's political stands gave the publishers more ammunition. They declared that they would not turn over the news to "any group already committed as an organization on highly controversial public questions." They claimed to speak for the highest ideals of journalism:

We do not deny that causes require champions, and that progress springs from the genius of advocates. Equally important to society, however, are those who report the controversial scene. It is the newspaperman's job to do that, not as a partisan but as an objective observer.[103]

While the publishers used the ideal of objectivity in criticism of the Guild, there is no reason to suppose publishers responsible for its development. They appealed to a standard whose independent authority had already been established.

While objectivity, by the 1930s, was an articulate professional value in journalism, it was one that seemed to disintegrate as soon as it was formulated. It became an ideal in journalism, after all, precisely when the impossibility of overcoming subjectivity in presenting the news was widely accepted and, I have argued, precisely *because* subjectivity had come to be regarded as inevitable. From the beginning, then, criticism of the "myth" of objectivity has accompanied its enunciation. Objectivity in journalism seems to have been destined to be as much a scapegoat as a belief and more an awkward defense than a forthright affirmation. The belief in objectivity is less central to American journalism than the ground in which it took root. That ground, on which both advocates and opponents of "objectivity" in journalism stand, is relativism, a belief in the arbitrariness of values, a sense of the "hollow silence" of modernity, to which the ideal of objectivity has been one response.

If we take as a working hypothesis the proposition that the history of ideas is a history of concepts identifying social conditions which have become problematic, then we can see the cultural currents of the 1920s and 1930s as a response to the crisis of the democratic market society. While democracy and the market continued to expand formally, the extension of the franchise and of capital ownership paradoxically seemed to separate people from power more than ever. Faith in democracy and in the market was shaken. With the questioning of these central institutions, there was also questioning of the implicit vision that independent individuals voting in a democracy would produce the right decision, and that independent individuals uncovering facts in a random fashion would reveal truth. The vision faded. The systems did not work. The independent individuals who were supposed to be the components of the system did not exist. Corporations, not individuals, controlled supply and demand; machines, not voters, controlled elections; powerful publishers and the needs of mass entertainment, not the pursuit of truth, governed the press.

That, at least, was the early perception, the view of the Progressive era. By the 1920s disenchantment was more thorough. Corporate power had replaced enterprise in the economy; indeed, even the vestiges of a vision of nineteenth-century capitalism were hard to find. Owners did not control what they owned—expert managers did, while citizens took part in the economy as consumers to be manipulated. In politics, where machines were beaten, they were replaced with political organizations more abstract, formal, and remote. Moreover, in politics and in business, liberal thinkers were coming to believe that this was the only way things could possibly work; liberal democrats became liberal elitists. One had to destroy democracy and the market, perhaps—or watch them destroy themselves—to save them.

The Progressive perception of American society was critical and troubled but hopeful; the postwar view was less critical, more accommodated, because it was also much less hopeful. People who had once taken progress for granted began to doubt it. There was a deep loss of confidence. Yet even that gave rise to new visions and new plans. The ideal of objectivity in journalism, like related ideals in law and the social sciences at the same time, was founded on a confidence that the loss of faith was irretrievable. This was a peculiar and unsteady dialectic, one for which Karl Marx may have found the appropriate metaphor in *The German Ideology:*

If in all ideology men and their circumstances appear upside down as in a *camera obscura,* this phenomenon arises just as much from their historical life-process as the inversion of objects on the retina does from their physical life-process.

Journalists came to believe in objectivity, to the extent that they did, because they wanted to, needed to, were forced by ordinary human aspiration to seek escape from their own deep convictions of doubt and drift. Ours is an age, Thomas Mann wrote, which affords no satisfying answer to the question of "why?" or "to what end?". That is not a pronouncement one can stare at for very long without blinking. Surely, objectivity as an ideal has been used and is still used, even disingenuously, as a camouflage for power. But its source lies deeper, in a need to cover over neither authority nor privilege, but the disappointment in the modern gaze.

159

CHAPTER 5

OBJECTIVITY, NEWS MANAGEMENT, AND THE CRITICAL CULTURE

IN THE 1960s "objectivity" became a term of abuse. In the thirties, critics who had attacked objectivity favored interpretive reporting as a way of maintaining professional standing in a world which had outgrown the blunt approach of "just getting the facts." But, in the sixties, the goal of professionalism itself had become suspect. Critics claimed that urban planning created slums, that schools made people stupid, that medicine caused disease, that psychiatry invented mental illness, and that the courts promoted injustice. Intellectuals, no longer seen as the source of dispassionate counsel, were dubbed the "new mandarins," while government policy makers were called "the best and the brightest" in a tone of most untender irony. And objectivity in journalism, regarded as an antidote to bias, came to be looked upon as the most insidious bias of all. For "objective" reporting reproduced a vision of social reality which refused to examine the basic structures of power and privilege. It was not just incomplete, as critics of the thirties had contended, it was distorted. It represented collusion with institutions whose legitimacy was in dispute. And there was an intense moral urgency in this view. By the late sixties, many found Walter Cronkite's nightly assurance that "that's the way it is" too smug and preferred the challenge to "tell it like it is"—as if the reality to be reported was too wild to be tamed by grammar.

"Objectivity is a myth," announced reporter Kerry Gruson of the *Raleigh Observer,* and many young journalists shared her view. Sydney Gruson, her father and the assistant to the publisher at the *New York Times,* claimed, in contrast: "Maybe I'm old-fashioned but I feel very strongly about the purity of the news columns. Pure objectivity might not exist, but you have to strive for it anyway." The remarks of the Grusons were brought together by Stanford Sesser in the *Wall Street Journal* in the fall of 1969. Sesser was reporting on antiwar activism among journalists. Sydney Gruson had turned down the request of 308 employees at the *Times* to use the company's auditorium for discussion during the October 15 moratorium against the war in Vietnam. Kerry Gruson believed her father's decision was wrong. She herself wore a black armband while covering stories on October 15.[1]

The *Journal* article was a set piece for the conflict of generations as it was seen in American journalism in the late sixties—a conflict between the old defending objectivity and the young attacking it, between those who had fought in World War II and those born to the affluence and anxiety of the cold war, between those reluctant to abandon support of American policy in Vietnam and those angry at it, between the institutional responsibilities of powerful newspapers and the individual bravado of young reporters. Not least, the *Journal* story was itself a part of the set: in the sixties, as never before, news writing was itself a topic for news coverage.

We have seen a conflict of generations in journalism before. Editors in the 1890s trained reporters to keep their opinions out of their stories, and young reporters rebelled at this discipline. Editors and reporters perennially have different tasks at hand, different interests to protect, and different ambitions to serve; younger journalists and older journalists are at different points in their careers and have different concerns. That these differences should yield correspondingly different attitudes toward reporting the news is not surprising.

But in the past, the resentment of young reporters against editors was occasioned *only* by a conflict of interests on the job. It was not connected to broader political currents, and it did not express itself in a political idiom. In the sixties, however, the generational rebellion was part of a general cultural crisis. Young reporters still wanted to express their passion and personal style in print, but the rebellion at the conventions of "straight news" emerged more as a serious political challenge than as an adolescent stage in the passage to professionalism. Young reporters not only called for a more active journalism, a "participant" journalism skeptical of official accounts of public affairs; they also claimed pointedly that journalism had long been *too* participant. "Straight news" was not only drab and constricting—it was in itself a form of participation, a complicity with official sources whose most alarming feature was that it so self-righteously claimed to be above partisan or political considerations.

In the sixties, one might still criticize a newspaper for following the bent of its publisher or the intentional biases of its editorial staff. And much of this criticism was deserved. But the most original critics of the past decade have stressed, instead, that journalists were "political" unwittingly or even unwillingly. Their political impact lay not in what they openly advocated but in the unexamined assumptions on which they based their professional practice and, most of all, in their conformity to the conventions of objective reporting. In this view, objectivity was not an ideal but a mystification. The slant of journalism lay not in explicit bias but in the social structure of news gathering which reinforced official viewpoints of social reality. Correspondingly, newspapers in the past decade—especially those most prestigious, most powerful, and with most resources to devote to news gathering—have sought autonomy from official views and promoted what Max Frankel of the *New York Times* called "an exploded concept of what is news."[2] There is more interpretive reporting or "news analysis," more investigative or "enterprise" journalism, and more tolerance for new varieties of feature writing. But why at this time should criticism of conventional news gathering have been so pointed, and why should new ideas and new institutions in journalism have found as much support as they have?

I will suggest in this chapter that two conditions made a new criticism of journalism possible and popular and so made changes in newspaper content seem desirable. First, there was increasing government management of the news and a growing awareness of it. It has been said too often and too glibly that all governments lie and that all presidents back to George Washington have tried to mislead the press and con the public.[3] The modicum of truth in such assertions obscures the fact that management of information has been an organized, funded, and staffed function of government for just sixty years. Indeed, only since World War II has the importance and relative isolation of a national security establishment and an "imperial presidency" made government news policy, especially on matters of foreign policy, the symbolic center of the relationship between the government and the press.

The second basis for new developments in journalism was the emergence, in the 1960s, of an "adversary culture." The adversary, or critical, culture denied to government a level of trust it had come to expect and provided an audience for a more aggressive and more skeptical journalism. The collision in the late sixties between news management and the adver-

163

sary culture over the Vietnam war changed journalism in significant and, I think, lasting ways, which the final section of this chapter will consider.

Government and the Press: "News Management"

The Paris Peace Conference of 1919 symbolized the modern relationship between government and the press. It undercut the self-image of the press as a key actor in decision making at exactly the moment the press was most enchanted with its own powers. Wars are good for journalists as for generals. After the war, however, editors and reporters found themselves not partners to government, but instruments of government. They were valued—and feared—not for their capacity to represent public opinion, but for their power to control it.

Ray Stannard Baker, onetime muckraker who was President Woodrow Wilson's aide in Paris running the American Press Bureau, expressed the high hopes of the fourth estate:

One fact stands out at the Paris Peace Conference as distinctive and determining: the fact that the people of the world, publics, were there represented and organised as never before at any peace conference. At the older congresses, the diplomats occupied the entire stage, bargained, arranged, and secretly agreed; but at Paris democracy, like the blind god in Dunsany's play, itself comes lumbering roughly, powerfully, out upon the stage.[4]

When Baker said "publics" and "democracy," he meant reporters from the newspapers and wire services. It was typical of liberal thought of the 1920s that the press was taken to be the very incarnation of democratic government. Press coverage of the Peace Conference, in Baker's view, was to open a new epoch in world diplomacy. From that moment on, national policy would have to be formulated in the presence of public opinion and with the need for public assent in view.

Baker himself was disappointed, then, that the negotiations at Paris turned out to be shrouded in secrecy. He knew that Wilson's promise of "open covenants of peace openly arrived at" meant only, as Wilson explained, "that no secret agreements should be entered into" and not that "there should be no private discussions of delicate matters."[5] Baker did not object to governments keeping some of their meetings confidential from the news-reading public, but he did criticize Wilson for keeping them secret from the press. "It had been proved over and over again," he asserted, "that no group of men can be more fully trusted to keep a confidence or use it wisely than a group of experienced newspaper correspondents—if they are honestly informed and trusted in the first place."[6]

Paris did not mark a new era in open diplomacy as decisively as Baker had hoped, but it did announce a new relationship between the press and the government in a way he had not anticipated, for it made publicity itself a key political issue. For the first time in the history of American foreign policy, political debate at home concerned not only the substance of decisions the government made but also the ways in which the government made decisions. Foreign policy began to be domesticated; the legitimacy of procedure, as well as the effectiveness of outcome, became an issue. In the first week of the Peace Conference, American correspondents wrote in protest to Wilson regarding rules of secrecy the peace commissioners had adopted, and Joseph Tumulty in Washington warned the President of the distrust his adherence to secrecy would engender. Five months later there was conflict over public release of the treaty draft, and the Senate passed a resolution calling on Wilson to transmit the draft to the Senate. From beginning to end, publicity was a political issue of the first importance.[7]

This peacetime resort to managing the news was a milestone in the relations of government and the press. Just a few years before, in 1913, the Congress had forbidden government agencies to hire public relations personnel. Even the government's investment in publicity with the Committee on Public Information was viewed as exceptional, a wartime emergency, and the Committee was dismantled when the fighting stopped. But at the Paris Peace Conference the government "controlled" the news in an organized, self-conscious fashion. This dramatized, as nothing before could have, that government management of news would be a permanent condition of modern society.

As government public relations expanded in the twenties and thirties, critics of Roosevelt and the New Deal attacked the government's growing involvement in publicity. *Handout,* a book published pseudonymously in 1935 by two Washington journalists, assaulted Roosevelt's "system of censorship and propaganda."[8] The charges were overblown and underdocumented, but Elmer Davis, in a *New York Times* review, still wrote:

The one valid point is this: that the Roosevelt administration, imitating big business in the boom years, has set up in every department a press bureau through which the news is channeled instead of permitting newspaper men to talk directly to subordinate officials. . . . This was not wholly unknown in Washington before 1933; but the present administration has enormously extended the practice and it has undoubtedly made it harder for newspaper men to get at the truth.[9]

Davis' apparent unhappiness with Roosevelt's press relations was common coin in the world of journalism—a grudging acceptance of government publicity. But acceptance it was. Publishers opposed Roosevelt, but reporters felt themselves well treated by him, and the Washington press corps was favorably disposed to both Roosevelt and his policies. It was left to a critic of Roosevelt, Henry Luce, the publisher of *Time, Life,* and *Fortune,* to suggest that the new relationship between the government and the press raised questions of far-reaching significance for freedom of the press. In 1942, Luce suggested to Robert M. Hutchins, Chancellor of the University of Chicago, that he undertake a study of freedom of the press. When the Commission on Freedom of the Press was established in 1944, Luce told *Editor and Publisher* that the meaning of "freedom of the press" was no longer self-evident. Luce's main concern was that "big government" controlled the news through its publicity acitivities, not so much by censoring the news as by flooding the press with information. Could a press dominated by the public relations efforts of big government still be considered a free press? Luce hoped the Commission would explore the question.[10]

But the Commission did not do so. Its general statement, *A Free and Responsible Press,* did not deal with the question at all. Its *Government and Mass Communications,* a two-volume study written by Zechariah Chafee, devoted seven hundred pages to the use of government powers to suppress communication or to encourage it, but less than seventy pages to the topic of the government itself as a party to communications. Even here, Chafee focused as often on government's direct communication to the citizenry, especially through films, as on communication to the people through the press. Nowhere did the Commission discuss the ways in which, day to day, the social reality represented in the newspaper is constructed and reconstructed through the interaction of journalists and public officials.

The bizarre case of Senator Joseph McCarthy made the relations of reporters and officials a center of attention in journalism. According to many of the Senator's critics at the time and later, McCarthy made his brief and tawdry political career by a shrewd manipulation of the reporters' reliance on public officials for news and on the norms of objectivity as a guide to news writing. Douglass Cater, for instance, criticized "frozen patterns" of the press coverage of McCarthy, which gave McCarthy more coverage than he merited. One of these "frozen patterns" was the distinction between straight reporting and interpretive reporting. While the interpretive reporter seeks the background to a story, uncovers motives for actions, and tracks down side issues, the straight reporter passively accepts the public record. Straight news was the stock in trade of the wire services and most reporters; interpretive reporting was the work of a "privileged few." Cater observed that there was good interpretive reporting on McCarthy but that it was rarely picked up and reprinted, since it was regarded not as hard news but as "the writer's private property." The straight reporters provided most of the country with its news about McCarthy, writing up McCarthy's lies and accusations without commenting on whether or not his charges were true. The straight reporter, Cater concluded, is a "strait-jacketed reporter."[11]

Most observers agreed with this assessment. Richard Rovere, who covered McCarthy for the *New Yorker,* later wrote of McCarthy's mastery of publicity, his skill in manipulating reporters "like Pavlov's dogs." Reporters were angry that the conventions of their work required them to publish "news" they knew to be false, but they did not abandon the conventions, and, indeed, Rovere concluded that the press had done well to stand by its traditions:

... I suspect there is no surer way to a corrupt and worthless press than to authorize reporters to tell the readers which "facts" are really "facts" and which are not. Certainly in those countries where this is the practice, the press serves the public less well than ours does.[12]

The McCarthy phenomenon caused a tremor in the press but did not unsettle established patterns in reporting. Indeed, the great and growing concern in the 1950s and 1960s was not with the legacy of a demagogic senator but with the increasingly centralized management of the news in the executive branch. Here, while there was no question of demagoguery, there was still a sense of menace in the rapid rise, after 1945, of the "national security state." The national security state, as Daniel Yergin has defined it, is a "unified pattern of attitudes, policies, and institutions" designed to prepare the nation for permanent international conflict, the cold war.[13] Yergin focuses on the national security state as a "Commanding Idea," more a doctrine than a set of institutions. But it is, of course, both. Over the past thirty years, the doctrine of preparedness against an external (and sometimes internal) communist threat has promoted and in turn been reinforced by several powerful institutions. These include the military, and the industrial and scientific clients increasingly dependent on it; the intelligence agencies, without precedent before World War II, as important in enacting foreign policy as in providing information for policy makers; and the presidency itself, never before as overwhelming a force, as autonomous of Congress, or as "imperial" in scope and ambition.

Not only was foreign policy more centrally organized than ever before in the executive branch of government, but it was more centrally located in national affairs. The United States was finally fully and willingly the world's premier power. There was little tolerance for postwar isolationism; foreign affairs had assumed a salience that the appearance of peace could not turn aside. Thus, at the very time the public and the press had growing reason to be interested in foreign policy, the new institutions of national security frustrated efforts to understand it. The American government, long noted for its openness in comparison to the governments of Europe, removed control of foreign policy to the agencies most remote from public observation. There was agreement on the good sense of this. The press, like the Congress, sympathized with cold war ideology and rarely questioned the presuppositions of national security doctrine. But again, like the Congress, the press wanted to get into the game and was not content on the sidelines of power.

In 1955, James Reston, testifying before a congressional committee on government information, coined the term "news management."[14] Many found the term suitable for the Eisenhower administration's handling of the press. When Eisenhower was in a Denver hospital recovering from coronary thrombosis, members of his cabinet flew to Denver ostensibly to consult with him. In fact, they were in Denver only to present to the public the misinformation that the president was still able to perform the duties of office. The press knew of the deception but did not report it. Russell Baker observed:

Because the tradition of the American newspaper compels it to report with straight face whatever is said by anyone in high office, it was unable to suggest any element of charade in the parade of Cabinet officers to Denver. And so, in a sense, the press was seduced by its own morality.[15]

The master of news management under Eisenhower was press secretary James Hagerty. In a portrait for *Esquire* in 1959, Joseph Kraft wrote of "the dangerous precedent of James Hagerty." He described Hagerty's bag of tricks for getting the administration reported in the most favorable light, such as announcing successful missile tests at the White House and failures at the proving grounds. Kraft seemed to find this menacing but could not say just why.[16] Hagerty "managed" the news—and Kraft used the still novel term in quotes—but Kraft, while finding this unsavory, had no language in which to pronounce it wrong. There was *ressentiment* here, but no rebellion.

Another addition to the lexicon of journalism came in 1961 when the historian Daniel Boorstin suggested the term "pseudo-event" to refer to happenings that are planned "for the immediate purpose of being reported or reproduced." Thus a train accident is a real event, but an interview is a pseudo-event. A pseudo-event, Boorstin explained, might be intended to persuade, but its logic was quite different from that of propaganda:

Pseudo-events appeal to our duty to be educated, propaganda appeals to our desire to be aroused. While propaganda substitutes opinions for facts, pseudo-events are synthetic facts which move people indirectly, by providing the "factual" basis on which they are supposed to make up their minds. Propaganda moves them directly by explicitly making judgments for them.[17]

In the United States, as we have seen, pseudo-events can be traced to the late nineteenth century and the "journalism that acts" of Hearst and Pulitzer. But for Boorstin the public relations work of Edward Bernays was the archetype of pseudo-events. He suggested that it is only since the early twentieth century that "a larger and larger proportion of our experience, of what we read and see and hear, has come to consist of pseudo-events."[18]

Journalists complained, but they did not challenge the routines of government news management and the creation of pseudo-events. Concern about these issues was episodic, not cumulative, and produced no institutionalized responses. In the 1960s, however, something changed, not all at once and by no means altogether. But some journalists were shocked by the government's lies about the U-2 flights over the Soviet Union in 1960; some were troubled by the tortured acquiescence of the *New York Times* to the Kennedy administration in soft-pedaling coverage of the impending invasion of the Bay of Pigs in 1961; and many reporters and editors were appalled at the statements of Arthur Sylvester, spokesman for the Pentagon under Kennedy (and later Johnson) who defended news management in the Cuban missile crisis of 1962. In a news briefing on October 30, 1962, Sylvester argued that "In the kind of world we live in, the generation of news by actions taken by the government becomes one weapon in a strained situation. The results justify the methods we used."[19] A month later, speaking to the New York chapter of Sigma Delta Chi, the honorary fraternity in journalism, he put it even more strongly: "I think the inherent right of the government to lie—to lie to save itself when faced with nuclear disaster—is basic, *basic*."[20]

The fourth estate was outraged.[21] But why? The press itself was used to—if not lying—at least cooperating in not telling the truth to serve the national interest. In 1956 American newspapers refused a Chinese government invitation to send correspondents to China because, as *New York Times* editor Clifton Daniel recalled, "We did not want to embarrass our government."[22] Editors and reporters at the *Washington Post* and other papers knew about aerial spying over the Soviet Union well before the U-2 incident, but, in the interests of national security as they understood it, they chose to write nothing.[23] The *Times* sat for weeks on a story on "Project Argus," a government program involving the detonation of nuclear devices in outer space, before the testing actually began. The *Times* finally published it only after the tests were completed and it seemed as if *Newsweek* would publish first.[24] In 1961, editors of the *Miami Herald* asked reporter David Kraslow to clear his story on the training of Cuban exile forces in Florida with C.I.A. chief Allen Dulles. Kraslow's story was never published.[25] The cooperation of the *New York Times* with the Kennedy administration in playing down the story of the forthcoming Bay of Pigs invasion is well known.[26] Why, then, if the press was used to acting on its own and in cooperation with government officials to suppress or shade the news, should Sylvester's declaration of a government right to lie have been so offensive?

In part, the answer is simply that Sylvester's statement threatened the role of the press as the "fourth branch of government."[27] News management in itself was not disquieting—news management, after all, is the daily business of the press, and reporters have long published much less than they know about politics and public life.[28] *Government* news management is what the press resisted. For the press to cooperate with government in keeping news from the public was one thing; for the government to keep information from the press was something else.

What made Sylvester's comment even more troubling was that it crossed a thin moral line the press felt an obligation to patrol. It was perhaps bad for the government to keep information from the press by dodging; it was certainly bad for the government to lie outright; but it was worse still for the government to announce its "right" to lie. There was at least this virtue to hypocrisy when the government lied while claiming to be truthful: that if the press discovered the lie, it could embarrass the government. The Sylvester statement placed the government beyond embarrassment.

In the middle and late 1960s, reporters began to suspect that Sylvester's crude philosophy had actually become everyday government practice. Most of all, it was Vietnam that drained the reservoir of trust between the government and the press. "The fruits of Sylvesterism in Vietnam are public knowledge," wrote Staughton Lynd and Tom Hayden.[29] This was so. Even a man who served as public information officer for the American Mission in Saigon in 1962 and 1963, John Mecklin, acknowledged in *Mission in Torment* (1965) that while he did not believe any responsible American official in Saigon ever told a newsman "a really big falsehood," it was nonetheless true that "there were endless little ones."[30] Mecklin held that the American Mission was in a particularly difficult position for dealing with the press. For one thing, the American officials were themselves misled; they placed too much faith in the Diem government and retailed the bad information they got from Diem. Further, the American position was unusually delicate because American support for Vietnam had never been popular, because the American intervention in Vietnam in 1961 clearly violated the Geneva Agreement of 1954, and because—especially after the Bay of Pigs—there was fear of feeding anti-imperialist anti-American propaganda. Finally, Mecklin observed, the American efforts to deal with the press were hobbled by the attitude of the Diem regime which "reacted to newsmen as though they were a foreign substance in the bloodstream, in uncontrollable convulsions."[31] All this made American officials wary of reporters, at best, and sometimes openly hostile, well before there was any sentiment in the press against American involvement in Vietnam. What was distinctive, at first, was not the performance of the press but the attitude of the government.[32] In this setting, reporters simply pursuing their conventional duties were bound to run afoul of the government.

An instance that attracted great attention was the visit of *New York Times'* correspondent Harrison Salisbury to Hanoi in December, 1966. For Salisbury, going to Hanoi meant another "first": he had been the first American journalist to visit post-Stalin Siberia and central Asia and the first to visit Albania after World War II. But it was not merely another "first." For one thing, the only other prominent visitors from the United States to Hanoi in the mid-sixties were antiwar activists. Herbert Aptheker, Thomas Hayden, and Staughton Lynd were in Hanoi, for example, in a well-publicized visit a year before Salisbury. For another, Salisbury's reports from Hanoi, unlike his writings from Siberia or Albania, were not only about Hanoi but about the United States; they were not delivered to an untutored public but to one that had been regularly informed about North Vietnam by the American government. And Salisbury's stories, at the very least, cast doubt on the veracity of the government's statements. The Defense Department had insisted repeatedly that the bombing of North Vietnam involved military targets. Salisbury wrote that civilian targets had been badly damaged by bombing:

Whatever the explanation, one can see that United States planes are dropping an enormous weight of explosives on purely civilian targets. Whatever else there may be or might have been in Nam-dinh, it is the civilians who have taken the punishment.

If that was not clear enough, Salisbury went further:

President Johnson's announced policy that American targets in North Vietnam are steel and concrete rather than human lives seems to have little connection with the reality of attacks carried out by U.S. planes.[33]

Salisbury's reports were disputed by the government and, indeed, Salisbury did not escape censure in the *Washington Post* and the *Washington Star* as a tool of Hanoi's propaganda. Still, his reporting altered what he called "the pattern of acceptability" in what could be legitimately regarded as news. Within a year, the wire services could quote "intelligence sources" that the bombing of the North damaged civilian structures.[34]

In the 1960s every journalistic feat that evaded news management called attention to news management. More than ever before, the continuing story in the press was the story of the press itself in its efforts to gather news. The power of Salisbury's reporting was as much in its revelation of the lies of the American government as in its description of the sufferings of the Vietnamese people. The content of the Pentagon papers was shocking enough, but the Nixon administration's efforts to suppress their publication were just as devastating. The events leading up to the break-in of Democratic National Committee headquarters at Watergate were appalling, but the attempted "cover-up" was more frightening still.

When Walter Lippmann wrote *Public Opinion* in 1922, he argued that the function of news is to "signalize an event," while the function of truth is to "bring to light the hidden facts and set them into relation with each other." [35] Only where social conditions take recognizable and measurable shape, he wrote, do truth and news coincide. Lippmann felt the newspapers had no special access to truth—their responsibility was to print news, and they would be able to print better news only if government and independent agencies of intelligence could provide them with more reliable data. But from the twenties on, it became more and more clear that this is too narrow a view of what news should be, especially if "credibility" of the government and "independent agencies" is in doubt. If events are spontaneous, random occurrences, if they are a relatively unbiased sampling of the "hidden facts," then a newspaper could be content to report the news and feel it had done an important job responsibly. But if events themselves are constructed, and constructed by the individuals and institutions with the greatest wealth and power in society, then reporting the news is not just an incomplete approach to the truth but a distorted one. With the rise of public relations in the 1920s, with the growing awareness of government that it can serve itself better by managing the news, and with the growing consciousness in the press that it has to contend with the manipulation of news on a grand scale, it grew more difficult for the conscientious journalist to be satisfied that getting the news is sufficient. With Washington and foreign policy more and more the symbolic center of public affairs, Washington and foreign correspondence provided the most prestigious work in journalism, and the frustrations of reporting foreign policy moved to the core of journalism's sense of itself.

The Rise of a Critical Culture

The term "adversary culture" was used by Lionel Trilling in 1965 to describe "the subversive intention" that distinguishes modern writing. From the late eighteenth century on, according to Trilling, literature in the West has had the "clear purpose of detaching the reader from the habits of thought and feeling that the larger culture imposes, of giving him a ground and a vantage point from which to judge and condemn, and perhaps revise, the culture that produced him." [36] This impulse in literature reached its height in the early twentieth century. The change since then has been one of scale: since the 1930s, large numbers of people have come to take the idea of the adversary culture for granted.

This account of adversary culture bears on the political and cultural ferment of the 1960s. Trilling's emphasis on size is important: after World War II, enrollment in higher education grew tremendously; by the late fifties, after the shock of Sputnik, educational excellence became a social goal of high priority; by the early sixties, the college professor had attained a status and a salary unknown to previous generations of scholars. When the children of the postwar baby boom entered colleges in the middle sixties, more people were being offered "a ground and a vantage point from which to judge and condemn, and perhaps revise" than ever before.

The acceptability of that vantage point was made possible by a development of central importance: the intensity of the cold war declined after the Cuban missile crisis. [37] The signing of the nuclear test ban treaty in the summer of 1963 enabled people who had been holding their breath for twenty years to sigh. The flagging cold war provided the space for criticism to appear and find an audience, and the time to form institutions of its own. The national concussion of the assassinations of John Kennedy, Martin Luther King, Jr., and Robert Kennedy made criticism seem not only possible but vital. An understandable world was coming apart at the "seems"—appearances could not be trusted. The assassinations made no sense. Symbols of security against a communist threat—the C.I.A. and the F.B.I.—increasingly seemed a menace themselves. They were a source of anxiety and insecurity, not only for radical students, but for moderate legislators. Even President Lyndon Johnson was persuaded that the C.I.A. was implicated in John Kennedy's murder. Even the American

177

flag changed its meaning and became more a partisan than a national symbol.

Younger people, whose antipathy to communism had been inherited, not earned, could question their feelings or turn away from them. And they found, as they began to criticize the government and especially the institutions of foreign policy, that they had a responsive audience. It was a reading audience. It was a college audience. The first widely noted dissent to the war in Vietnam surfaced in the teach-ins sponsored by students and faculty at colleges and universities. But distrust of government was by no means confined to the young and educated. Distrust grew dramatically in all groups during the sixties. In 1958, 24 percent of the population felt "you cannot trust the government to do right," while 57 percent felt that way in 1973; in 1958, 18 percent felt government was run for the benefit of the few, while 67 percent felt that way in 1973.[38] At the same time that voters became more attentive to politics, participated more in political campaigns, and developed more consistent or sophisticated views on political issues, there was a marked decline in identification with political parties. This was especially true among younger voters. As political scientist Norman Nie and his collaborators have pointed out, the new voters who joined the electorate in the 1960s were less tied to party than the new voters of any earlier period: 53 percent of voters aged twenty-one to twenty-five, in 1974, called themselves "independents," compared to just 25 percent of the comparable group in 1952.[39] And the key political issues of the 1960s, rather than encouraging these new voters to identify with parties, weakened their commitment to conventional parties and conventional politics. In Nie's view, racial conflict, Vietnam, and Watergate led the public away from parties and made the public antagonistic to the political system.[40]

Thus, while a culture of criticism was finding more leaders and more followers in higher education in the 1960s, there was also an apparently long-term trend toward greater political sophistication and critical scrutiny of government on the part of a substantial portion of the population. Higher education does not of itself promote dissidence—certainly it did not do so in the fifties. Why, then, did distrust of government grow in the sixties? The students of public opinion polls are not sure. They are sure only that the distrust was greatest among the young, and they are inclined to believe that a chief cause of declining trust in government was that government demonstrated itself less deserving of trust.

It is a mistake, therefore, to define the "adversary" culture of the late sixties as an essentially hostile attitude toward government or to identify it with a small, willful group of students and leftists. Daniel Patrick Moynihan made both errors in an essay in *Commentary,* in 1971, where he argued that the muckraking tradition in American journalism had been mightily reinforced by the "adversary culture" of middle- and upper-class young people who were increasingly being recruited to journalism. The result of the rising social status of journalism, Moynihan went on, was "that the press grows more and more influenced by attitudes genuinely hostile to American society and American government."[41] But "hostile" is not to be confused with "critical" or even "adversarial." Further, if the upper classes were growing more critical of government, so were the lower classes. The adversary culture is not an antinomian culture, though no doubt it has provided fertile ground for irresponsibility and irrationalism. Nor is it exclusively an elite culture, although it gained a high level of acceptance in elite groups in the sixties and is sustained there by the modernist art and literature of which Trilling writes.

The critical culture deeply affected journalism. There was a direct effect: journalists were citizens, too, susceptible to the same cultural currents as anyone else. Younger journalists, like younger people in general, were more affected, having

less memory of, and less investment in, the cultural presuppositions of the cold war. And journalists, especially those
covering national politics, were more deeply affected than
most citizens because they had trusted more in, and cared
more about, government. While a muckraking tradition has
long been honored in the press, actual muckraking has always
been exceptional, and even muckrakers have typically focused
on the hypocrisies and corruptions of government, rather than
on underlying assumptions or structures of power. Journalists, in general, have tended to feel politically involved and
efficacious—less, rather than more, alienated than the population at large.[42] The division in American political culture
touched all citizens deeply but journalists with special force.
For them, it was a trauma of the heart and, at the same time,
a constantly irritating rash on the skin of their working lives.

The critical culture touched journalists in indirect ways,
too. For one thing, young people recruited to the government
service in the sixties *also* distrusted government. Journalists
did not "impose" an adversary culture on their reporting of
politics—they responded to a critical stance they found in
their sources. Indeed, *Washington Post* national editor Richard Harwood has argued that the press did not become
notably more "adversary" in the past decade but that, rather,
a "New Establishment" came to power which took a stance
adversary to itself.[43] Thus there was an adversary journalism
within the halls of government itself. A group of employees at
the Department of Housing and Urban Development, for
instance, published a newsletter called *Quest*, which accused
department officials of racism, encouraged antiwar protest,
and urged employees to vote against Nixon in 1972. Similar
publications in other departments of government, in business
corporations, the universities, the professions, and the military
attested to the widespread appeal of a critical culture.[44] For
the press, which had long pictured itself as a loyal opposition
to government, the stress on "loyal" was muted, while the

emphasis on "opposition" was fueled by, and in turn helped feed, the critical culture arising in the government itself.

The extent to which the press independently promoted an adversarial culture has been overemphasized, while the extent of the wider and growing adversarial culture's influence on the culture of the press has perhaps not been emphasized enough. Not only did reporters find their sources in government increasingly critical, but the most visible evidences of an adversary culture became topics of news which younger reporters were frequently assigned to and affected by. Several journalists I interviewed in 1977 recalled that young reporters recruited to journalism in the 1960s frequently covered the civil rights movement and the antiwar movement. Young people, more likely to fit into the youth culture of casual manners and language, open sexuality, and rock music, covered the campuses and social movements and were influenced by them. They often felt uncomfortable in their reportorial roles, almost as if they were agents of "straight" society spying on a subversive culture. They found themselves sympathetic to the ideas and values of the people they wrote about and increasingly skeptical, uneasy, or outraged at the transformation of their stories between copy desk and printed page.[45]

The rebellion of young reporters in the sixties, then, was no mere repetition of perennial generational conflict in journalism; it was one manifestation of a social and cultural movement. The movement affected younger journalists first and most profoundly, but this, in turn, influenced older and more powerful journalists. Editors and publishers in the sixties had good reason to be receptive to their young colleagues' hopes for more interpretive and investigative reporting: the papers were feeling the competition of television. Television news, which had been of slight importance and of slighter quality in the 1950s, became intent on exploring its opportunities for vivid and immediate coverage of the news. It became less a radio with pictures, more a distinctive medium. In 1963, the same year in which the network evening news changed from a fifteen-minute to a half-hour format, the Roper survey of public attitudes toward television found for the first time that more people listed television as a chief source of news than newspapers. By 1974, 65 percent surveyed mentioned television as one of their chief sources of news, while only 47 percent mentioned newspapers. In that year, for the first time, more college-educated respondents mentioned television than newspapers.[46]

Correspondent Jules Witcover espoused the common view that newspapers turned to investigative and interpretive reporting in the late sixties to compete with television's advantage in covering spot news. But within a year, writing again in *Columbia Journalism Review,* he complained that the competition-with-television argument was more fashionable than true and that, in fact, "an informal survey of Washington news chiefs indicates most pay little attention to the television 'threat.' They are more concerned with the changing scope of news reporting itself and how they are coping with it." He added that the *New York Times* felt more pressure from the *Washington Post* and the *Wall Street Journal* than from television.[47]

Even this, however—the competition among leading newspapers in different cities with one another, with the wire services, and with the news magazines—may be a by-product of television. If the national security state and the centralization of economic policy on the federal level has made Washington a focal point for the mass media, television news coverage itself has accentuated Washington's prominence. Because network news depends on a national audience and must rely on expensive and cumbersome camera equipment, television reports disproportionately on the capital. This has encouraged newspapers to see their Washington correspondence as the most significant and competitive field of work.

The argument that competition with television led newspapers away from objective reporting repeats an argument of the 1930s that the advantage of radio in presenting spot news forced newspapers to become more interpretive. It may be that in both the thirties and the sixties publishers *believed* they had to change news policy to compete with the new media, and this belief opened the way for journalists to experiment with more interpretive work. On the other hand, in both radio and television, particularly in television, there was also a strong interest in going beyond the conventions of objectivity. In the late sixties, television itself moved away from straight news. "Editorials" appeared on local news programs and "commentary" (especially the work of Eric Sevareid for CBS) became a regular feature of network news. The introduction, in 1968, of the CBS news program "60 Minutes," and its extraordinary success in magazine journalism for television, suggest that the "exploded" sense of news was more than a competitive strategy—television, too, responded to a changing culture which welcomed critical perspectives in journalism.[48]

The Critique of Conventional Journalism—and Its Consequences

An adversary culture must be adversary *to* something. But leaders of the major institutions of society appeared to deny any substance to their own culture: problems of government were said to be technical, not political; social science was a "value-free" guide to policy; professionals and managers, coming to prominence in the occupational structure and the power structure of society, were "neutral" or "detached" or "objective" in their decisions. To the increasingly numerous and vocal critics, the rhetoric of objectivity seemed hypocriti-

183

cal or deceitful, or in Vietnam, criminal. The adversary culture's attack on objectivity conjured up a more unified and univocal Establishment culture than in fact existed. Still, there *was* an ideology of technique and neutrality, and it *did* conceal other values that, the critical culture demanded, should be open to question.

In journalism this critique of objectivity took many institutional and intellectual forms. It is the sum of these, not the novelty of any single one of them, that was most important and original. Still, one can distinguish three kinds of criticism which attacked the notion of objectivity.

First, there is the position that *the content of a news story rests on a set of substantive political assumptions,* assumptions whose validity is never questioned. Journalists acquire these assumptions from their own upbringing, from fellow journalists who constantly check and tutor their "news judgments," and from the officials they regularly report on. These assumptions are the hidden message of "objectivity." Jack Newfield articulated this point of view:

So the men and women who control the technological giants of the mass media are not neutral, unbiased computers. They have a mind-set. They have definite life styles and political values, which are concealed under a rhetoric of objectivity. But those values are organically institutionalized by the *Times.* by AP, by CBS . . . into their corporate bureaucracies. Among these unspoken, but organic, values are belief in welfare capitalism, God, the West, Puritanism, the Law, the family, property, the two-party system, and perhaps most crucially, in the notion that violence is only defensible when employed by the State. I can't think of any White House correspondent, or network television analyst, who doesn't share these values. And at the same time, who doesn't insist he is totally objective.[49]

This first view, then, holds that form conceals content in the news story. A second position is that form constitutes content, that *the form of the news story incorporates its own bias.* This is illustrated in an essay by Paul Weaver on "The Politics of a News Story." Weaver argues that the typical news story is politically biased—but not toward right, left, or center. Rather the bias is toward statements of fact which are observable and unambiguous; toward broad, categorical vocabulary—"say," rather than "shout" or "insist"; toward impersonal narrative style and "inverted pyramid" organization which force a presentation of facts with "as little evocation of their real-world context" as possible; toward conflicts rather than less dramatic happenings; toward "events" rather than processes. Weaver argues that this makes the news story a story about conflict from the point of view of the different parties actively engaged in it—and only those parties.[50]

Other critics contend that the news-story format Weaver outlines reinforces existing structures of power. It favors institutions which are most oriented to, and best able to control, "events" or stage pseudo-events. Powerful institutions, and particularly the government, are attuned to the "event-orientation" of reporters and so can manipulate them, while social movements and reformers holding to an "issue-orientation" tend to be ignored by journalists, at least until they, too, can gain the power to stage or participate in "events." [51]

A third criticism, closely related, sees the form of a news story, not as a literary form, but as a social form tightly constrained by the routines of news gathering. Here the argument is that *the process of news gathering itself constructs an image of reality which reinforces official viewpoints.* One analyst after another has made the point that the tradition of objectivity in journalism has favored official views, making journalists mere stenographers for the official transcript of social reality. Here again, the emphasis is not on intentional bias but on the consequences, intended or not, of social forms and processes. According to this perspective, "objectivity" is not a strong conviction of journalists. It is not even, as I have portrayed it for the twenties and thirties, a precarious faith in procedure where agreement on the substantial reality of facts and values cannot be counted on. Instead it is a practice rather than a belief. It is a "strategic ritual," as sociologist Gaye Tuchman puts it, which journalists use to defend themselves against mistakes and criticism. In this view, objectivity is a set of concrete conventions which persist because they reduce the extent to which reporters themselves can be held responsible for the words they write. Thus one can quote speakers in positions of recognized authority; one cannot independently evaluate what they say except by quoting another acknowledged authority. Adherence to these routines, Tuchman writes, is "compulsive." Like Douglass Cater writing in 1950 on the coverage of McCarthy, Tuchman sees journalists as strait-jacketed. And she offers a plausible account of why journalists are willing to put on the strait-jackets: they want to protect themselves from self-inflicted wounds. They do not want to make mistakes which would threaten their jobs or careers.[52] Perhaps more important, it seems to me, editors and publishers do not want their subordinates to make mistakes which would jeopardize *their* careers and institutions.

In the past decade critics of objectivity in journalism have often pictured themselves as lonely exponents of a viewpoint without support in the traditions of journalism. In fact, however, critics were able to draw on, and draw out, what Bernard C. Cohen called the "bootleg" roles in journalism. Cohen found in interviews with foreign correspondents in 1953–1954 and 1960 that journalists held two conceptions of their role, one as neutral observer and one as participant. Curiously, the reporters' overt ideology preached only neutrality. Participant journalism, "like illicit liquor . . . is found everywhere," but it is rarely acknowledged.[53]

This raises two important points. First, it suggests that if a shift in the ideals of journalism occurs, it will have submerged traditions to support it. Forces in and around journalism play *against* the ideal of objectivity and its conventions and have done so even when objectivity seemed most completely to have captivated the profession. Second, it indicates that some rituals and routines of occupational practice will be defended in an overarching ideology, while others may not be linked to any comprehensive or comprehensible world view. Whatever the reasons for this, it suggests at least that there is a problem to be investigated: if social contents do not automatically find expression or justification in cultural forms, then we need to consider how and why they do when they do.[54]

Two submerged traditions in journalism which stand against objectivity found renewed support in the sixties—a literary tradition and a muckraking tradition. The literary tradition has deep roots in journalism. It honors the desire to write a good story, not a safe story or an objective story, but one finely crafted and forceful in its emotional impact. Nat Hentoff described the "new journalism" in 1968 as a journalism "powered by feeling as well as intellect," the kind of journalism which "can help break the glass between the reader and the world he lives in."[55] In the sixties, the tradition of fine writing sailed under the flag of "new journalism." It found expression primarily in magazines rather than newspapers, including a number of new magazines, like *Rolling Stone*, which took for granted an audience fully sympathetic to voices of an adversary culture. It also found its way into book form, most notably in Norman Mailer's account of the 1967 march on the Pentagon, *Armies of the Night*. Whatever else "new journalists" wrote about, they were always implicitly writing about reporting itself. In traditional journalism, form is just a vehicle for the report, but in the new journalism, or "metajournalism" as David Eason calls it, "the form itself is part of the subject of the report."[56] In the thirties, there had also been a nascent sense that the activity of reporting itself was problematic and that the experience of reporting should be included in the report—James Agee's *Let Us Now Praise Famous Men* is the chief example.[57] But in the sixties this sensibility was more richly elaborated and more widely endorsed. It responded to, and helped create, the audience of the critical culture.

While "new journalism" did not have much direct impact on news-writing in daily papers, it did have indirect effects. It fed the imaginations of daily reporters—*Rolling Stone,* for instance, came to be read in newsrooms across the country.[58] More recently, newspapers have turned more to feature or magazine writing. The *New York Times* and the *Chicago Tribune* and other papers now have special semimagazine sections for different days of the week. There has been a corresponding shift in the character of journalistic labor since papers rely more on free-lance writers than on regular staff members for magazine writing. This rewards flair, personality, style, and insight and trains the tastes of journalists and their readers away from objective reporting.

The second tradition which expanded in the sixties, the muckraking tradition, had greater impact on the "hard news" of the papers. Muckraking or "investigative reporting" or "enterprise journalism" came most prominently to public attention with the *Washington Post*'s investigation of Watergate and the romance that grew up around it through the book and film *All the President's Men.* In their account of their own reporting, Bob Woodward and Carl Bernstein insisted that they did nothing exceptional. They denied that their manner of reporting was distinctive; to them, "investigative reporting" is just plain reporting. They were, in short, just doing their job.[59] If *All the President's Men* is read as a set of instructions, a handbook for aspiring journalists (and unquestionably it is being read that way), it provides a counsel of caution. Where Woodward and Bernstein took liberties with law or rules of confirming information they received, they apologize. Where they followed rules—like the guideline they established of confirming every important charge with the testimony of at least two informants—they are proud. They make a case for a journalism true to an ideal of objectivity and false to the counterfeit conventions justified in its name. It is not a personal journalism and not a journalism of advocacy; if there is a personal element in it, it is not opinion or conviction but energy. Where literary journalism contrasts passion to "cold" objectivity, the investigative tradition distinguishes its aggressiveness from objective reporting's passivity.

In the sixties investigative journalism established important institutional beachheads in the media. Journalism reviews provided a forum for journalistic criticism and self-criticism. Beginning with the *Chicago Journalism Review* in 1968, more than two dozen journalism reviews appeared within the space of a few years. Except for *More* in New York, founded in 1971, the reviews did not survive the decline of radical political activity in the early seventies. But *More* is read widely; a new review, *Washington Journalism Review,* began publishing in 1977; and some of the "underground" weeklies that began in the sixties and became well-established and prosperous in the seventies regularly publish criticism of local newspapers and television.[60]

Another institutional change was the development of teams of investigative reporters at many of the country's major metropolitan dailies, several years before the Watergate investigation. In February, 1967, *Newsday* established a team of three reporters, an editor, and a secretary-researcher to pursue investigative work exclusively. The team had its own office and files. It produced three major reports a year, each report running in the paper over five days. The *Boston Globe* in 1970 inaugurated its "spotlight" team on the model of the *Newsday* group. Investigation at the *New York Times,* according to Washington correspondent Robert Semple, proceeded in the late sixties from a "catch as catch can" basis to a "full-time proposition." The *Cleveland Plain-Dealer* had a team from 1974 until 1977 but abandoned it then as too expensive. The *Chicago Tribune* established its investigative task force in 1968 which still has its separate identity, office space, and mission.[61]

There was a corresponding change even at the Associated Press. With the establishment of the *Washington Post-Los Angeles Times* News Service in the early sixties and the growth of the older *New York Times* News Service, AP felt pressure to move away from conventional reporting. In 1967 AP created a "special assignment team" to report on "the submerged dimension" in government activity. In 1968, the group produced 268 stories, including the bungling of the development of the M-16 rifle and the revelation of a secret report on government corruption in Saigon.[62] Not only did news organizations invest time and talent in investigative work, but investigative reporters began to see themselves as an interest group in their own right. In 1975, a number of investigative reporters formed Investigative Reporters and Editors to share information and to protect investigative reporting from becoming a "fad" and "attracting reporters seeking notoriety." I.R.E., amidst considerable criticism, even undertook its own collaborative investigation into the death of one of its members, Arizona reporter Don Bolles.[63]

Another institution for nonconventional journalism is the Fund for Investigative Journalism, founded in 1969 "for the purpose of increasing public knowledge about the concealed, obscure or complex aspects of matters significantly affecting the public." The Fund pledged to aid writers who would "probe abuses of authority or the malfunctioning of institutions and systems which harm the public." Its grants are small—five hundred dollars is typical. While most of the writing the Fund supports appears in magazines, the Fund aided Seymour Hersh in his investigation of My Lai in 1969; it supported him again in 1970 with a study of conflicting claims of the United States and North Vietnam regarding American prisoners of war; it supported James Polk in 1971 in a study of political campaign contributions that uncovered

Robert Vesco's transactions and won for Polk a 1974 Pulitzer Prize. The Fund is by no means a major influence in American journalism. Nevertheless, it is a permanent organization and a potent emblem suggesting that the development in the late sixties of a nonconventional journalism may be sustained.[64]

The Watergate stories capped, rather than inaugurated, the wave of investigative journalism, but they did so in such a stunning fashion that Watergate may turn out to be a symbol of enduring importance for newspaper work. That the Woodward and Bernstein stories, their book about the Watergate investigation, and the film from the book have glamorized "investigative reporting" beyond all bounds and have been a factor in attracting increasing numbers of young people to schools of journalism is a short-term phenomenon with conceivably long-range consequences. For now there is a common point of reference, "Watergate," which confirms the importance of enterprise journalism. It gives to the patchwork of provisional institutional changes leading away from the conventions of objectivity, a cultural identity of considerable force. Never before has there been a national symbol of enterprise reporting of even remotely comparable substance and scope—and effect.

Investigative reporting remains a very precarious enterprise. It is expensive but must survive inside newspapers increasingly cost-conscious. It sets up a reportorial elite potentially in conflict with the generally democratic newsroom.[65] It is very hard work, with results rarely as glamorous as an impeachment. Many investigators get disillusioned. That investigative work has been to some degree institutionalized in the past decade is no assurance it will survive. While investigators may have a place in the newsroom, they do not have an equally permanent spot in the newspaper itself. In that sense, the great innovation of the thirties—the columnist—secured a safer position in journalism than the enterprise journalism of the sixties. The columnist is supported by a reputation among readers in the local or national community; investigative reporters rarely have a public following and are supported only by the climate within journalism itself. Only that, and the continued potency of the symbol "Watergate."

What is likely to happen in schools of journalism and in newsrooms around the country as new recruits enter the field is that they will be told to forget the romance of newspaper work and to learn the same old basics of who, what, where, when reporting. They will be encouraged to reenact the rituals of objective reporting. Enterprise journalism, like interpretive reporting, may have its traditions and may have its rewards, but it will not have its handbooks. It requires mature subjectivity; subjectivity tempered by encounters with, and regard for, the views of significant others in the profession; and subjectivity aged by encounters with, and regard for, the facts of the world. There is no text for this. Even Curtis MacDougall's classic *Interpretative Reporting* actually devoted but one short chapter to problems of interpretation; the book's title is a philosophy but not a program.

The exercise of judgment is not something editors want to entrust to cub reporters. Even veteran journalists who believe in the necessity of interpretation urge young reporters to begin at a city news bureau or wire service learning to write straight news according to the most stringent rules of objective journalism. Separating facts from opinion is still one of the first things young reporters learn and one of the only things they can be taught in catechismic form. This is not likely to change.

But this does not mean the changes of the past decade will not lastingly influence journalism.

> We've so little faith that anyone
> ever makes anything better,

Robert Lowell wrote in "For Eugene McCarthy." Despite the passionate political commitments of the late sixties, even then it did not come naturally to very many people to believe that anyone ever makes anything better. That made McCarthy such a perfect symbol, for he was a man who so obviously had difficulty in believing himself. After the wave of the sixties has passed, we wonder again if anyone ever makes anything better and whether, in fact, anything did get more than momentarily better out of the elations and despairs, the courage and the folly of the past decade.

In journalism, the decline of the social movements of the sixties depleted the psychic and organizational resources that sustained a high pitch of journalistic criticism and reform. There is little support now for the kind of mobilized, advocacy journalism that flourished in the underground papers. Most journalism reviews have died. Incipient efforts at "newsroom democracy" have disappeared.[66] But the residue of reform remains impressive. Short of an intensified cold war or some other cultural and political muzzle on dissent, we can expect a critical culture to continue as a voice in journalism and as a market for its products. There is no new ideal in journalism to successfully challenge objectivity, but there is a hope for something new, a simmering disaffection with objective reporting. There has been no magical leap beyond the difficult understanding that human perceptions are subjective and no easy solution to the problem that the events one reports have been prefabricated by powerful institutions, and yet there is more tolerance and encouragement for a variety of ways of knowing and writing.

The *Boston Herald,* an early penny paper, wrote in 1847 that its leading purpose was to "give expression to the spirit of the age." It hoped to be "a zealous historian of the hour" and proclaimed its intention to *"group* and *picture* the events of the passing time, and daguerreotype them for the public eye, in unfading lines." Today we suspect the bias of grouping and the rhetoric of picturing; we see the lies in photography and the astigmatism of the public eye. Even the *Herald*'s promise of a "faithful and unflattering likeness" of society would be questioned in our self-conscious age, where skepticism about mottos extends to mottos that proclaim skepticism. What prospectus could one write for a newspaper today?

I do not know. I know only that it matters. Journalists, like other seekers, must learn to trust themselves and their fellows and the world enough to take everything in, while distrusting themselves and others and the appearances of the world enough not to be taken in by everything. They would refuse, then, as some of them do now, either to surrender to relativism or to submit uncritically to arbitrary conventions established in the name of objectivity. This requires both personal and institutional tolerance of uncertainty and acceptance of risk and commitment to caring for truth. If this is difficult in journalism, it is nonetheless most vital, for the daily persuasions of journalists reflect and become our own.

NOTES

Introduction

1   John W. C. Johnstone, Edward J. Slawski, and William M. Bowman, "The Professional Values of American Newsmen," *Public Opinion Quarterly* 36 (Winter 1972-1973): 522-540; and, by the same authors, *The News People* (Urbana: University of Illinois Press, 1976).

2   Donald L. Shaw, "News Bias and the Telegraph: A Study of Historical Change," *Journalism Quarterly* 44 (Spring 1967): 3-12, 31.

3   Shaw suggests this in Shaw, "News Bias and the Telegraph" and in "Technology: Freedom for What?" in Ronald T. Farrar and John D. Stevens, *Mass Media and the National Experience* (New York: Harper and Row, 1971), pp. 64-86. James W. Carey cautiously voices the same position in "The Communications Revolution and the Professional Communicator," *Sociological Review Monograph* 13 (1969): 23-38. Bernard Roscho espouses the same view in *Newsmaking* (Chicago: University of Chicago Press, 1975), p. 31.

4   From the seventeenth century until the past several decades, Wayne Booth wrote in 1974, "it grew increasingly unfashionable to see the universe or world or nature or 'the facts' as implicating values." But he argues that it is only in the twentieth century that "the fact-value split became a truism *and* that the split began to entail the helplessness of reason in dealing with any values but the calculation of means to ends." (See Wayne C. Booth, *Modern Dogma and the Rhetoric of Assent* [Chicago: University of Chicago Press, 1974], pp. 14-15.) Booth argues forcefully against a radical disjunction of facts and values as does the philosopher Alasdair MacIntyre in *A Short History of Ethics* (New York: Macmillan, 1966) and *Against the Self-Images of the Age* (New York: Schocken Books, 1971), especially the essay, "Hume on 'Is' and 'Ought,' " pp. 109-124.

5   Two influential recent statements regarding the social construction of reality are Thomas Kuhn, *The Structure of Scientific Revolutions* (Chicago: University of Chicago Press, 1962); and Peter Berger and Thomas Luckmann, *The Social Construction of Reality* (Garden City, N.Y.: Doubleday, 1966).

6   This is the leading version of objectivity in science. Israel Scheffler has defined it as follows: "Commitment to fair controls over assertion is the basis of the scientific attitude of impartiality and detachment; indeed, one might say that it constitutes this attitude. For impartiality and detachment are not to be thought of as substantive qualities of the scientist's personality or the style of his thought; scientists are as variegated in these respects as any other group of people. . . . What is central is the acknowledgment of general controls to which one's dearest beliefs are ultimately subject." (Israel Scheffler, *Science and Subjectivity* [Indianapolis: Bobbs-Merrill, 1967], p. 2.)

Chapter 1

1 James Fenimore Cooper, *A Letter to His Countrymen* (New York: John Wiley, 1834), p. 11.
2 George Dekker and Larry Johnston, "Introduction" in James Fenimore Cooper, *The American Democrat* (Baltimore: Penguin Books, 1969), p. 26.
3 James Fenimore Cooper, *The American Democrat*, edited with an Introduction by George Dekker and Larry Johnston (Baltimore: Penguin Books, 1969), p. 183. Originally published 1838.
4 Statistics on journalism in this period are from Alfred McClung Lee, *The Daily Newspaper in America* (New York: Macmillan, 1937), pp. 705–753.
5 Glyndon G. Van Deusen, *Thurlow Weed* (Boston: Little, Brown, 1947), pp. 108, 360.
6 Philip Hone, *The Diary of Philip Hone*, ed. Bayard Tuckerman, 2 vols. (New York: Dodd, Mead, 1889), I: 30 (April 20, 1831). Lambert A. Wilmer cataloged duels and fights between editors in his diatribe on the American press, *Our Press Gang* (Philadelphia: J. T. Lloyd, 1859), pp. 294–325.
7 Isaac Clark Pray, *Memoirs of James Gordon Bennett* (New York: Stringer and Townsend, 1855), p. 84. Pray wrote this biography of Bennett under the name, "A Journalist." On Pray and his relation to Bennett, see William A. Croffut, *An American Procession 1855–1914* (Boston: Little, Brown, 1931), pp. 9–23.
8 Newspaper names and dates of publication for this period can be found in Clarence S. Brigham, *History and Bibliography of American Newspapers 1690–1820* (Worcester, Mass.: American Antiquarian Society, 1947); and S. N. D. North, *The Newspapers and Periodical Press* (Washington: Government Printing Office, 1884).
9 Walter Lippmann, "Two Revolutions in the American Press," *Yale Review* 20 (March 1931): 433–441.
10 Willard G. Bleyer, *Main Currents in the History of American Journalism* (Boston: Houghton Mifflin, 1927), p. 166.
11 Ibid., pp. 171–180. Bleyer's information comes from the newspapers' own claims of their circulation and so surely overestimates the actual circulation.
12 See James Harvey Young, *The Toadstool Millionaires* (Princeton: Princeton University Press, 1961); and James Harvey Young, *The Medical Messiahs* (Princeton: Princeton University Press, 1967), for a history of patent medicines in America.
13 P. T. Barnum, *Struggles and Triumphs: Or, Forty Years' Recollections of P. T. Barnum* (New York: American News, 1871), p. 67.
14 *Boston Daily Times*, October 11, 1837, quoted in Bleyer, *Main Currents*, p. 175.
15 *New York Tribune*, December 20, 1841, quoted in Bleyer, *Main Currents*, p. 217.
16 *New York Times*, July 17, 1852.
17 *New York Herald*, November 21, 1837.
18 *New York Sun*, December 9, 1833.
19 *New York Transcript*, July 4, 1834.
20 *Baltimore Sun*, quoted in Bleyer, *Main Currents*, p. 180.
21 Horace Greeley, *Recollections of a Busy Life* (New York: J. B. Ford, 1868), p. 137.
22 *New York Transcript*, June 23, 1834, quoted in Bleyer, *Main Currents*, p. 165. The "cotemporary" referred to is the *New York Sun*.
23 *New York Herald*, December 8, 1837.
24 Pray, *Memoirs*, p. 251.

25 James Gordon Bennett, quoted in Frederic Hudson, *Journalism in the United States* (New York: Harper and Brothers, 1872), p. 286. Bennett's self-report of his innovation is corroborated in Ben: Perley Poore's recollections, which recall Bennett's "lively" letters which "abounded in personal allusions" about politicians and their families as an important new development in Washington correspondence. Ben: Perley Poore, *Perley's Reminiscences of Sixty Years in the National Metropolis*, 2 vols. (Philadelphia: Hubbard Brothers, 1886), I:58.

26 John Quincy Adams, *The Diary of John Quincy Adams*, ed. Allan Nevins (New York: Frederick Ungar Publishing, 1969), p. 543.

27 James Parton, "The New York Herald," *North American Review* 102 (April 1866): 376.

28 *New York Herald*, September 30, 1840. Stansbury is Arthur J. Stansbury, an important figure in the early development of Washington correspondence, who wrote out his accounts of speeches with his own contractions of longhand. See L. A. Gobright, *Recollections of Men and Things at Washington During the Third of a Century* (Philadelphia: Claxton, Remson, and Haffelfinger, 1869), p. 401.

29 *New York Herald*, December 24, 1841.

30 *New York Herald*, November 21, 1840.

31 Hudson, *Journalism*, p. 470.

32 Erich Auerbach, *Mimesis* (Princeton: Princeton University Press, 1953), p. 31.

33 Frank Luther Mott, *American Journalism: A History 1690–1960* (New York: Macmillan, 1962), pp. 196–197.

34 *New York Herald*, March 12, 1837.

35 *New York Herald*, March 17, 1837.

36 Hone, *The Diary*, II:13. (February 25, 1840.)

37 *New York Herald*, March 2, 1840.

38 *New York Herald*, December 28, 1837.

39 Gobright, *Recollections of Men and Things*, pp. 73–76.

40 Hannah Arendt, *The Human Condition* (Garden City, N.Y.: Doubleday Anchor Books, 1958), p. 33.

41 New York's position as the focal point of the nation's commerce, transportation, and communication is documented in Allan R. Pred, *Urban Growth and the Circulation of Information: The United States System of Cities, 1790–1840* (Cambridge: Harvard University Press, 1973).

42 It forms the basis for Alfred McClung Lee's study of the daily newspaper, *The Daily Newspaper in America* (New York: Macmillan, 1937). It is a close cousin to the idea of a "transportation revolution" that historian Lee Benson hopes will provide a unifying explanation for early nineteenth-century American history in *The Concept of Jacksonian Democracy* (Princeton: Princeton University Press, 1961; New York: Atheneum, 1964), pp. 337–338.

43 For this account of technological change I have relied on Lawrence C. Wroth and Rollo G. Silver, "Book Production and Distribution from the American Revolution to the War Between the States" in Hellmut Lehmann-Haupt, *The Book in America* (New York: R. R. Bowker, 1951); Sean Jennett, *Pioneers in Printing* (London: Routledge and Kegan Paul, 1958); S. H. Steinberg, *Five Hundred Years of Printing* (Harmondsworth, England: Penguin Books, 1961); John Tebbel, *A History of Book Publishing in the United States*, vol. 1 (New York: R. R. Bowker, 1972); James Moran, *Printing Presses* (Berkeley: University of California Press, 1973); and Rollo G. Silver, *The American Printer 1787–1825* (Charlottesville: University Press of Virginia, 1967).

44 John F. Stover, *American Railroads* (Chicago: University of Chicago Press, 1961), pp. 264–269.

45 Jennett, *Pioneers in Printing*, p. 159. See also Moran, *Printing Presses*, p. 222.

46 Frank M. O'Brien, *The Story of The* Sun (New York: D. Appleton, 1928), pp. 4, 26, 32. Lee, *Daily Newspaper,* p. 116, gives a figure of eight thousand, rather than twenty thousand, for the *Sun*'s circulation just before it converted to steam. See the *New York Sun,* September 5, 1853, for its own useful anniversary history of itself.

47 George Rogers Taylor, *The Transportation Revolution 1815-1860* (New York: Rinehart and Co., 1951), p. 152.

48 Gerald Johnson, Frank Kent, H. L. Mencken, and Hamilton Owens, *The Sunpapers of Baltimore* (New York: Alfred A. Knopf, 1937), pp. 67-71.

49 Robert Luther Thompson, *Wiring a Continent: The History of the Telegraph Industry in the United States 1832-1866* (Princeton: Princeton University Press, 1947), p. 219.

50 Mott, *American Journalism,* p. 304, invokes literacy in a reflexlike way. Richard Altick automatically adopts the same position in his history of reading in England: "Everybody knows that in the nineteenth century the number of English readers, and therefore the production of the press, multiplied spectacularly." Richard D. Altick, *The English Common Reader* (Chicago: University of Chicago Press, 1957), p. 1. The "therefore" in that sentence is the suspect word.

51 There is some evidence that for every two persons who could write, three or four could read. Robert K. Webb, "Working Class Readers in Early Victorian England," *English Historical Review* 65 (1960): 350.

52 Ian Watt, *The Rise of the Novel* (Berkeley: University of California Press, 1965), pp. 39-40.

53 Webb, "Working Class Readers," p. 334, suggests the importance of various inducements to literacy and recalls a story by Harriet Martineau in which a boy relearns reading, which he had forgotten, by studying advertising posters.

54 See Jack Goody and Ian Watt, "The Consequences of Literacy" in *Literacy in Traditional Societies,* ed. Jack Goody (Cambridge: Cambridge University Press, 1968), pp. 27-68.

55 Paulo Freire, *Cultural Action for Freedom* (Cambridge: *Harvard Educational Review* Monograph Series, 1970), p. 13.

56 Thomas Hamilton wrote on his travels to America, "The influence and circulation of newspapers is great beyond anything ever known in Europe." (*Men and Morals in America,* 2 vols., 2: 74.) [Edinburgh: William Blackwood, 1833]. See Carlo M. Cipolla, *Literacy and Development in the West* (Harmondsworth, England: Penguin Books, 1969), p. 94; and Daniel Boorstin, *The Americans: The National Experience* (New York: Vintage Books, 1965), pp. 280, 328.

57 E. P. Thompson, *The Making of the English Working Class* (New York: Vintage Books, 1963), p. 718; and J. F. C. Harrison, *Learning and Living 1790-1960* (London: Routledge and Kegan Paul, 1961), p. 41.

58 Freire, *Cultural Action,* p. 4. For more recent discussion of Freire's work, see Nan Elsasser and Vera P. John-Steiner, "An Interactionist Approach to Advancing Literacy," *Harvard Educational Review* 47 (August 1977): 355-369. There is support for Freire's view that people learn better when they feel power to act in their own lives from some work in social psychology: see Melvin Seeman, "Alienation, Membership, and Political Knowledge: A Comparative Study," *Public Opinion Quarterly* 30 (Fall 1966): 353-367.

59 Kenneth A. Lockridge, *Literacy in Colonial New England* (New York: W. W. Norton, 1974).

60 Lippmann, "Two Revolutions," p. 440.

61 Robert E. Park, "The Natural History of the Newspaper," *American Journal of Sociology* 29 (November 1923): 273-289.

62 Mott, *American Journalism,* p. vii.

63 Ibid., pp. 215, 304.

64 Allan Nevins and Henry Steele Commager, *A Pocket History of the United States* (New York: Washington Square Press, 1967), p. 167.

65 See Edward Pessen, "The Egalitarian Myth and the American Social Reality: Wealth, Mobility, and Equality in the Era of the Common Man," *American Historical Review* 76 (October 1971): 989–1034. For a review of historiography of the Jacksonian era critical of Pessen's work, see Lee Benson, "Middle Period Historiography: What Is to Be Done?" in Lee Benson, *Toward the Scientific Study of History* (Philadelphia: J. B. Lippincott, 1972), pp. 190–224.

66 Douglas T. Miller, *Jacksonian Aristocracy* (New York: Oxford University Press, 1967), pp. 124–125.

67 Margaret G. Myers, *The New York Money Market*, vol. 1 (New York: Columbia University Press, 1931), pp. 17, 18, 32. When the exchange began in 1817 only the stocks of federal and state governments, banks, and insurance companies were traded. In the 1820s the usual volume of trading was one hundred or so shares a day. In 1830–1831, when the first railroad stock was traded on the exchange, a daily volume of one thousand shares was not uncommon. By the middle 1830s, there was a great amount of railroad trading, and volume averaged five thousand shares a day.

68 Bray Hammond, *Banks and Politics in America* (Princeton: Princeton University Press, 1957), p. 9.

69 Stephen Salsbury, *The State, The Investor, and the Railroad* (Cambridge: Harvard University Press, 1967), pp. 140–141. When the shares of the Baltimore and Ohio Railroad were offered in 1827, more than 22,000 people subscribed for 36,788 shares at one hundred dollars a share. Edward Hungerford, *The Story of the Baltimore and Ohio Railroad 1827–1927* (New York: G. P. Putnam's, 1928), p. 30.

70 Taylor, *The Transportation Revolution 1815–1860*, p. 102.

71 Paul Starr, "Medicine, Economy and Society in Nineteenth Century America," *Journal of Social History* 10 (Summer 1977).

72 Pray, *Memoirs*, p. 199.

73 J. A. Scoville, quoted in Robert G. Albion, *The Rise of New York Port 1815–1860* (New York: Charles Scribner's, 1967), p. 244. For other evidence of the changing values of businessmen see Paul Goodman, "Ethics and Enterprise: The Values of a Boston Elite, 1800–1860," *American Quarterly* 18 (Fall 1966): 437–451. A more general statement describing the shift from an economy governed by community needs to one led by individualistic entrepreneurs can be found in Oscar Handlin and Mary Handlin, "Origins of the American Business Corporation," *Journal of Economic History* 5 (May 1945): 1–23. The Handlins show that the corporation in America, in the period before the War of 1812, was conceived as an agency of government serving a "social function." They write, "Turnpikes, not trade, banks, not land speculations were its province because the community, not the enterprising capitalists, marked out its sphere of activity."

74 Chilton Williamson, *American Suffrage From Property to Democracy 1760–1860* (Princeton: Princeton University Press, 1960), p. 260. For discussion of the transformation of American party politics in this era see Richard P. McCormick, *The Second American Party System* (Chapel Hill: University of North Carolina Press, 1966); and also William Nisbet Chambers, "Party Development and the American Mainstream;" Walter Dean Burnham, "Party Systems and the Political Process;" and Paul Goodman, "The First American Party System;" all in William Nisbet Chambers and Walter Dean Burnham, *The American Party Systems* (New York: Oxford University Press, 1967).

75 McCormick, *Second American Party System*, p. 30.

76 Richard Hofstadter, *The Idea of a Party System* (Berkeley: University of California Press, 1972), p. 242. See also Robert V. Remini, *Martin van Buren and*

the Making of the Democratic Party (New York: W. W. Norton, 1970), p. 193.

77   That they resembled each other greatly is the point of Lee Benson, *The Concept of Jacksonian Democracy.* That they were both distinct from earlier parties is a different point, one made by both Richard McCormick and Richard Hofstadter.

78   William Appleman Williams, *The Contours of American History* (New York: Franklin Watts New Viewpoints, 1973), p. 229.

79   Ronald Formisano, "Michigan and the Party System, Mass Party Loyalty 1835–1852" in *Political Ideology and Voting Behavior in the Age of Jackson,* ed. Joel H. Silbey (Englewood Cliffs, N.J.: Prentice-Hall, 1973), p. 153. It is one thing to know that party loyalty became important in the 1830s, quite another matter to understand it. For all historians know of the institutional developments in parties in this period, we know very little about how they came to *matter* to people. The question Ronald Formisano raises is a good one: "How did parties become reference groups for various subcultures in the 1830s?" See Ronald Formisano, "Political Character, Antipartyism and the Second Party System," *American Quarterly* 21 (Winter 1969): 688.

80   *Springfield Republican,* June 7, 1872, quoted in Bleyer, *Main Currents,* pp. 208–209.

81   *New York Herald,* quoted in Bleyer, *Main Currents,* p. 187.

82   *New York Herald,* September 6, 1836.

83   Ibid.

84   Ibid. Bennett also charged that his penny rivals were read by Negroes, an indication to Bennett that they were poor papers indeed. See, for instance, the *Herald* of December 27, 1837, where Bennett claims that the *Sun* circulated "principally among the negroes of this city."

85   *New York Herald,* May 22, 1837.

86   The *Evening Chronicle* was published from May 22, 1837, to July 11, 1837, and, under the name *Evening Herald,* continued to be published until March 30, 1839.

87   *New York Herald,* April 13, 1840. This was a standard theme with Bennett from the beginning. On May 26, 1835, the *Herald* proclaimed that it was "diffused among all classes—but principally among the business and commercial, private families, and men of leisure. In this respect, it differs from the other small daily papers." Quoted in Bleyer, *Main Currents,* p. 187.

88   Pray, *Memoirs,* pp. 256–257, 474.

89   This announcement was reprinted daily in the *New York Herald* from February 28 through March 12, 1838.

90   *New York Herald,* January 30, 1837.

91   *New York Herald,* October 28, 1836.

92   *New York Herald,* January 30, 1837.

93   *New York Herald,* September 28, 1837, and April 13, 1840.

94   *Albany Argus,* quoted in the *Commercial Advertiser,* June 11, 1840.

95   *New York Courier and Enquirer,* June 4, 1840.

96   *New York Courier and Enquirer,* June 9, 1840.

97   My account of the "Moral War" relies on Pray, *Memoirs,* pp. 263–270; Hudson, *Journalism,* pp. 456–462; and the contemporary newspapers themselves.

98   Joseph Gusfield, *Symbolic Crusade* (Urbana: University of Illinois Press, 1963), p. 36.

99   David Donald, *Lincoln Reconsidered* (New York: Vintage Books, 1956), p. 36.

100   William Charvat, "American Romanticism and the Depression of 1837," *Science and Society* 2 (1937): 67.

101 Robert Nisbet, *The Sociological Tradition* (New York: Basic Books, 1966), p. 47.

102 Louis Wirth, "Urbanism as a Way of Life," *American Journal of Sociology* 44 (July 1938): 21.

103 See Reinhard Bendix, "Traditon and Modernity Reconsidered," *Comparative Studies in Society and History* 9 (April 1967): 292–346.

104 Richard Sennett, *The Fall of Public Man* (New York: Alfred A. Knopf, 1976), p. 39.

105 See Sennett, *The Fall of Public Man* and Lionel Trilling, *Sincerity and Authenticity* (Cambridge: Harvard University Press, 1972).

Chapter 2

1 Irvin S. Cobb, *Exit Laughing* (Indianapolis: Bobbs-Merrill, 1941), pp. 251–264. Cobb divides American newspaper history into the "Time of the Great Editor," the "Time of the Great Reporter" in the 1890s, the "Age of the Publishers," and finally an age of the columnists.

For the account of the Olivette affair, I have read the New York newspapers of the day and also relied on Charles H. Brown, *The Correspondents' War* (New York: Scribner's, 1961). There is information on Richard Harding Davis' reports from Cuba in Charles Belmont Davis, ed., *Adventures and Letters of Richard Harding Davis* (New York: Scribner's, 1917); Richard Harding Davis, *Cuba in War Time* (New York: R. H. Russell, 1897); Fairfax Downey, *Richard Harding Davis: His Day* (New York: Scribner's, 1933); and Gerald Langford, *The Richard Harding Davis Years* (New York: Holt, Rinehart, and Winston, 1961). Other relevant accounts of this period in New York journalism include Gerald Linderman, *The Mirror of War* (Ann Arbor: University of Michigan Press, 1974); W. A. Swanberg, *Citizen Hearst* (New York: Scribner's, 1961); and W. A. Swanberg, *Pulitzer* (New York: Scribner's, 1967). Besides the accounts in the *World* and the *Journal,* the only contemporary account which deals with the Olivette affair in any detail is a story in the *New York Times* of March 2, 1897, "Cuban Women Ill Treated."

The story of Hearst's telegram has often been retold. Whether it is true or not is not clear, but it has been part of the mythology of journalism for a long time, beginning at least as far back as James Creelman, *On the Great Highway* (Boston: Lothrop Publishing, 1901), pp. 177–178.

2 Edwin A. Perry, *The Boston Herald and Its History* (Boston: 1878), p. 13.

3 See Culver Smith, *The Press, Politics, and Patronage: The American Government's Use of Newspapers, 1789–1875* (Athens, Ga.: University of Georgia Press, 1977), pp. 219–234. Smith discusses both the establishment of the Government Printing Office in 1860, which eliminated the government's need to patronize a newspaper, and President Buchanan's decision near the end of his term to abandon the use of a Washington paper as a personal and party organ. The way for Lincoln's decision was well paved.

4 *New York Herald,* March 13, 1852.

5 *New York Times,* November 1, 1860.

6   There is disagreement on who deserves credit, if credit is due, for the first interview. Oliver Carlson attributes it and nearly every other important innovation in nineteenth-century journalism to James Gordon Bennett in *The Man Who Made News: James Gordon Bennett* (New York: Duell, Sloan and Pearce, 1942). Carlson reprints part of a Bennett story in the *Herald* of April 16, 1836, in which a question and answer session between Bennett and Rosina Townsend, the madam who ran the brothel where Ellen Jewett was murdered, appears. However, Townsend denied that the interview ever took place. At any rate, the interview did not at that time become a regular feature in the press. F. B. Marbut suggests that the first interview may have been Horace Greeley's conversation with Brigham Young as reported in the *Tribune* on August 20, 1859. The form was clearly unusual then, for Greeley felt the need to explain it: "Such is, as nearly as I can recall, the substance of nearly two hours of conversation, wherein much was said incidentally that would not be worth reporting, even if I could remember and reproduce it. . . ." Marbut notes that Andrew Johnson was the first president to grant interviews. See F. B. Marbut, *News From the Capital* (Carbondale: Southern Illinois University Press, 1971), pp. 134, 167.

7   Bernard Weisberger is most forthright: "The Civil War was a turning point for reporting." (*The American Newspaperman* [Chicago: University of Chicago Press, 1961], p. 118.) Edwin Emery is more careful but leaves a similar impression: "The War Between the States affected all aspects of journalism. Reporting, editing, circulation, printing, advertising, and illustration were all modified during the conflict." (*The Press and America* [Englewood Cliffs, N.J.: Prentice-Hall, 1972], p. 231.) Havilah Babcock listed the main consequences of the Civil War for journalism in "The Press and the Civil War," *Journalism Quarterly* 6 (March 1929): 1–5. The list is stretched to include developments like yellow journalism—which the author claims had "its inception in conditions arising from the war" (conditions which are not identified)—which the war had nothing to do with.

8   This brief sketch of journalism in the Civil War relies on Louis M. Starr, *Bohemian Brigade* (New York: Alfred A. Knopf, 1954); and J. Cutler Andrews, *The North Reports the Civil War* (Pittsburgh: University of Pittsburgh Press, 1955), especially pp. 1–34.

9   Frederic Hudson, *Journalism in the United States* (New York: Harper's, 1872), p. 719.

10   Julius Chambers, *News Hunting on Three Continents* (New York: Mitchell Kennerly, 1921), p. 3.

11   "Our 17th 'Special,' " *The Journalist* 28 (December 15, 1900).

12   Isaac F. Marcosson, *David Graham Phillips and His Times* (New York: Dodd, Mead, 1932), p. 101.

13   Richard Hofstadter, *The Age of Reform* (New York: Vintage Books, 1955), p. 191, reports that the salaries of reporters doubled between 1870 and 1890.

14   See, for instance, the editorial "Working on Space," *The Journalist* 7 (March 31, 1888).

15   Margheita Arlina Hamm, "The Journalist's Birthday," *The Journalist* 23 (April 23, 1898).

16   On the Whitechapel Club, see Willis J. Abbot, *Watching the World Go By* (Boston: Little, Brown, 1933), pp. 87–92; and Elmer Ellis, *Mr. Dooley's America* (New York: Alfred A. Knopf, 1948; reprint ed., New York: Archon Books, 1969), pp. 48–54. On "Doc" Perry's see Abbot, *Watching the World Go By*, pp. 22–23. Allen Churchill, *Park Row* (New York: Rinehart, 1958; reprint ed., Westport, Conn.: Greenwood Press, 1973), provides a colorful sketch of New York newspaper life in this period.

17   See William H. Freeman, *The Press Club of Chicago: A History* (Chicago: Press Club of Chicago, 1894); and Duncan Aikman, "Prehistory" in *Dateline:*

Washington, ed. Cabell Phillips (Washington: National Press Club, 1949; New York: Greenwood Press, 1968), pp. 9–25.

18   E. L. Godkin, "Newspapers Here and Abroad," *North American Review* 150 (February 1890): 198.

19   See, for instance, Edwin L. Shuman, *Steps Into Journalism* (Evanston, Ill.: Correspondence School of Journalism, 1894), an outgrowth of the author's Chautauqua course on journalism. A new edition under the title, *Practical Journalism* (New York: D. Appleton, 1903), appeared later. Robert Luce, *Writing for the Press* (Boston: Writer Publishing, 1891), had editions published in 1886, 1888, 1889, and 1891.

20   On the rise of the expert, see Richard Hofstadter, *Anti-intellectualism in American Life* (New York: Alfred A. Knopf, 1964), pp. 197–229. On scientific management, see Samuel Haber, *Efficiency and Uplift: Scientific Management in the Progressive Era* (Chicago: University of Chicago Press, 1964). On realism, see Alfred Kazin, *On Native Grounds* (New York: Reynal and Hitchcock, 1942); George J. Becker, ed., *Documents of Modern Literary Realism* (Princeton: Princeton University Press, 1963); Malcolm Cowley, "A Natural History of American Naturalism," *ibid.,* pp. 429–451; Wallace Stegner, ed., *American Prose: The Realistic Movement 1841–1900* (New York: Holt, Rinehart, & Winston, 1958); and Erich Auerbach, *Mimesis* (Princeton: Princeton University Press, 1953). On the revolt against formalism, see Morton White, *Social Thought in America: The Revolt Against Formalism* (Boston: Beacon Press, 1957), and also see the challenging new interpretation in Thomas L. Haskell, *The Emergence of Professional Social Science* (Urbana: University of Illinois Press, 1977).

21   Quoted in Robert Bremner, *From the Depths* (New York: New York University Press, 1956), p. 140.

22   On Baker, see Robert C. Bannister, *Ray Stannard Baker* (New Haven: Yale University Press, 1966), pp. 30–40. On Steffens, see Lincoln Steffens, *The Autobiography of Lincoln Steffens* (New York: Harcourt, Brace, 1931), pp. 149–152; and Justin Kaplan, *Lincoln Steffens* (New York: Simon & Schuster, 1974), pp. 34–52. On Dreiser, see Theodore Dreiser, *Newspaper Days* (New York: Horace Liveright, 1922), p. 457; and Robert H. Elias, *Theodore Dreiser: Apostle of Nature* (Ithaca: Cornell University Press, 1970), pp. 80–83. On London, see the passion for Spencer of the character Martin Eden in London's autobiographical novel, *Martin Eden* (New York: Macmillan, 1957), pp. 98–107; for Cahan, see Abraham Cahan, *The Education of Abraham Cahan* (Philadelphia: Jewish Publication Society of America, 1969), pp. 369, 404–405. See, in general, Richard Hofstadter, *Social Darwinism in American Thought* (New York: George Braziller, 1959).

23   Cahan, *Education,* p. 405.

24   Clarence Darrow, "Realism in Literature and Art" in *The Land of Contrasts: 1880–1901,* ed. Neil Harris (New York: George Braziller, 1970), p. 286. The essay originally appeared in *The Arena* 9 (December 1893): 98–109, 111–113.

25   Everett Carter, *Howells and the Age of Realism* (Philadelphia: J. B. Lippincott, 1954), p. 102.

26   Larzer Ziff, *The American 1890s* (New York: Viking Press, 1966), p. 159.

27   Quoted in Fred C. Kelly, *George Ade* (Indianapolis: Bobbs-Merrill, 1947), p. 110.

28   Becker, *Documents,* p. 31.

29   See note 20 above for references on realism in literature.

30   Quoted in Carter, *Howells,* p. 89.

31   Kazin, *On Native Grounds,* p. 10.

32   Ibid., p. 15.

33   See Perry Miller, *The Life of the Mind in America* (New York: Harcourt,

Brace, 1965); and also Michael Schudson, "Origins of the Ideal of Objectivity in the Professions: Studies in the History of American Journalism and American Law 1830–1940" (Ph.D. diss. Harvard University, 1976).

34 Charles Rosenberg, *The Cholera Years* (Chicago: University of Chicago Press, 1962), p. 232.

35 For early "democratic" science, see George Daniels, "The Pure-Science Ideal and Democratic Culture," *Science* 156 (June 30, 1967): 1699–1705. Discussions of the kind of science democratic culture is conducive to are: Alexis de Tocqueville, *Democracy in America*, ed. Phillips Bradley, 2 vols. (New York: Vintage Books, 1945), pp. 42–49; and Karl Mannheim, *Essays on the Sociology of Culture* (London: Routledge and Kegan Paul, 1956), pp. 171–246. Mannheim's essay here, "The Democratization of Culture," is especially suggestive.

36 Julius Chambers, *News Hunting on Three Continents* (New York: Mitchell, Kennerly, 1921), p. 7.

37 Steffens, *Autobiography*, p. 179.

38 Joseph H. Appel, *Growing Up With Advertising* (New York: Business Bourse, 1940), p. 23.

39 Dreiser, *Newspaper Days*, p. 52.

40 Ibid., p. 467.

41 Edwin L. Shuman, *Steps Into Journalism* (Evanston, Ill.: Correspondence School of Journalism, 1894), p. 66.

42 Ibid., p. 123.

43 Ibid., p. 66. My emphasis.

44 Edwin L. Shuman, *Practical Journalism* (New York: D. Appleton, 1903), p. 102. Shuman was more circumspect in his comments about the "journalistic imagination" in this later edition. He observed that the use of the journalistic imagination existed "to some degree on every enterprising paper," but he was hesitant to recommend it to his readers: "The ethics of the subject may be left to the individual reader." (p. 104). Robert Luce in *Writing for the Press* (Boston: Writers Publishing, 1891) qualified the separation between fact and opinion in this way: " 'Never put an editorial opinion into a news paragraph,' is a standard rule and, interpreted correctly, a good one. Theoretically it is not the province of the reporter or correspondent to express opinions, but too strict an application of the theory makes news columns prosy. Descriptive matter especially it is next to impossible to make entertaining without putting in opinions. Most of these and other sorts of opinions are harmless. The rule would be better modified to read, 'Never put into a news paragraph, a special article, or correspondence, any personal opinion that will hurt anyone's feelings, or that is of moment enough to cause discussion.' This excludes opinions that might cause libel suits, and opinions that might differ from the 'policy' of the paper or compel the paper to adopt an unwelcome policy." (p. 82).

45 H. L. Mencken, *Newspaper Days (1899–1906)* (New York: Alfred A. Knopf, 1941), pp. 14, 23.

46 Arthur Reed Kimball, "The Invasion of Journalism," *Atlantic Monthly* 86 (July 1900): 119–124. Leading magazines until the 1890s had had small circulations, high prices, conservative publishing houses, and editors whose interests were primarily literary and who thought of a magazine as a book in periodical form. *McClure's* and the other magazines that sprouted in the 1890s sold for ten or fifteen cents, not thirty-five, and had circulations not hovering around 100,000 but ranging from 400,000 to a million. The publishers were businessmen, not literary men, and they regarded newspapers, not books, as the appropriate model for the magazine. The gulf that separated the world of the newspapers from the world of the magazines was bridged in the 1890s. The revolution the penny press initiated in daily newspapers in the 1830s—cheaper prices, large circulation, and a focus on news— was repeated exactly for magazines in the 1890s. For general discussions of this shift

in magazine journalism, see Hofstadter, *The Age of Reform,* pp. 192–194; and Ziff, *American 1890s,* pp. 120–123. A very useful and more detailed discussion is Theodore Greene, *America's Heroes* (New York: Oxford University Press, 1970).

47 Harold S. Wilson, McClure's Magazine *and the Muckrakers* (Princeton: Princeton University Press, 1970), p. 191.

48 Ibid., p. 192.

49 Ibid., p. 192.

50 Jacob Riis, *The Making of an American* (New York: Grosset and Dunlap, 1901), p. 266.

51 Ibid., p. 223.

52 Ibid., p. 204.

53 Steffens, *Autobiography,* p. 375, discusses his own intentions for reporting on cities "scientifically."

54 Ibid., p. 223.

55 Ibid., p. 312.

56 Hugh Dalziel Duncan, *Culture and Democracy* (Totowa, N.J.: Bedminster Press, 1965), p. 53.

57 Dreiser, *Newspaper Days,* p. 151.

58 Hugh Dalziel Duncan, *The Rise of Chicago as a Literary Center from 1885 to 1920* (Totowa, N.J.: Bedminster Press, 1964), p. 114.

59 Quoted in Duncan, *The Rise of Chicago,* p. 117.

60 Dreiser, *Newspaper Days,* p. 396.

61 *New York World,* February 17, 1897, p. 2.

62 Quoted in Wilson, McClure's Magazine, p. 196.

Chapter 3

1 George Herbert Mead, "The Nature of Aesthetic Experience," *International Journal of Ethics* 36 (July 1926): 390. John Dewey made a similar point: ". . . the newspaper is the only genuinely popular form of literature we have achieved. The newspaper hasn't been ashamed of localism, it has revelled in it, perhaps wallowed is the word. I am not arguing that it is high-class literature, or for the most part good literature, even from its own standpoint. But it is permanently successful romance and drama, and that much can hardly be said for anything else in our literary lines." ("Americanism and Localism," *The Dial* 68 [June 1920]: 686.)

2 Walter Benjamin, *Illuminations* (New York: Schocken Books, 1969), pp. 88–89.

3 Alvin Gouldner, *The Dialectic of Ideology and Technology* (New York: Seabury Press, 1976); and Basil Bernstein, "Elaborated and Restricted Codes" in "The Ethnography of Communication," ed. John Gumperz and Dell Hymes, *American Anthropologist* 66 (1964), pt. 2: 55–69. See also Basil Bernstein, *Class, Codes, and Control* (New York: Schocken Books, 1974).

4 Julian S. Rammelkamp, *Pulitzer's* Post-Dispatch *1878–1883* (Princeton: Princeton University Press, 1967), p. 109.

5 Ibid., p. 239.

6 *New York World,* September 30, 1884, quoted in Willard G. Bleyer, *Main Currents in the History of American Journalism* (Boston: Houghton Mifflin, 1927), p. 333.

7 Frank Presbrey, *The History and Development of Advertising* (Garden City, N.Y.: Doubleday, Doran, 1929), p. 356.

8 Daniel Boorstin, *The Americans: The Democratic Experience* (New York: Random House, 1973), p. 139. It is perhaps difficult to conceive of the absence of any standard, continuous relationship between periodicals and advertisers before the 1880s, but this was even more true in magazines than in newspapers. *Harper's* contained primarily ads for its own Harper's Publishing; it rejected a sewing machine company's $18,000 offer for a regular back page advertisement. Presbrey, *History and Development of Advertising*, p. 466.

9 On department stores, see George Juergens, *Joseph Pulitzer and the New York World* (Princeton: Princeton University Press, 1966), pp. 135–136. See also Charles Edward Russell, *These Shifting Scenes* (New York: George H. Doran, 1914), p. 309, where Russell, a reporter and, from 1894 to 1897, city editor of the *World*, remarks that at the end of the nineteenth century the newspaper became "an appendage of the department store." On the growth of national manufacturing and its impact on advertising, see Neil Borden, *The Economic Effects of Advertising* (Chicago: Richard D. Irwin, 1942), p. 37. Borden observes that manufacturers of consumer goods who advertised, beginning in the 1880s, gained a new control over the merchants who bought and sold their products. They won security by becoming dependent not on the small group of intermediate purchasers but on the large group of ultimate consumers. This allowed them more control than ever before over the selling and pricing of their products. The main clients of N. W. Ayer in the 1870s and 1880s were retailers; by 1890 manufacturers were their main accounts. David Potter, *People of Plenty* (Chicago: University of Chicago Press, 1954), p. 171.

Newspapers in markets less competitive than New York could lag behind in changing advertising policy. The *Baltimore Sun*, for instance, prohibited advertisers from breaking column-rules or including illustrations until after 1898. Gerald W. Johnson, Frank R. Kent, H. L. Mencken, and Hamilton Owens, *The Sunpapers of Baltimore* (New York: Alfred A. Knopf, 1937), p. 213.

10 Juergens, *Joseph Pulitzer*, p. 136. This book is an excellent study and, as my footnotes indicate, I have relied heavily on it in this chapter.

11 William S. Rossiter, "Printing and Publishing" in *U.S. Census Reports* 9 (12th census), 1902, pp. 1041–1042. Advertising revenue represented 66 percent of newspaper income in 1970, according to the 1972 U.S. Census of Manufactures.

12 Boorstin, *The Americans*, p. 150.

13 Edwin Emery, *History of the American Newspaper Publishers Association* (Minneapolis: University of Minnesota Press, 1950; Westport, Conn.: Greenwood Press, 1970). Emery's data indicate that advertising revenue rose from 49 percent of total newspaper income in 1879 to 64 percent in 1909 (p. 29).

14 *The Journalist* (August 22, 1885), quoted in Juergens, *Joseph Pulitzer*, p. 95.

15 Robert Taft, *Photography and the American Scene* (New York: Macmillan, 1942), p. 428.

16 Juergens, *Joseph Pulitzer*, pp. 98–105.

17 Ibid., p. 27. Juergens stresses the conservatism of *World* typography in Pulitzer's first years.

18 Harold U. Faulkner, *The Decline of Laissez Faire: 1897–1917* (New York: Holt, 1962), pp. 4–5.

19 Juergens, *Joseph Pulitzer*, p. 239.

20 Robert Park, *The Immigrant Press and Its Control* (New York: Harper, 1922; Westport, Conn.: Greenwood Press, 1970), p. 103.

21 *New York World*, October 11, 1891, quoted in Bleyer, *Main Currents*, p. 352.

22 On Ochs, see Meyer Berger, *The Story of the New York Times 1851–1951* (New York: Simon and Schuster, 1951), p. 424; on Hearst, see Gerald Linderman,

The Mirror of War (Ann Arbor: University of Michigan Press, 1974), p. 167; on Bennett, see An Insider, "New York Editors and Daily Papers" (in the pamphlet file on journalism, Widener Library, Harvard University). For discussion of the decline of the editorial, see *The Journalist* 28 (March 30, 1901): 419–420. This includes an editorial on "The Newspaper Editorial" and an article by Henry Watterson, editor of the *Louisville Courier-Journal,* on the same topic. Paul Starr, in a personal communication, makes the good point that one reason these editors chose, after all, to keep the editorial page may have been that they understood the existence of the editorial page is living proof that there is a distinction between news and editorial and that that vouchsafes the credibility of the news columns.

23   Quoted in W. A. Swanberg, *Citizen Hearst* (New York: Charles Scribner's, 1961), p. 90. The statement appeared in a *Journal* editorial on November 8, 1896.

24   Melville Stone, *Fifty Years a Journalist* (Garden City, N.Y.: Doubleday, Page, 1921), pp. 53, 107.

25   Juergens, *Joseph Pulitzer,* pp. 56–57.

26   Charles Dana, *The Art of Newspaper Making* (New York: D. Appleton, 1900), p. 84. From a lecture delivered at Cornell University, January 11, 1894.

27   Juergens, *Joseph Pulitzer,* p. 57.

28   Ibid., pp. 132–174.

29   Ibid., pp. 145–149.

30   Ibid., p. 148.

31   Michael Young and Peter Willmott, *Family and Kinship in East London* (Harmondsworth: Penguin Books, 1957), p. 160.

32   Ibid., p. 164. Note that they refer to the impersonal judge of social status with the possessive pronoun "her."

33   It should not be surprising, then, that the classic work by an economist on social status was written in this period; Thorstein Veblen's *The Theory of the Leisure Class* (New York: New American Library Mentor Books, 1953) was originally published in 1899.

34   See Theodore Hershberg et al., "The 'Journey-to-Work': An Empirical Investigation of Work, Residence and Transportation, Philadelphia, 1850 and 1880" in *Toward an Interdisciplinary History of the City: Work, Space, Family and Group Experience in Nineteenth-Century Philadelphia,* ed. Theodore Hershberg (New York: Oxford University Press, forthcoming).

35   Juergens, *Joseph Pulitzer,* pp. 39, 47.

36   Charles Dickens, *American Notes* (Paris: Baudry's European Library, 1842), p. 100.

37   Walt Whitman, *Calamus* (Boston: Laurens Maynard, 1897), pp. 41–42. Whitman recalled the pre-Civil War days, however, as the "flush" era of the omnibus. See his recollections in *Specimen Days* (Boston: David Godine, 1971), p. 10. *Specimen Days* was first published in 1882.

38   Theodore Dreiser, *Newspaper Days* (New York: Horace Liveright, 1922), p. 139.

39   Mabel Osgood Wright, *My New York* (New York: Macmillan, 1926), p. 37. Wright's passion for fires dates to the early 1870s when she was in her early teens. But her account suggests that her mother would have taken her to the fires had she not had callers or sewing to do when the fire bell rang. The interest in fires was not just child's play.

40   Quoted in Fred H. Matthews, *Quest for an American Sociology: Robert E. Park and the Chicago School* (Montreal: McGill-Queen's University Press, 1977), pp. 9–10.

41   *The Journalist* 32 (December 27, 1902).

42   Will Irwin, "The American Newspaper. VI: The Editor and the News," *Colliers* 47 (April 1, 1911).

43   *New York Times,* September 19, 1926.

44   Presbrey, *History and Development of Advertising,* p. 354.

45   *The Journalist* 22 (December 4, 1897): 46.

46   John Lee Mahin, quoted in Chester S. Lord, *The Young Man and Journalism* (New York: Macmillan, 1922), p. 211.

47   Meyer Berger, *The Story of the* New York Times *1851–1951* (New York: Simon and Schuster, 1951; reprint ed., New York: Arno Press, 1970), p. 109.

48   Elmer Davis, *History of the* New York Times: *1851–1921* (New York: The New York Times, 1921), p. 193.

49   *The Journalist,* quoted in Berger, *Story of the* New York Times, p. 125.

50   Berger, *Story of the* New York Times, pp. 70–106. See also the biography of Ochs, Gerald W. Johnson, *An Honorable Titan* (New York: Harper, 1946).

51   Berger, *Story of the* New York Times, p. 112.

52   Davis, *History of the* New York Times, p. 218.

53   Berger, *Story of the* New York Times, p. 124.

54   *The Journalist* 32 (December 20, 1902).

55   Davis, *History of the* New York Times, pp. 223–224.

56   *New York Times,* February 16, 1897.

57   *New York Times,* March 4, 1897. The *Evening Post* urged all libraries and clubs to follow Newark's precedent in an editorial entitled "The Way to Reform in Journalism," March 3, 1897. Trustees of the General Society of Mechanics and Tradesmen removed the *World* and the *Journal* from their library; Princeton Theological Seminary did the same; leading men's clubs in New York stopped putting the *World* and the *Journal* out on tables and kept one copy of each to be seen privately and only upon request. All this was reported in the *New York Sun,* March 3, 1897.

58   *New York Times,* September 18, 1911, and September 18, 1926. (These were special anniversary issues of the paper.)

59   Quoted in Berger, *Story of the* New York Times, p. 126.

60   R. C. Cornuelle, "Remembrance of the *Times:* From the Papers of Garet Garrett," *The American Scholar* 36 (Summer 1967): 429–445.

61   Benjamin Stolberg, "The Man Behind *The Times,*" *Atlantic Monthly* 138 (December 1926): 721–731.

62   Gary Steiner, *The People Look at Television* (New York: Alfred A. Knopf, 1963); and Harold Wilensky, "Mass Society and Mass Culture: Interdependent or Independent?" *American Sociological Review* 29 (April 1964): 173–196.

63   Quoted in Juergens, *Joseph Pulitzer,* p. 17.

64   E. L. Godkin, "Journalistic Dementia," *The Nation* 60 (March 14, 1895): 195. This editorial criticized sensationalism in general but focused especially on the attention the yellow journals paid to the private lives of the rich.

65   Edmund Wilson, *Patriotic Gore* (London: Oxford University Press, 1962), pp. 635–669, discusses the shift in American tastes in prose and in oratory from the well-embroidered to the efficient and plain-spoken in the mid-nineteenth century.

66   See Christopher Driver, "Why Newspapers Have Readers" in Alan Casty, comp., *Mass Media and Mass Man* (New York: Holt, Rinehart and Winston, 1973), pp. 199–207. Driver discusses the ways in which London newspapers organize the experience of their readers. The *Express,* he writes, organizes everything as a surprise, "a present from the inexhaustible galaxy of random happenings." The *Times* and the *Telegraph* are instances of a kind of paper which "reduces the apparent randomness of the world's events, and satisfies the educated, conservative reader's longing to find order in the universe." See also the exchange between H. L. Mencken and Ralph Pulitzer in the *Atlantic Monthly* in 1914. Mencken attacked newspapers generally for trying to be interesting. Morality is at essence, he wrote, "the control of impulse by an ideational process, the subordination of the immediate

desire to the distant aim." The morality the newspapers appeal to is morality of the liver, not the head or heart. H. L. Mencken, "Newspaper Morals," *Atlantic Monthly* 113 (March 1914): 289–297. Pulitzer, who had taken over the *World* from his father, defended the press in "Newspaper Morals: A Reply," *Atlantic Monthly* 113 (June 1914): 773–778.

Chapter 4

1 See Alvin W. Gouldner, *The Coming Crisis of Western Sociology* (New York: Avon Books, 1970), for a discussion of "utilitarian culture." For observations on the shift from what we could call a superego culture to an ego culture, see Christopher Lasch, *Haven in a Heartless World* (New York: Basic Books, 1977), p. 23; and Allen Wheelis, *The Quest for Identity* (New York: W. W. Norton, 1958). A work which strongly influenced the orientation of this chapter to the intellectual history of the twenties and thirties is Edward Purcell, *The Crisis of Democratic Theory* (Lexington: University Press of Kentucky, 1973).

2 Quoted in James Wechsler, *The Age of Suspicion* (New York: Random House, 1953), p. 16.

3 See John Diggins, *Mussolini and Fascism: The View from America* (Princeton: Princeton University Press, 1972), on Mussolini's popularity in the United States in the twenties.

4 Walter Lippmann, *The Phantom Public* (New York: Harcourt, Brace, 1925), p. 58.

5 Idem., *Drift and Mastery* (New York: Mitchell Kennerly, 1914), pp. 275–276.

6 Felix Frankfurter, "Democracy and the Expert," *Atlantic Monthly* 146 (November 1930): 649.

7 Harold J. Laski, "The Present Position of Representative Democracy," *American Political Science Review* 26 (August 1932): 630, 632.

8 *The New Republic* 90 (April 7, 1937).

9 White and Baker are quoted respectively on pp. 98 and 179 of Otis L. Graham, Jr., *An Encore for Reform: The Old Progressives and the New Deal* (New York: Oxford University Press, 1967).

10 On optimistic currents in the 1920s, see Arthur M. Schlesinger, Jr., "Theology and Politics from the Social Gospel to the Cold War: The Impact of Reinhold Niebuhr" in *Intellectual History in America,* edited by Cushing Strout, vol. 2 (New York: Harper and Row, 1968), pp. 158–181, who takes the Social Gospel and Deweyan pragmatism in the twenties to have been important sources of optimism. A very important article is Henry F. May, "Shifting Perspectives on the 1920's," *Mississippi Valley Historical Review* 43 (December 1956): 405–427. May distinguishes three contemporary views of the 1920s—that of business, which was very optimistic; that of social scientists, which also was optimistic; and that of literary intellectuals, which saw the twenties as an age of decline. May concludes that, in one fashion or another, "disintegration" of old values and old structures was the common theme of the time.

11 Roscoe Pound, "The Cult of the Irrational," *Wellesley Alumnae Magazine* 13 (August 1929): 368.

12 Leon Bramson, *The Political Context of Sociology* (Princeton: Princeton University Press, 1961), p. 62.

13   Edward L. Bernays, *Biography of an Idea: Memoirs of Public Relations Counsel Edward L. Bernays* (New York: Simon and Schuster, 1965), pp. 290–291.

14   Quoted in J. D. Y. Peel, *Herbert Spencer* (New York: Basic Books, 1971), p. 70. See Cecil S. Emden, *The People and the Constitution* (Oxford: Clarendon Press, 1933), pp. 312–315, for an account of the changing meaning of "the people."

15   Peel, *Herbert Spencer,* p. 70.

16   Chilton Williamson, *American Suffrage from Property to Democracy 1760–1860* (Princeton: Princeton University Press, 1960), p. 185. Williamson quotes the *Connecticut Courant*'s use in 1817 of a distinction between "the people"—meaning the middle class—and "the populace."

17   Donald Fleming, "Attitude: The History of a Concept," *Perspectives in American History* 1 (1967): 287–365.

18   H. J. Dyos and Michael Wolff, "The Way We Live Now" in *The Victorian City,* edited by H. J. Dyos and Michael Wolff, vol. 2 (London: Routledge and Kegan Paul, 1973), p. 396.

19   Seymour I. Toll, *Zoned American* (New York: Grossman Publishers, 1969), p. 193.

20   Quoted in Toll, *Zoned American,* p. 224.

21   See John Higham, *Strangers in the Land* (New York: Atheneum, 1963), pp. 271, 278, 302. See also William Greenbaum, "America in Search of a New Ideal: An Essay on the Rise of Pluralism," *Harvard Educational Review* 44 (August 1974): pp. 411–440.

22   John Dewey, *The Public and Its Problems* (New York: Henry Holt, 1927).

23   Adolph A. Berle and Gardiner C. Means, *The Modern Corporation and Private Property* (New York: Harcourt, Brace, and World, 1968), pp. 64–65, 116.

24   Vincent P. Carosso, *Investment Banking in America: A History* (Cambridge: Harvard University Press, 1970), p. 237. On the democratization of stock ownership, see also Edward C. Kirkland, *A History of American Economic Life* (New York: F. S. Crofts, 1941), pp. 656–657; and Forrest McDonald, *Insull* (Chicago: University of Chicago Press, 1962), pp. 185, 203–205.

25   John Dewey, *Individualism Old and New* (New York: Minton, Balch, 1930), p. 44.

26   Robert S. Lynd with Alice C. Hanson, "The People as Consumers" in the President's Research Committee on Social Trends, *Recent Social Trends* (New York: McGraw-Hill, 1933), pp. 862–864.

27   The phenomenological implications of living in a "consumer society" have not received much scholarly attention. Peter d'A. Jones has written an economic history of the United States entitled *The Consumer Society* (Harmondsworth: Penguin Books, 1965) and finds the United States becoming a fully "consumer" society by the 1920s, but he refuses to say very much about what this meant besides an increase in disposable personal income. More suggestive is Daniel Bell, *The Cultural Contradictions of Capitalism* (New York: Basic Books, 1976), pp. 65–72. Bell's attention to installment buying takes up Dewey's theme. Also still of great interest is David Riesman, Nathan Glazer and Reuel Denney, *The Lonely Crowd* (New Haven: Yale University Press, 1961).

28   These included *New Republic* editors Walter Lippmann and Walter Weyl. See Charles Forcey, *The Crossroads of Liberalism* (London: Oxford University Press, 1961), pp. 82, 165.

29   Edwin L. Shuman, *Practical Journalism* (New York: D. Appleton, 1903), p. 36, gives an instance of this in his account of the "typical" education of a reporter.

30   Ray Eldon Hiebert, *Courtier to the Crowd: The Story of Ivy Lee and the Development of Public Relations* (Ames: Iowa State University Press, 1966), p. 57.

31   Quoted in Hiebert, *Courtier to the Crowd,* p. 50.

32   Ivy Lee, *Publicity* (New York: Industries Publishing, 1925), p. 21. See the

critical editorial, "Lee and Publicity," *Journalism Bulletin* 2 (June, 1925): 16; and also the generally favorable review "The Case for Publicity," by John Cunliffe, dean of the Columbia School of Journalism, in *Journalism Bulletin* 2 (November 1925): 23–26.

33 Lee, *Publicity*, p. 38.

34 Edward L. Bernays, *Crystallizing Public Opinion* (New York: Horace Liveright, 1923), p. 122.

35 Ibid., p. 214.

36 Ibid., p. 215.

37 Bernays, *Biography of an Idea*, p. 288.

38 Stanley Walker, "Playing the Deep Bassoons," *Harper's* 164 (February 1932): 365.

39 Ibid., p. 370.

40 Nelson Antrim Crawford, *The Ethics of Journalism* (New York: Alfred A. Knopf, 1924), p. 160. Muckraking had also prodded business into a concern about publicity and inspired efforts to develop public relations. See Silas Bent, *Ballyhoo* (New York: Boni and Liveright, 1927), p. 134.

41 Henry Pringle, quoted in Hiebert, *Courtier to the Crowd*, p. 302.

42 Quoted in Hiebert, *Courtier to the Crowd*, p. 114.

43 Bernays, *Crystallizing Public Opinion*, p. 195.

44 Crawford, *Ethics of Journalism*, p. 162.

45 Quoted in Walter Lippmann, *Public Opinion* (New York: Macmillan, 1922), p. 218.

46 F. B. Marbut, *News From the Capital* (Carbondale: Southern Illinois University Press, 1971), pp. 192–196.

47 Leo C. Rosten, *The Washington Correspondents* (New York: Harcourt, Brace, 1937), pp. 67–77, noted the vast increase in the use of handouts in Washington, observed that reporters complained about them and had done so at least since 1923, but concluded that, on the whole, they improved journalism.

48 Eric Goldman, *Two-Way Street* (Boston: Bellman Publishing, 1948), p. 19.

49 Quoted in Hiebert, *Courtier to the Crowd*, p. 307.

50 Ibid., p. 307.

51 Dewey, *Individualism Old and New*, p. 43.

52 Lee's personal doubts were reinforced by widespread public criticism. Senator LaFollette referred to his work as a "monument of shame" and introduced a bill which would have made it illegal to attempt to influence the Interstate Commerce Commission by letters, articles, or any other form of communication as an effort to thwart Lee's work. Lee's publicity for the Rockefellers following the Ludlow Massacre had early made him a target of critics and earned for him from Upton Sinclair the nickname, "Poison Ivy." Most devastating of all, in the early thirties Lee, along with a number of other prominent public relations agents, was investigated by the House Un-American Activities Committee for advising German industry and giving counsel to the Nazi government. See Hiebert, *Courtier to the Crowd*, for further discussion.

The contemporary literature in social science and in popular periodicals and in trade journals in journalism on public relations and propaganda is enormous. Useful bibliographic sources include Harold D. Lasswell, "Propaganda," *Encyclopedia of the Social Sciences* (New York: Macmillan, 1934) 12:521–528, which has an extensive bibliography; and Linda Weiner Hausman, "Criticism of the Press in U. S. Periodicals, 1900–1939: Annotated Bibliography," *Journalism Monographs* No. 4 (August 1967). There is an excellent bibliography in Leila A. Sussmann, "The Public Relations Movement in America," (M. A. diss., University of Chicago, 1947). There are a number of useful articles in Harwood L. Childs, ed., "Pressure Groups and Propaganda," *Annals of the American Academy of Political and Social Science*

179 (May 1935). *Public Opinion Quarterly,* an academic journal devoted to the study of public opinion, began in 1937 and is a useful source. Journalism trade journals, particularly *Editor and Publisher,* are replete with discussions of public relations in this period.

53 Edward L. Bernays, *Propaganda* (New York: Horace Liveright, 1928), p. 27.

54 John Luskin, *Lippmann, Liberty, and the Press* (University, Ala.: University of Alabama Press, 1972), pp. 38–39; and Michael Stockstill, "Walter Lippmann and His Rise to Fame, 1889–1945," (Ph.D. diss., Mississippi State University, 1970), pp. 152, 178.

55 See George Creel, *How We Advertised America* (New York: Harper and Row, 1920); James R. Mock and Cedric Larson, *Words That Won the War* (Princeton: Princeton University Press, 1939); Carol Oukrop, "The Four Minute Men Became National Network During World War I," *Journalism Quarterly* 52 (Winter 1975): 632–637.

56 The *Times* is quoted in Hiebert, *Courtier to the Crowd,* p. 243. Jack J. Roth, *World War I: A Turning Point in Modern History* (New York: Alfred A. Knopf, 1967), p. 109.

57 Bent, *Ballyhoo,* p. 134; Scott M. Cutlip, *Fund Raising in the United States: Its Role in America's Philanthropy* (New Brunswick, N.J.: Rutgers University Press, 1965); Robert S. Lynd and Helen Merrell Lynd, *Middletown* (New York: Harcourt, Brace, 1929), pp. 458–470; Will Irwin, "If You See It in the Paper, It's—?" *Colliers* 72 (August 18, 1923): 27.

58 Forrest McDonald, *Insull* (Chicago: University of Chicago Press, 1962), p. 185.

59 Ernest Gruening, *The Public Pays* (New York: The Vanguard Press, 1931), p. 235.

60 Lasswell in his article on "Propaganda" in the *Encyclopedia of the Social Sciences* lists a number of propaganda institutions and writes, "Perhaps five hundred rather important propaganda institutions are organized nationally and usually have offices in Washington, D.C. or New York City." Some institutions with a national presence had international sponsorship. Diggins, *Mussolini and Fascism,* pp. 49–50, discusses Italy's establishment of an American press service to counter antifascist stories in 1927.

61 O. H. Archambault, quoted in Lee William Huebner, "The Discovery of Propaganda: Changing Attitudes Toward Public Communication in America 1900–1930" (Ph.D. diss., Harvard University, 1968), p. iv.

62 Harold D. Lasswell, *Propaganda Technique in the World War* (New York: Alfred A. Knopf, 1927), p. 4.

63 Lippmann, *Public Opinion,* p. 218.

64 Bent, *Ballyhoo,* p. 123.

65 Personal interview, September 17, 1977.

66 Peter Odegard, *The American Public Mind* (New York: Columbia University Press, 1930), p. 132.

67 I examined the front page of the *New York Times* for the first week in January every four years from 1920 to 1944. The results are as follows:

Number of By-lines	
1920	6
1924	2
1928	16
1932	8
1936	20
1940	35
1944	37
1964	62

In 1920 and 1924, none of the by-lines were on domestic stories. In 1928 the Albany correspondent had by-lined stories, and in 1932 both the Albany correspondent and the science writer had by-lined stories. Turner Catledge noted the growing status of reporters relative to the copy desk began in the 1930s and was evident in a proliferation of by-lines at the time. My brief sampling bears him out. See Turner Catledge, *My Life and The Times* (New York: Harper and Row, 1971), p. 165.

68 Kent Cooper, *Kent Cooper and the Associated Press; An Autobiography* (New York: Random House, 1959), pp. 104, 110. Contemporary note of the increased use of by-lines was made by Elmo Scott Watson in "The Return to Personal Journalism," an address to the University Press Club of Michigan, November 21, 1931, reprinted in Frank L. Mott and Ralph D. Casey, *Interpretations of Journalism* (New York: F. S. Crofts, 1937). See also Victor Rosewater, "Sees Wire Services Freed of Routine," *Editor and Publisher* 66 (January 20, 1934): 7.

69 *Journalism Bulletin* 1 (1924): 16.

70 Edwin Emery, *The Press and America* (Englewood Cliffs, N.J.: Prentice-Hall, 1972), pp. 563–565. On specialization, see also "Williams Says Day of Specialization in News Writing Here," the report of a speech by Dean Walter Williams, head of the School of Journalism at the University of Missouri, in *Quill* 13 (March 1925): 20. *Quill* 14 (September 1926): 14–15, editorialized on the question of specialization. Curtis MacDougall, *Interpretative Reporting* (New York: Macmillan, 1938), p. 65, wrote, "The trend in the news room is definitely in the direction of specialized reporting."

71 Herbert Brucker, *The Changing American Newspaper* (New York: Columbia University Press, 1937), pp. 11–12.

72 MacDougall, *Interpretative Reporting*, p. v.

73 Ibid., p. 251.

74 Raymond Gram Swing, comment in panel on "The Big News in Europe, What It Means and How to Get It" at the 13th Convention of the American Society of Newspaper Editors, April 18–20, 1935, in *Problems of Journalism* (American Society of Newspaper Editors, 1935), p. 92.

75 *Problems of Journalism* (American Society of Newspaper Editors, 1933), p. 74. The Associated Press moved toward interpretation, too. See Kent Cooper, "Report of the General Manager," Associated Press, *32nd Annual Report of the Board of Directors to the Members*, 1932, p. 6.

76 Walter Trohan, *Political Animals* (Garden City, N.Y.: Doubleday, 1975), p. 30. Trohan served for many years as Washington correspondent for the *Chicago Tribune*.

77 The New Deal, of course, concentrated political initiative in Washington as never before, but even before Roosevelt came to power the centralization of power in Washington was clear. See Leonard D. White, "Public Administration" in the President's Research Committee on Social Trends, *Recent Social Trends* (New York: Macmillan, 1933), pp. 1393–1397.

78 Quoted in W. A. Swanberg, *Luce and His Empire* (New York: Charles Scribner's, 1972), pp. 142–143. See also Robert T. Elson, *Time Inc.* (New York: Atheneum, 1968).

79 MacDougall, *Interpretative Reporting*, p. 18. In 1904 Robert Park collaborated with John Dewey and Franklin Ford on *Thought News*, a publication they intended as a newspaper in which journalism would be guided by philosophy. Park wrote later in his career that *Time* embodied the ideal of *Thought News*. See Fred H. Matthews, *Quest For an American Sociology: Robert E. Park and the Chicago School* (Montreal: McGill–Queen's University press, 1947), p. 28.

80 C. L. Edson, *The Gentle Art of Columning* (New York: Brentano's, 1920); and Hallam W. Davis, *The Column* (New York: Alfred A. Knopf Borzoi Handbooks of Journalism, 1926).

81 Emery, *Press and America*, p. 491.

82 Mrs. Raymond Clapper, biographical sketch of her late husband in Raymond Clapper, *Watching the World*, ed. Mrs. Raymond Clapper (London: Whittlesey House, 1944), p. 21.

83 "The Press and the Public," special section of *The New Republic* 90 (March 17, 1937): 185.

84 Robert S. Lynd and Helen Merrell Lynd, *Middletown in Transition* (New York: Harcourt, Brace, 1937), pp. 377–378.

85 "The Press and the Public," *The New Republic* 90 (March 17, 1937): 188. The spread of syndicated Washington columns was not universally applauded. The Lynds were wary about its influence on independent local thought in Middletown. See *Middletown in Transition*, pp. 377–378. Raymond Clapper, in a column in 1936, felt that syndicated columns were "a mixed blessing to the editor," increasing the inclination of editorial page writers to leave judgment to the commentators. See Clapper, *Watching the World*, pp. 36–37. At the 16th convention of the American Society of Newspaper Editors in 1938, the following resolution was proposed and debated though, finally, voted down: "This Society sees in the increasing use in the press of syndicated columns of opinion and interpretation—for which individual papers assume no responsibility—a threat to the independent thought of the newspaper public. It fears that predigested opinion, sweetened with rhetoric and garnished with Olympian pronouncements, may come to be accepted by too many readers as an easy substitute for fact and individual thought." See *Problems of Journalism* (American Society of Newspaper Editors, 1938), pp. 157–162.

86 Lippmann, *Public Opinion*, p. 256.

87 Walter Lippmann, *Liberty and the News* (New York: Harcourt, Brace, and Hone, 1920), pp. 5, 54–55.

88 Ibid., p. 67.

89 Ibid., p. 82.

90 Joseph Pulitzer, "The College of Journalism," *North American Review* 178 (May 1904): 657. See also Pulitzer's original memo of August, 1902, in Richard Terrill Baker, *A History of the Graduate School of Journalism* (New York: Columbia University Press, 1954), pp. 23–25.

91 Walter Lippmann and Charles Merz, "A Test of the News," supplement to *The New Republic* 23 (August 4, 1920): 3.

92 Ibid., pp. 41–42. See also H. L. Mencken, "Journalism in America" (1927) in H. L. Mencken, *The American Scene*, ed. Huntington Cairns (New York: Alfred A. Knopf, 1965). Mencken argued, "Most of the evils that continue to beset American journalism today, in truth, are not due to the rascality of the owners nor even to the Kiwanian bombast of business managers, but simply and solely to the stupidity, cowardice, and Philistinism of working newspapermen." There was not unanimity on this point. Lippmann's views were criticized in John Macy, "Journalism" in *Civilization in the United States*, edited by Harold Stearns (New York: Harcourt, Brace, 1922), pp. 35–51. Macy, a literary editor of the *Boston Herald*, argued that employers, not the reporters, were responsible for the plight of American journalism. "Paradoxically," he wrote, "the journalist is the one man who can do little or nothing to improve journalism."

93 Walter Lippmann and Charles Merz, " 'A Test of the News': Some Criticisms," *The New Republic* 24 (September 8, 1920): 32.

94 Ibid., p. 33.

95 Walter Lippmann, "The Press and Public Opinion," *Political Science Quarterly* 46 (June 1931): 170.

96 Walter Lippmann, *American Inquisitors* (New York: Macmillan, 1928), p. 46.

97   Walter Lippmann, *A Preface to Morals* (New York: Macmillan, 1929; reprint ed., Time Incorporated, 1964), pp. 222–224.

98   Leo C. Rosten, *The Washington Correspondents* (New York: Harcourt, Brace, 1937), p. 351.

99   Ibid., pp. 149–150.

100   Robert T. Elson, *Time Inc.* (New York: Atheneum, 1968), p. 319.

101   Quoted in Herbert Harris, *American Labor* (New Haven: Yale University Press, 1938), p. 185. The Supreme Court upheld the National Labor Relations Board position. See Associated Press v. National Labor Relations Board 301 U.S. 1–147 (1937).

102   *Editor and Publisher* 70 (July 3, 1937), p. 3.

103   Ibid., p. 4.

Chapter 5

1   Stanford Sesser, "Journalists: Objectivity and Activism," *Wall Street Journal*, October 21, 1969. Reprinted in full in *Quill* 57 (December 1969): 6–7.

2   Quoted in Leon V. Sigal, *Reporters and Officials* (Lexington, Mass.: D. C. Heath, 1973), p. 68.

3   Here I disagree equally with statements like that of Joe McGinniss: "Politics, in a sense, has always been a con game;" and Richard J. Barnet: "The tradition of news management in the United States goes back to the days of George Washington." See Joe McGinniss, *The Selling of the President 1968* (New York: Trident Press, 1969; Pocket Books, 1970), p. 19; and Richard J. Barnet, *The Roots of War* (Baltimore: Penguin Books, 1972), p. 271.

4   Ray Stannard Baker, *Woodrow Wilson and World Settlement*, 2 vols. (London: William Heineman, 1923), 1:116.

5   Quoted in Baker, *Woodrow Wilson*, p. 137.

6   Ibid., p. 150.

7   See Baker, *Woodrow Wilson*, pp. 139ff. for a discussion of the issue of publicity at the opening of the conference. For the controversy over release of the draft treaty, see Frederic L. Paxson, *American Democracy and the World War. Postwar Years: Normalcy, 1918–1923* (New York: Cooper Square Publishers, 1966; Berkeley: University of California Press, 1948), p. 108.

8   "George Michael," *Handout* (New York: G. P. Putnam's, 1935), p. 233.

9   Elmer Davis, "The New Deal's Use of Publicity," review of George Michael, *Handout* (New York: G. P. Putnam's, 1935) in *New York Times*, May 19, 1935. See also Arthur Krock, "Press vs. Government—A Warning," *Public Opinion Quarterly* 1 (April 1937): 45–49.

10   *Editor and Publisher* 77 (April 8, 1944): 7, 56.

11   Douglass Cater, "The Captive Press," *The Reporter* 2 (June 6, 1950): 18.

12   Richard Rovere, *Senator Joe McCarthy* (New York: Harcourt, Brace, 1959), p. 166. See also Ronald May, "Is the Press Unfair to McCarthy?" *The New Republic* 127 (April 20, 1953).

13   Daniel Yergin, *Shattered Peace* (Boston: Houghton Mifflin, 1977), p. 5. See also Francis E. Rourke, "The United States" in *Government Secrecy in Democracies,* ed. Itzhak Galnoor (New York: Harper Colophon, 1977), pp. 113–128; Arthur

Schlesinger, Jr., *The Imperial Presidency* (New York: Popular Library, 1974); David Wise, *The Politics of Lying* (New York: Random House, 1973); Geoffrey Hodgson, *American in Our Time* (Garden City, N.Y.: Doubleday, 1976); and Robert Borosage, "The Making of the National Security State" in *The Pentagon Watchers,* edited by Leonard S. Rodberg and Derek Shearer (Garden City, N.Y.: Doubleday, 1970), pp. 3–63.

14   Reston used the phrase "manage the news" in testimony before a congressional committee: "Most of my colleagues here," he said, "have been talking primarily about the suppression of news. I would like to direct the committee, if I may, to an equally important aspect of this problem which I think is the growing tendency to manage the news." *Availability of Information from Federal Departments and Agencies* pt. I, Hearings before a subcommittee of the Committee on Government Operations, House of Representatives, November 7, 1955 (Washington: Government Printing Office, 1956), p. 25. Reston takes credit in a January 28, 1965, interview for having coined the phrase—credit which other authorities seem to think he deserves. For the interview, see George H. Berdes, *Friendly Adversaries: The Press and Government* (Milwaukee: Center for the Study of the American Press, Marquette University College of Journalism, 1969), p. 92. See also "U.S. Suppression of News Charged," *New York Times,* November 8, 1955, which quotes *Washington Post* editor J. Russell Wiggins' view that secrecy at the Defense Department and the National Security Council was "ominous."

15   Russell Baker, *An American in Washington* (New York: Knopf, 1961), pp. 81–83.

16   Joseph Kraft, "The Dangerous Precedent of James Hagerty," *Esquire* 51 (June 1959): 94. See also Baker, *American in Washington,* pp. 75–84.

17   Daniel Boorstin, *The Image* (New York: Harper and Row, 1961; Harper Colophon, 1964), p. 34.

18   Ibid., p. 12.

19   Quoted in *Editor and Publisher* (November 10, 1962): 12. See also "Use of Press As Weapon In Blockade Is Debated," *Editor and Publisher* (November 3, 1962): 11, 59.

20   Sylvester's statement appeared in a number of variants in a wide range of publications. For an evaluation of the way the quotation has been used and abused in the press, see Martin Gershen, "The 'Right to Lie' " *Columbia Journalism Review* 5 (Winter, 1966–1967): 14–16.

21   See, for instance, the frequent references to Sylvester in *Nieman Reports* 16 (December 1962); and the symposium on "news management" in *Nieman Reports* 17 (March 1963). On the other hand, when Sylvester finished responding to questions at his "right to lie" talk, the audience of journalists stood and cheered. See *Editor and Publisher* (December 15, 1962): 54.

22   Clifton Daniel, "Responsibility of the Reporter and Editor," *Nieman Reports* 15 (January 1961): 14.

23   Chalmer M. Roberts, *First Rough Draft* (New York: Praeger, 1973), p. 171.

24   William L. Rivers, *The Opinionmakers* (Boston: Beacon Press, 1965), pp. 84–85.

25   "The CIA's 3-Decade Effort to Mold the World's Views," *New York Times,* December 25, 1977, p. 12.

26   See, for instance, Gay Talese, *The Kingdom and the Power* (New York: World Publishing, 1969; Bantam Books, 1970), pp. 5–6, 8, 28.

27   Douglass Cater, *The Fourth Branch of Government* (Boston: Houghton Mifflin, 1959).

28   An early statement is in O. O. Stealey, *Twenty Years in the Press Gallery* (New York: Publishers Printing, 1906), p. 4, where Stealey writes that Washington

correspondents know more than they print but that they keep confidences.

29 Staughton Lynd and Tom Hayden, *The Other Side* (New York: New American Library, 1966), p. 11.

30 John Mecklin, *Mission in Torment* (Garden City, N.Y.: Doubleday, 1965), p. 113. Later there were big lies, too. For instance, the idea that American withdrawal would precipitate a "blood bath" was a horror story planted in the press by the CIA and "conjured out of the air" according to Frank Snepp, former CIA analyst, quoted in Seymour Hersh, "Ex-Analyst says CIA in Saigon Gave False Reports to Newsmen," *New York Times,* November 21, 1977.

31 Mecklin, *Mission in Torment,* p. 107.

32 Philip Geyelin, "Vietnam and the Press: Limited War and an Open Society" in *The Vietnam Legacy,* ed. Anthony Lake (New York: New York University Press, 1976), p. 172.

33 New York Times, December 27, 1966. For Salisbury's account of his travels, see Harrison E. Salisbury, *Behind the Lines—Hanoi* (New York: Harper and Row, 1967).

34 James Boylan, "A Salisbury Chronicle," *Columbia Journalism Review* 5 (Winter, 1966–1967): 10–14. See also James Aronson, *The Press and the Cold War* (Indianapolis: Bobbs-Merrill, 1970), p. 254–261.

35 Walter Lippmann, *Public Opinion* (New York: Macmillan, 1922; Free Press Paperback, 1965), p. 226.

36 Lionel Trilling, *Beyond Culture* (New York: Viking, 1965), pp. xii–xiii.

37 David Halberstam makes this point in "Press and Prejudice," *Esquire* 81 (April 1974): 114.

38 Norman H. Nie, Sidney Verba, and John R. Petrocik, *The Changing American Voter* (Cambridge: Harvard University Press, 1976), p. 278.

39 Ibid., p. 60.

40 Ibid., p. 350. Other relevant considerations of the changing American voter include: Philip E. Converse, "Change in the American Electorate" in Angus Campbell and Philip E. Converse, *The Human Meaning of Social Change* (New York: Russell Sage Foundation, 1972), pp. 263–337; Arthur H. Miller, "Political Issues and Trust in Government: 1964–1970," *American Political Science Review* 68 (September 1974): 951–972; and Jack Citrin, "Comment: The Political Relevance of Trust in Government," ibid., pp. 973–988; and Arthur H. Miller's rejoinder, ibid., pp. 989–1001.

41 Daniel Patrick Moynihan, "The Presidency and the Press," *Commentary* 51 (March 1971): 43.

42 For views critical of the press for not being critical enough, see Tom Bethell, "The Myth of an Adversary Press," *Harper's* 254 (January 1977): 33–40 and Nicholas von Hoffman, "Dining Out in Medialand," *More* (February 1978): 24–25. For data that journalists are more trusting of government than the public at large, see E. Barbara Phillips, "Journalistic Versus Social Science Perspectives on Objectivity" in *Methodological Strategies for Communications Research,* edited by Paul Hirsch, Peter V. Miller, and F. Gerald Kline, vol. 6 (Beverly Hills: Sage Publishers, 1978) and E. Barbara Phillips, "The Artists of Everyday Life: Journalists, Their Craft, and Their Consciousness," Ph.D. diss., Syracuse University, 1975. For the position that the press has long been trusting of government and that this has been a strength, not a fault, of the American journalistic tradition, see Paul Weaver, "The New Journalism and the Old—Thoughts After Watergate," *Public Interest* 35 (Spring 1974): 68–74 and Irving Kristol, "Is the Press Misusing Its Growing Power?" *More* (January 1975): 26, 28.

43 Richard Harwood, "The Fourth Estate" in *The Washington Post Guide to Washington* edited by Laura Longley Babb (New York: McGraw-Hill, 1976), p. 85.

44 On *Quest,* see *Wall Street Journal,* October 29, 1971. See also Joann S. Lublin, "Underground Papers in Corporations Tell It Like It Is—Or Perhaps Like It Isn't," *Wall Street Journal,* November 3, 1971.

45 This point was raised by several journalists I interviewed in New York, Chicago, and Washington in 1977.

46 On the changing character of television news and a provocative argument about the "dispatriating" political effect of television news, see Michael J. Robinson, "American Political Legitimacy in an Era of Electronic Journalism: Reflections on the Evening News" in *Television as a Social Force* edited by Douglass Cater and Richard Adler (New York: Praeger, 1975). For the survey data, see Burns W. Roper, *Trends in Public Attitudes Toward Television and Other Mass Media 1959–1974* (New York: Television Information Office, 1975). The Roper survey overestimates the reliance of the population on television for news, according to University of North Carolina researchers Robert L. Stevenson and Kathryn White. See Chris Welles, "At Issue," *Columbia Journalism Review* 16 (January-February 1978): 12–13.

47 Jules Witcover, "The Press and Chicago: The Truth Hurt," *Columbia Journalism Review* 7 (Fall 1968): 6; and idem., "Washington: The News Explosion," *Columbia Journalism Review* 8 (Spring 1969): 25.

48 On "60 Minutes" see Donovan Moore, "60 Minutes," *Rolling Stone* (Jan. 12, 1978), pp. 43–46. On the prominence of controversial documentaries, programs of political satire, and "relevant" situation comedies on television in the past decade, see Erik Barnouw, *Tube of Plenty* (London: Oxford University Press, 1977).

49 Jack Newfield, "Journalism: Old, New and Corporate" in *The Reporter as Artist: A Look at the New Journalism,* edited by Ronald Weber (New York: Hastings House, 1974), p. 56. Originally in *The Dutton Review,* ed. Susan Stern (New York: E. P. Dutton, 1970).

50 Paul Weaver, "The Politics of a News Story" in *The Mass Media and Modern Democracy,* edited by Harry M. Clor (Chicago: Rand McNally, 1974), pp. 85–112.

51 Gaye Tuchman, "The Exception Proves the Rule: The Study of Routine News Practices" in *Methodological Strategies for Communications Research,* edited by Paul Hirsch, Peter V. Miller, and F. Gerald Kline, vol. 6 (Beverly Hills: Sage Publishers, 1978). A study which makes a closely related point very well is Harvey Molotch and Marilyn Lester, "Accidents, Scandals, and Routines: Resources for Insurgent Methodology" in *The TV Establishment,* edited by Gaye Tuchman (Englewood Cliffs, N.J.: Prentice-Hall, 1974), pp. 53–65. This first appeared in *The Insurgent Sociologist* 3 (1973): 1–11.

52 Gaye Tuchman, "Objectivity as Strategic Ritual: An Examination of Newsmen's Notions of Objectivity," *American Journal of Sociology* 77 (January, 1972): 660–679. There is now a vast literature which in various ways makes the point that the content of the news is a function of the social structure of news gathering and news organizations. Most of this literature observes that the process of "newsmaking" favors official points of view. See, inter alia, the articles in Gaye Tuchman, ed., *The TV Establishment;* Edward Jay Epstein, *News From Nowhere* (New York: Random House, 1973); E. Barbara Phillips, "The Artists of Everyday Life: Journalists, Their Craft, and Their Consciousness," (Ph.D. diss. Syracuse University, 1975); Leon V. Sigal, *Reporters and Officials* (Lexington, Mass.: D. C. Heath, 1973); Bernard Roshco, *Newsmaking* (Chicago: University of Chicago Press, 1975); David L. Altheide, *Creating Reality* (Beverly Hills: Sage Publications, 1976); Lou Cannon, *Reporting: An Inside View* (Sacramento: California Journal Press, 1977).

53 Bernard C. Cohen, *The Press and Foreign Policy* (Princeton: Princeton University Press, 1963), p. 20.

54 For a useful discussion of how social institutions are—and must be—

governed by conflicting sets of norms rather than by a single consistent set, see Robert
Merton, *Sociological Ambivalence and Other Essays* (New York: Free Press, 1976).
Merton offers no counsel, however, on why one set of norms, rather than another, is
dominant.

55 Nat Hentoff, "Behold the New Journalism—It's Coming After You!" in
Weber, *Reporter as Artist*, p. 52. From *Evergreen Review* (July 1968). That this
tradition of valuing well-written stories with emotional impact is a significant one is
indicated by the fact that the 1945–1946 Nieman fellows at Harvard, asked to select
a news story to illustrate their ideal of the best reporting, chose a highly subjective,
personal, and moving piece from the *New York Herald Tribune* by Vincent Sheean
on the treatment of Negro defendants by Southern courts. See *Nieman Reports* 1
(April 1947): 16–17; and the correspondence in the following issue, *Nieman Reports*
1 (July 1947): 29–30.

56 David L. Eason, "Metajournalism: The Problem of Reporting in the
Nonfiction Novel," (Ph.D. diss. Southern Illinois University, 1977). See also John
Hollowell, *Fact and Fiction* (Chapel Hill: University of North Carolina Press,
1977).

57 James Agee and Walker Evans, *Let Us Now Praise Famous Men* (New
York: Ballantine Books, 1966; Boston: Houghton Mifflin, 1941). See the fine
commentary on the book in William Stott, *Documentary Expression and Thirties
America* (New York: Oxford University Press, 1973).

58 Cannon, *Reporting*, p. 54.

59 Bob Woodward and Carl Bernstein, *All the President's Men* (New York:
Simon and Schuster, 1974; Warner Books Edition, 1975). See also the speech by Carl
Bernstein accepting the degree of doctor of laws at Boston University (April 1975),
printed in Walter Lubars and John Wicklein, eds., *Investigative Reporting: The
Lessons of Watergate* (Boston: Boston University School of Public Communication,
1975), pp. 9–13. For a discussion of the work habits and journalistic ideas of
Woodward, Bernstein, and other prominent contemporary investigative reporters, see
Leonard Downie, *The New Muckrakers* (Washington: New Republic Books, 1976).
All the President's Men and *The New Muckrakers* are reviewed by Michael
Schudson in "A Matter of Style," *Working Papers for a New Society* 4 (Summer,
1976): 90–93.

60 Cannon, *Reporting*, p. 54, testifies to *More*'s wide readership. The *Chicago
Reader* and the *Village Voice* (a publication which predates the sixties by a few
years) are among the publications with regular columns of press criticism. The
Columbia Journalism Review, which began in 1962, is the only serious journal of
press criticism which is not intimately connected to the adversary culture of the
sixties. A good discussion of the growth of journalism reviews in the late sixties is in
James Aronson, *Deadline for the Media* (Indianapolis: Bobbs-Merrill, 1972), pp.
93–122, 299–300.

61 On *Newsday*, see Carey McWilliams, "Is Muckraking Coming Back?"
Columbia Journalism Review 9 (Fall 1970): 12. On the *Boston Globe*, see the
discussion of "City and State Investigative Reporting" in Lubars and Wicklein,
Investigative Reporting, p. 38. On the *New York Times*, see Robert B. Semple, Jr.,
"The Necessity of Conventional Journalism: A Blend of the Old and the New" in
Liberating the Media: The New Journalism, edited by Charles C. Flippen (Wash-
ington: Acropolis Books, 1974), pp. 89–90. On the *Cleveland Plain-Dealer* and for
general discussion of the topic of investigative teams, see John Consoli, "Investigative
Reporters Debate Use of Teamwork," *Editor and Publisher* (June 25, 1977): 5, 13.
Information on the *Chicago Tribune* from interview with a *Tribune* editor, January,
1978.

62 Jules Witcover, "Washington: The Workhorse Wire Services," *Columbia
Journalism Review* 8 (Summer 1969): 13. On the pressures on the wire services to

expand their "straight news" coverage to more interpretive and even investigative reporting, see the article on the wire services in *Wall Street Journal,* January 28, 1969. The sixties spawned several new, small news services devoted to aggressive journalism. The State News Service began in 1973 in Washington. Later the same year the Capitol Hill News Service was born, subsidized at first by Ralph Nader, and dedicated to "nonpassive" reporting. The two groups merged in May, 1978. Together they provide in-depth coverage of Washington affairs keyed to the special concerns of the localities of the 77 small and medium-sized papers they serve. See John S. Rosenberg, "Imperiled Experiment: Capitol Hill News Service," *Columbia Journalism Review* 16 (September–October, 1977): 59–64 and "Sale of Small News Service in Capital to Have a Big Effect," *New York Times,* May 12, 1978.

63 Melvin Mencher, "The Arizona Project: An Appraisal," *Columbia Journalism Review* 16 (November, December, 1977): 38–42, 47. See also Michael F. Wendland, *The Arizona Project* (Kansas City: Sheed Andrews and McMeel, 1977).

64 From Fund for Investigative Journalism report (mimeo, 1977) on its grants and from the publicity pamphlet explaining the Fund. In 1976 the Sabre Foundation, organized in 1969, established The Journalism Fund to provide small grants to journalists who investigate government abuses and publish their work in member publications. Member publications include *The New Republic, Inquiry, Washington Monthly, Progressive, Human Events, Reason,* and *National Enterprise*—a most ecumenical grouping.

65 See Consoli, "Investigative Reporters," p. 5.

66 Peter Dreier, "Newsroom Democracy: A Case Study of an Unsuccessful Attempt at Worker Control," mimeo, 1977.

INDEX

Abell, Arunah, 18
Abolitionism, 56
Accuracy: facts and, 78–81, 204; in news (1890s), 62–64; in penny press, 25; of information and story journalism, 118–19
Action journalism, 105–6
Adams, John, 47
Ade, George, 73
Advertisers, 93–94
Advertising, 206; decency of, 109–10; directly to consumers, 133; and drop in price for the *Times*, 114–15; and expansion of market, 46; financial, 108; page one (1850s), 66; and penny press, 18–20; percent revenue from (1880–1900), 93; self, 95–97, 106, 112–13, 118; sold on basis of circulation, at fixed price, 93; timely, 26; and women's consciousness of social status, 100–1
Advertising agency: first modern, 94; *see also* Public relations
Advertising Club of New York, 135
Aesthetic function, 89
Agee, James, 187
Agnew, Spiro, 3
Albany Argus, 15, 54
Albany Evening Journal, 15
Alger, Horatio, 6, 101
American Association of Teachers of Journalism, 135
American Newspaper Guild, 156–57
American Newspaper Publishers Association, 94, 157
American Political Science Review (magazine), 125
American Press Bureau, 164
American Society of Newspaper Editors, 147, 148, 157
Appel, Joseph, 78, 85
Aptheker, Herbert, 174
Arnold, Matthew, 117

Associated Press, 4–5, 145, 146, 156, 184, 190
Atlantic Monthly (magazine), 116, 151
Attitude: modern use of term, 129
Authority: problem of loss of, 124–25

Baker, Ray Stannard, 72, 73, 126, 164–65
Baker, Russell, 170
Baltimore *American and Commercial Daily Advertiser*, 17
Baltimore *Federal Gazette and Baltimore Daily Advertiser*, 17
Baltimore *Federal Republican and Baltimore Telegraph*, 17
Baltimore *Morning Chronicle and Baltimore Advertiser*, 17
Baltimore *Patriot and Mercantile Advertiser*, 17
Baltimore Sun, 18, 22, 34, 80
Bancroft, George, 67
Barnum, P. T., 19
Bay of Pigs invasion (1961), 171, 172
Beach, Moses, 34
Becker, George, 73
Bennett, James Gordon, 16, 18, 50–55, 128; advertising and, 20, 26, 93; influence of, 91; as journalist, 24; pioneering work of, 65; political independence and, 21; self-advertising and, 95; use of telegraph and, 34
Bennett, James Gordon, Jr., 98
Bent, Silas, 144
Berle, Adolf A., 132
Bernays, Edward L., 128, 134, 136–38, 141, 171
Bernstein, Basil, 90
Bernstein, Carl, 188, 191
Bierce, Ambrose, 73
Birth announcements, 29

221

Index